HOW DO WE LEARN?

T0284806

HOW DO WE LEARN?

A SCIENTIFIC APPROACH TO LEARNING AND TEACHING

(EVIDENCE-BASED EDUCATION)

Héctor Ruiz Martín

JB JOSSEY-BASS™
A Wiley Brand

Library of Congress Control Number is Available

Cover Design: Wiley
Cover Image: © malerapaso/Getty Images

English translation: Oriol Solé Mula
Illustrators: Sandra Villa Valenzuela and Isabel Soler Chorro
Photographs: 123rf.com and Wikimedia Commons

SKY10072784_041524

To those who dedicate their lives to education

CONTENTS

FOREWORD

I first read (or perhaps, more precisely, started reading) *How Do We Learn?* after hearing Héctor Ruiz Martín speak at a researchED conference in Santiago, Chile, in November 2022.

Having now read the book fully, twice, I am convinced that it will prove to be one of the most important books in education for the foreseeable future, destined to enter the pantheon of must-read books on the science of learning. If you work in education, you simply cannot afford not to read this book. It is indispensable, full stop.

But let me return to my introduction to Héctor and his work. It might not seem especially remarkable to point out that hearing him speak in Santiago caused me to instantaneously buy and read his book, save for the fact that, at the time, it was available only in Spanish (under the title *¿Como Aprendemos?*) and my Spanish was rudimentary at best.

Reading *¿Como Aprendemos?* the first time entailed six months of hard cognitive labor for me. I struggled phrase by phrase and sometimes word by word. But I persisted. Even through the haze of my partial understanding, the book offered up one insight after another.

Still, I ask myself now, what about Héctor's presentation might have driven me to go to such lengths to read his book in Spanish? After all, I had listened to informed presentations on cognitive psychology before; in fact, I knew a lot of the science Héctor was discussing to some degree or another. I had read dozens of other books on the topic and there were ones in my native language that I could have read in a fraction of the time.

Ironically, some of the things that were so effective about his presentation, and that might also be said about this book, might at first sound insufficiently dramatic to warrant a six-month personal translation odyssey.[1] It was *carefully explicated*. It was *thorough and logically and progressively organized*. And its style was *calm and patient*.

Let me begin with this last point, which was remarkable because Héctor, there on the stage, as he often is in this book, was engaged at least in part in quietly dismantling a series of common misconceptions and distortions about how people

---

[1] I should note here, in case you had any questions, that this book is professionally translated by first-rate experts, and my only role has been to read their work and say, "Wow, that's really good."

learn—*edu-myths*, as you might call them—and this sort of work is often done elsewhere in a style that tends toward judgment and rancor, as if it was a deliberate choice of people who held incorrect ideas about learning to do so.

But Héctor proceeded in Santiago, as he does here, with patience and without judgment, steadily helping his audience to reconceptualize first one key idea and then another. Gradualism, I am reminded, has been a more productive force in the history of ideas than revolution, and that's how Héctor's work plays out. You don't realize at first that he is preparing to shift your worldview. You merely follow as he goes steadily from point to point until the ideas start to coalesce and suddenly you realize that you understand something very well and quite differently than you did previously.

The ideas are not just clear, they are connected, and through those connections a model emerges. It is powerful because it is cohesive. Suddenly you understand not just bits and pieces but something bigger.

Interestingly, this exact topic, conceptual change, or how to change the minds of learners who already believe something else—possibly something erroneous—is a topic Héctor writes about explicitly in this book, and he notes that it requires time and patience.

But also more than patience. Something like trust must also be built up. As Jonathan Haidt points out in *The Righteous Mind: Why Good People Are Divided by Politics and Religion,* we are most likely to change our opinions not when confronted by someone who disparages us but in discussion with someone who understands us, whom we have come to trust and feel connected to. The motive in a book like this has to be truth and not ideology, and you feel that right from the outset. "I am a scientist first," Héctor told me in Santiago, and his is a book for people who are motivated to seek the best, clearest, and comprehensive summary of our aggregated knowledge about human cognition. It's a book for people who want to know what the evidence tells us, whether it's what they expected or not.

The phrase "well-organized" might also seem at first unprepossessing as a term of praise, but like patience, it too is profoundly important. We can only aspire to guide people to understand differently by "building the concepts" one by one, Héctor writes. We have to make sure people understand all the research, but then also connect the pieces together.

In seeking to understand how people learn we are not seeking to understand a handful of useful ideas, but to grasp a body of knowledge, and that means understanding how it fits together. To facilitate that, sequence is highly relevant. The order, the thoroughness, the organization of the knowledge is really, really important. Durable and useful learning, as I learned from reading this book, is built on the *connections between* the ideas we understand. An organized methodical presentation of connected ideas from an interlocutor whose motives you trust leads to a systematic understanding of the big picture. That perhaps is what this book gives its readers more than any other—the comprehensiveness of it, the thoroughness, the linkages among ideas.

But the gradual, progressive, impeccably organized flow of ideas in the book is important in another way too. "Properly sequencing learning goals and adjusting task difficulty not only has positive consequences for the effectiveness of our memory . . . but also indirectly affects our motivation. Cognition and motivation are interconnected," Héctor explains in this book. When you feel things coming together, you grasp that you are building a substantive and useful understanding. Success at learning is one of the greatest sources of motivation to a learner. That you feel yourself understanding deeply and connecting the dots causes you to persist. This is yet another powerful lesson for our classrooms that Héctor will explain in this book. Take it from a guy who read his book in a language he didn't speak.

Earlier I used another potentially unprepossessing term not generally heard in the arts of marketing and persuasion to praise Héctor's work: *carefully explicated.*

You can count on Héctor to know the science from just about every angle, but one of the best parts of his presentation in Santiago—and which is also true of this book—was the way he not just explained the principles of cognitive psychology but brought them to life. He didn't just tell us why the brain worked the way it did and leave it at *useful abstraction*; he demonstrated it there in the hall with 400 participants or so, causing us, for example, to remember more from a list of words whose meaning we thought deliberately about and connected to our prior knowledge than from a list we thought deliberately about but didn't try to link to prior knowledge. He ran a live experiment on us to prove the point, in other words. And it worked!

Active learning, he showed us, entailed the brain actively making connections between knowledge that was already encoded in long-term memory and the object of present inquiry.

As he explains it in this book, in one of the most profoundly insightful passages:

> The simple yet powerful idea that emphasizes the importance of students actively seeking meaning in what they are learning, trying to relate it to their prior knowledge, reflecting on its implications for what they already know, and ultimately, thinking about it forms the basis of what is known as active learning.
>
> Active learning is often confused with educational practices in which the student "does things"—or what is known as learning by doing. But active learning could be better defined as learning by thinking. It encompasses any learning experience in which the student actively thinks about the learning object, seeking meaning and comparing it with their prior knowledge.

His ability to help his listeners conceptualize ideas through images is another theme you will notice. A photo of Héctor on stage in Santiago shows him making this idea profoundly accessible by presenting it visually.

Memory and learning, he is telling us here, come from the connections created between new information and existing knowledge (or between ideas already present in our memory that had never been connected before). It's the connections—the lines between and among the dots—that represent the building of durable meaningful knowledge.

As his ability to demonstrate—with an ad hoc experiment, with an image to crystallize an abstract idea—shows, he is able to combine vast knowledge with a pragmatic bent, and this is a rare thing. The "curse of knowledge" or the "expert's blind spot" is yet another idea that you will encounter in this book. It is the idea that the more you know about something, the harder it is to explain what you know to a novice or even understand why and how it became clear to you.

So while he is a research scientist of encyclopedic knowledge, he also "speaks teacher" and can translate his knowledge into practical suggestions of what it might look like on Monday morning with 30 14-year-olds.

All of which I suppose explains why I persisted with my ad hoc translation project and why, though I was expecting big things when I at last read the English translation, I was stunned again by its breadth, depth, and cohesion.

We live in a time of promise—when we know far more about how learning works than ever before—and by a wide margin—and when a broad awakening to the importance of that knowledge has begun to sweep the education sector, and this trend has the capacity to radically change the depth and scope of learning that happens in a thousand settings across society. This is both an incredible opportunity for teachers of all stripes but also an immense responsibility.

The knowledge is there—and so is the need. "Returns to education," the benefits people get from learning more in school, are higher than they have ever been. By necessity then, the converse of this is also true. The costs borne by students of not learning are ever greater. There is a lot of discussion these days about educational equity. In many ways the greatest form of equity lies in whether students get access to teaching that applies the science of learning as well as it can be by teachers who understand it well enough to make decisions to adapt and adjust their lessons for maximum benefit.

And in *How Do We Learn?*, that body of knowledge is present, all in one place, carefully and patiently explained, organized in a logical and sequential manner with real-world examples to help bring it to life. This book is a gift—an immensely powerful one—that Héctor Ruiz Martín has provided, now, too, to readers in English. I am convinced as I have said that it will prove to be one of the most important books in this new era: a, if not *the*, standard work on learning science.

And so now, the rest of the task is ours: to read it and study it and to think deliberately about its implications so that we can bring them to life for the students we serve.

DOUG LEMOV
AUTHOR, *TEACH LIKE A CHAMPION*, AND
MANAGING DIRECTOR OF UNCOMMON SCHOOLS

INTRODUCTION

"Learning results from what the student does and thinks and only from what the student does and thinks. The teacher can advance learning only by influencing what the student does to learn."

Herbert A. Simon (1916–2001)
Researcher in politics and cognitive science

Once, a journalist asked me if learning was an instinct. I responded, "Would you say that seeing is an instinct?" Indeed, learning, like seeing, is something our brain does continuously, whether we want it or not. Evolution has endowed us with an organ that not only allows us to interact with our surroundings but also to adapt and optimize our responses by learning from each and every experience.

Learning occurs in the learner's brain. Therefore, in the educational context, the primary protagonist of learning is the student. In fact, learning happens without the need for formal teaching. Nevertheless, regarding the type of knowledge and skills offered in school (literature, mathematics, history, science, reading, writing, etc.), teaching is the most effective way to promote learning (Geary, 2007). Teaching occurs when the teacher creates conditions and provides or facilitates experiences that trigger learning in students, always in relation to specific goals. But the teacher does not "generate" learning; their role is to provide optimal circumstances for it to unfold and encourage students to engage in actions that lead to achievement. Therefore, teaching is a facilitation of learning.

Although the brain learns from all experiences, not everything we experience is remembered in the same way. The way the brain has evolved shapes which experiences or actions are more effective in producing lasting learning. Interestingly, we are not born knowing how the brain learns; we do it spontaneously, and at most, some instincts may promote it. For example, curiosity prompts us to pay attention and explore the new, but we do not inherently know which actions optimize learning—even those inferred from personal experience may not necessarily be the most optimal (Karpicke et al., 2009). It could be compared to many other things we can do but do not know how to do optimally. For example, while we all know how to jump, it took decades of professional athletics to discover that jumping as high as possible requires a specific technique (backward flip, known as the Fosbury flop) which is neither intuitive nor obvious. Similarly, knowing how the brain learns can enable us to develop techniques or methods that optimize our capacity to learn. It can also make us much more effective as teachers.

This book starts with the premise that the processes of learning and teaching can be analyzed through the lens of the scientific method, and we can use the evidence derived from this research to guide decisions aimed at improving educational practices. Without a doubt, there is a significant artistic element in teaching, much like in medicine; and like in medicine, teaching has a scientific aspect—one that we have barely developed and transferred to classrooms. Of course, there are organizational and economic factors in educational systems that influence the success of their mission (as with healthcare). Still, this book primarily focuses on the processes of teaching and learning—that which happens inside classrooms and is, to a greater or lesser extent, in the hands of both students and teachers.

In recent decades, science has significantly advanced its understanding of learning processes, at both the neurological and the psychological levels. Additionally, educational research has gathered multiple pieces of evidence regarding the potential of the transfer of scientific knowledge about how the brain learns to teaching and learning processes in education. This line of research, in turn, has analyzed educational practices that yield better results, aiming to identify reproducible patterns.

In this sense, my goal with this book is to contribute to disseminating, especially among teachers, what research has revealed about how learning occurs and the factors that have a greater impact, in order to promote it in the academic context. My commitment has been to do so in an engaging and accessible manner, while also maintaining the necessary rigor for this task. Bearing in mind the evidence provided by research to date and its alignment with the scientific consensuses, I have stressed the need to exercise caution due to the demands of a science as inexact as this. Therefore, I would like readers to be aware that this is not a book intended to proclaim unequivocal, positivist, and exaggerated messages that distort reality—messages that gain popularity and contribute to book sales simply because they are messages we want to hear.

Because of the recent "fad" of neuroeducation, the rigorous science of learning proper is seeing a horde of opportunists disseminating messages that have nothing to do with its conclusions. Pseudoscience always spreads faster than science, likely because scientific explanations tend to be inherently more complex and nuanced. Science always demands doubt and requires multiple pieces of evidence to assert anything with a degree of certainty, while pseudoscience always asserts its claims with certainty from the outset. Nevertheless, this book aims to contribute to the realm of scientific dissemination with the double rigor demanded by such a crucial topic as education. Naturally, no one is entirely free from bias. So it may well be that, throughout this book, my objectivity may not have been as absolute as intended. Therefore, I apologize if, in any case, I have inadvertently been too extreme with any assertion. In any case, I have tried to adhere to the evidence and faithfully reflect the ideas of other researchers. I have also included references to scientific articles supporting each assertion; a text aiming to provide an evidence-based approach to teaching and learning would not be consistent if it did not provide such evidence. Readers will notice that many of these references are not recent; I have chosen to primarily cite foundational articles in each area, reflecting that educational research is nothing new.

The novelty lies not so much in what we scientifically know about learning but in bringing that knowledge into the classrooms.

While this book may shy away from sensationalism, it still, I hope, contains inspiring ideas. There is nothing more fascinating than synthesizing the key elements that, according to science, can genuinely impact education. In this sense, although in some cases I have ventured to translate certain research conclusions into specific actions that students and teachers can take to optimize learning—actions supported by empirical evidence—this is not a recipe book. In fact, it cannot be. If anything, educational research has taught us that there is no foolproof recipe. No educational method is universally effective for all students, purposes, or contexts. For example, is project-based learning effective? Is it beneficial to conduct exams? The answer, obviously, is that it depends. Didactic methods depend on too many variables for it to be reasonable to lump them all together just because they share some of them. Take online teaching, for example. In online teaching, students learn remotely using computer programs. However, this is not what determines whether or not this method is effective. Some online programs are remarkably effective, while others leave much to be desired. If we equate two online courses merely because they are online, we may be comparing apples and oranges from an educational perspective.

Therefore, this book focuses on the fundamentals, exploring the specific variables that make methods effective based on our understanding of how people learn. What factors contribute to team activity promoting meaningful learning? In what circumstances can exams be beneficial? What makes an online course effective? My main objective is to bring scientific models that explain the phenomenon of learning closer to teachers, empowering them to base their decisions on these models. This should always be in alignment with their own criteria, which must consider their students and their context. The transfer between theory and practice in a field like ours is typically neither straightforward nor direct. Fortunately, there are scientific disciplines that study learning phenomena relatively close to the real context, even within the classroom itself.

That said, it is important to clarify that this is not a book about neuroscience (or neurobiology). Although undoubtedly fascinating, neuroscience, in recent years, has made great strides in understanding the biological processes that constitute the physical substrate of learning. However, neurobiology can tell us little about what to do in the classroom (Anderson & Della Sala, 2012). The gap between the knowledge generated by this science and educational practice is too large. The intricacies of the brain captivate us, and knowing how it works is no doubt a major interest of ours. But let's not fool ourselves—understanding how neurons behave or which brain regions are involved in specific tasks will not help us in deciding how to organize an educational experience to achieve learning goals.

One of the scientific disciplines that is in a better position to contribute to the analysis and improvement of learning and teaching processes is cognitive psychology. As a deeply empirical branch of psychology, it studies how the brain obtains, manipulates, stores, and uses information initially received through the senses. Unlike neuroscience, which analyses the biological aspects of the brain, cognitive psychology draws conclusions by examining behavior and performance data. Cognitive psychology relies mainly on laboratory research, but it also draws insights from studies in everyday settings, such as the classroom. Recent advances in neurobiology have informed cognitive psychology and have helped validate models of how the mind processes information, including the mechanisms involved in learning. The truly beneficial scientific insights for educators, however, originate from psychology itself.

Within these pages, I present a cognitive perspective on the phenomenon of learning, precisely because this approach is considered by most scientists to better support the methodological decisions that teachers and students make daily. I also rely extensively on educational psychology, a multidisciplinary branch that draws on cognitive psychology, developmental psychology, and other related sciences to explore learning in its real context. Perhaps the most interesting thing about this discipline is that it conducts much of its research in the classroom, allowing hypotheses about which methods or measures will impact student performance to be tested in the most direct way possible, even if it comes at the expense of generalizability. Let's say it is the most direct bridge between basic research and its real-world application context.

Finally, it is crucial to emphasize that this book does not aim to define the goals of education. Science will never answer such a question because it is not a query that can be resolved through the scientific method. Instead, each educational community must establish its objectives based on the criteria it deems appropriate. However, once the goals are established, science can assist in revealing the methods more likely to help achieve them.

For historical reasons, this book revolves around how students can achieve meaningful, lasting, and transferable learning across any field of knowledge. It also addresses how they can improve their academic performance, an aspect not necessarily synonymous with meaningful learning. After all, these are the two major themes that science has investigated in greater depth. As we will see throughout this book, its conclusions validate the efficacy of certain practices that we have been conducting for decades. Still, they also reveal others that can significantly contribute to improving teaching and learning processes.

To conclude, my humble desire is that this book proves to be of use to teachers and students, as well as to all people interested in learning how learning works. After all, the journey of becoming a learner is an ongoing process.

HÉCTOR RUÍZ MARTÍN
ORIGINAL TEXT: DECEMBER 2019

THE SCIENCE OF HOW WE LEARN

Before delving into the topic of what we know about how people learn and what we can do to promote learning based on these ideas, the opening chapter explores how science has gained this knowledge and what precautions should be taken when applying it.

Thus, in the first section of the book, I explain how research is conducted in the field of teaching and learning processes and why this research provides unique insights to support the decisions we make daily, both as educators and as students. Furthermore, I advise on the nature and limitations of scientific knowledge, particularly in a field as complex as the one discussed here, and emphasize the importance of interpreting research results appropriately, with cautiousness and critical thinking.

The Scientific Study of Learning and Teaching

"It's unbelievable how much you don't know about the game you've been playing all your life."

Mickey Mantle (1931–1995)
Baseball player

Personal Experience and Cognitive Biases

As educators, we make countless decisions every day so that our actions and those of our students have a positive impact on their learning in all its dimensions. In addition to small day-to-day decisions, we also make important, high-impact choices when planning our teaching for the upcoming school year, selecting the educational materials we will use, or participating in decisions that define the educational project of our school.

Typically, we base all these decisions on our intuition, which is fueled by the knowledge and beliefs about education that we have built upon a vast body of personal experiences. The origin of these experiences that shape our conceptions of teaching and learning dates back to our time as students in the educational system, and for many educators, this extends uninterrupted into their professional careers. During this life journey through the educational system, first as students and then as educators, it is only natural that we accept the validity of many of its assumptions and, conversely, question others based on our personal experience.

However, how reliable are the intuitions we have developed about education based on our personal experience? If personal experience is the best way to determine what is best for our students, why do not all (equally experienced) teachers agree on which methods yield the best results? To begin with, each of us goes through different personal experiences, which can make comparisons challenging. Nonetheless, what truly compromises the reliability of our personal experiences is how we interpret them, which is influenced by the way our brain operates. And here lies the problem: the human brain exhibits multiple "biases" that distort its understanding of reality when it relies solely on personal experience. This is what we call *cognitive biases*.

To understand the problem of cognitive biases, take a look at the following images. Would you believe me if I told you that the horizontal lines in Figure 1 are straight and parallel? They are. Go ahead, take a sheet of paper and place it along each line and see for yourself.

FIGURE 1

FIGURE 2

Now look at Figure 2. Would you say that the tower at the right is more tilted? The truth is that both are identical, even in their inclination.

And what about Figure 3? Would you believe me if I told you that the squares marked with the letters *A* and *B* are exactly the same color? Well, they are.

These situations, like many more, prove that our brain normally operates by manipulating and altering sensory information. That is, we do not perceive things

FIGURE 3

as they are; the brain processes sensory information and "adjusts" it before placing it into our consciousness. Mechanisms that alter sensory information have obviously evolved over millions of years to make us more effective in interacting with the environment in which our species has developed—an environment that, by the way, was quite different from the one most of us inhabit today.

The fact is that the brain does not only "trick" us when it comes to what we perceive. Just as the brain modifies our perception, it also has mechanisms to "fine-tune" how we think and remember (Kahneman & Tversky, 1972). In other words, our reasoning and memories are subject to brain mechanisms that operate outside our consciousness and shape our thinking when we try to make sense of reality. We may not be aware of their existence, but these mechanisms play a role in the processes that help us interpret the world around us and make decisions. The problem is that they did not evolve so we could fully grasp the world as it is, but rather in a way that was practical for our survival and allowed our species to endure. We use these mechanisms to make immediate judgments and responses in situations that call for quick decisions, when it is not possible to process all available information, or when we lack information. These mechanisms divert us from logical thinking and steer us toward decisions fueled by our emotions—even when we think we are being rational. They also hinder our ability to appreciate the practical significance of statistical probability (why are we more afraid of flying than driving when many more people die in car accidents than in plane crashes?) and make us particularly vulnerable to fallacies, deceptive types of reasoning that may seem correct but are, in fact, flawed.

In summary, because of certain spontaneous cognitive "adjustment" mechanisms that our brain activates spontaneously, all humans exhibit various biases that influence

Note: Fallacies

Biases make us inclined to consider some types of reasoning as valid that, when carefully examined through the lens of logic, are not really so. These types of reasoning are called *fallacies*. Fallacies are powerful rhetorical tools for persuading others, which is why many politicians are quick to use them in their speeches. They are also effective for convincing oneself or reaffirming one's own ideas. The following are three of the most common fallacies:

Ad hominem **fallacy**. This occurs when an argument does not refute the interlocutor's position or claims, but instead seeks to discredit the interlocutor personally to undermine their position. For example, an *ad hominem* fallacy occurs when we say, "You say that this method is better, but you don't use it in your own classes," since it attempts to refute the proposition—the proposed method—by attacking the proponent. The fact that a person's actions are not consistent with their words does not mean that what they propose is not valid ("Do as I say, not as I do"). We also commit these fallacies when we disqualify the interlocutor's claims by referring to their education or profession: "You're not a teacher, so what you say is of no use to me."

Ad verecundiam **fallacy**. This is an argument that appeals to the prestige or authority of some individual or institution to support a claim, despite not providing evidence or reasons to justify it. For example, "Piaget, the renowned educational psychologist and father of constructivism, stated the same thing I just mentioned." Of course, it is interesting that he claimed it (whatever it was), but that does not mean it is true. Several of Piaget's ideas about children's cognitive development have actually been refuted by decades of research in developmental psychology.

Ad populum **fallacy**. This occurs when we attribute our opinion to the majority's opinion and then argue that if most people think something, it must be true. Just because most people in the 17th century believed the Sun revolved around Earth does not mean that this was true. Similarly, even if most teachers believe that memory can be improved in general by exercising it through memorizing academic content, this does not mean it is true.

how we understand the world, reason, and make decisions. These biases have nothing to do with our preferences, our likes, or our ethical or moral ideas. Cognitive biases are involuntary psychological phenomena that distort the way we process information—how we perceive it, how we interpret it, and how we remember it. For example, a common cognitive bias occurs when we think that the price of an item at $4.99 is much more appealing than one at $5.00, or when we perceive that a black object weighs more than the same object in white. These biases also come into play when we quickly establish cause-and-effect relationships based on a single experience.

Confirmation Bias and Cognitive Dissonance

Cognitive psychologists have identified dozens of biases influencing how we reason about reality. One of the most prominent biases that can clearly impact our decisions as teachers is confirmation bias—the tendency to notice, pay attention to, and remember information that confirms our beliefs, while disregarding information that contradicts them (Oswald & Grosjean, 2004). This bias causes us to interpret the same information in a completely different way than others would, seeing it as more aligned with our convictions. It even leads us to ignore evidence when it is right in front of us and preferentially perceive evidence that supports our views (Lord et al., 1979). To see this bias in action, just watch two fans of rival basketball teams watching the same game on TV.

Furthermore, this bias causes us to forget information that does not fit with our ideas in favor of information that does (Stangor & McMillan, 1992). Thus, confirmation bias acts when we remember situations that confirm our hypotheses but ignore or forget situations where they did not hold. For example, a person who believes that using technology in class is counterproductive to learning will preferably remember students' comments about the disadvantages of these tools and forget the positive comments. They will not consider whether the complaints are well founded or if they have a solution since they align with their ideas. In fact, it is when our beliefs are challenged that confirmation bias drives us to seek information that proves us right. However, we specifically seek the information that proves us right. We rarely decide to investigate further into the opposing view, and, in fact, when we do and come across information that supports the opposing hypothesis, we shamelessly dismiss it to continue searching for the one we want (Nickerson, 1998). As psychologist Ziva Kunda (1990) pointed out, "People are more likely to arrive at conclusions that they want to arrive at." In fact, Francis Bacon had already been aware of this in 1620 when he observed that "most people prefer to believe what they prefer to be true."

Therefore, confirmation bias is more evident when our beliefs are challenged. When that is the case, we may start feeling personally attacked. After all, the more deeply rooted our beliefs about how the world around us is and how it works, the more they become a part of our own identity. The inner conflict that arises when our ideas clash with information or experiences that contradict them is a phenomenon known as *cognitive dissonance* (Festinger, 1957).

Usually accompanied by an uneasy sensation, cognitive dissonance prompts us to react by trying to regain "balance" through confirmation bias, which helps us reaffirm our convictions, even leading us to ignore evidence. In a way, confirmation bias is an unconscious resistance to changing our ideas, an automatic system for protecting our identity.

Confirmation bias is reinforced by other biases, such as the so-called *bandwagon effect*, the tendency to do or believe something simply because many others do or believe it (Leibenstein, 1950). Indeed, there is an involuntary psychological tendency to follow or imitate the actions and thoughts of others to fit into the group we belong to. Undoubtedly, this bias also influences our understanding of education.

These cognitive biases, along with many others, make us very ineffective at analyzing reality without even realizing it. Therefore, when it comes to teaching and learning processes, we must go beyond personal experience and use strategies that help us free ourselves from our biases and discern between what most likely "works" and what does not, based on empirical evidence untainted by our minds. To this end, there is no better remedy than the scientific method.

The Scientific Method as a Remedy for Cognitive Biases

Think of the scientific method as a pair of glasses crafted by humanity to correct our cognitive biases when we look at the world around us. It invites us to collect data methodically and analyze it logically and systematically. In doing so, it allows us to establish cause-and-effect relationships with greater precision than our personal experiences alone. As Carl Sagan once said, it may not be a perfect method, but it is the best one we have for such purposes.

It is important to emphasize that the scientific method goes beyond just learning from direct experience. In this sense, it differs from personal experience in how it collects and analyzes data and how it uses that data to draw logical conclusions. Only then can direct experience break free from our cognitive biases.

For instance, someone may be convinced that presenting a concept in a particular way in primary education can lead to misconceptions hindering later learning in secondary education. This is their hypothesis, possibly based on intuition, later confirmed by observing cases in their classes (which they will readily remember). But how do we determine how widespread or anecdotal these misconceptions are in the classroom? And, most importantly, how can we tell if the presentation of the concept in primary education is indeed the cause of these misconceptions? Relying solely on spontaneous observation and subjective assessments will subject us to confirmation bias, making us see and remember what we already believe. Conversely, by choosing to analyze the situation scientifically, we can objectively shed more light on the matter.

Of course, this does not mean that every time we face a decision as teachers, we must conduct experiments and scientifically analyze them to find supporting evidence. Fortunately, several researchers (many of them also teachers) have already done this for us and published their results. Still, it is not necessary to consult scientific literature for every step we take. However, when it comes to significant decisions, especially those requiring substantial investments of resources—be it money, time, effort, enthusiasm, or opportunity (the opportunity cost of doing one thing is missing out on another potentially better option)—it is advisable to learn about what research has to offer, and not just to have our hypotheses supported! However, it is important to remember that science will never tell us what we should or should not do; it can only inform us about what is more likely to happen when we do this or that.

Levels of Research on Learning and Teaching

There are several scientific disciplines studying the processes of learning and teaching from different perspectives, focusing on complementary aspects.

First, neurobiology explores how learning occurs at the molecular, cellular, and organ system levels. In essence, it examines how the nervous system serves as the physical foundation for learning-related phenomena. In its studies, neurobiology employs animal models and, when possible, also works with human subjects—either *in post-mortem* settings, during surgical procedures, or with cell cultures. In recent decades, this field has greatly benefited from the ability to "observe" the brain of a healthy person in action while they engage in mental or motor activities. This milestone has been made possible through the development of neuroimaging technology, such as functional magnetic resonance imaging (fMRI), allowing us to observe which regions of the brain become more active than usual when individuals undertake various tasks. Figure 4 presents two examples of such images (although in black and white).

At a different level of study lies cognitive psychology, a deeply empirical branch of psychology that investigates how the brain acquires, processes, and stores information. However, it does not study the physiology of the brain. Instead, cognitive psychology models its operation by assessing the changes that certain sensory or motor experiences cause in people's behavior and performance. For example, an experiment in this discipline might explore whether individuals remember a story better when they read it or when it is explained to them. Consequently, cognitive psychology is much more equipped to guide us in educational practice than neurobiology. In fact, it draws on the advances of neurobiology to support its models and theories, thus acting as a link between scientific advancements in understanding how the brain works and education.

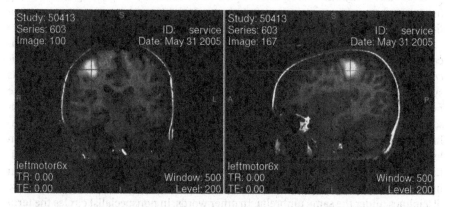

FIGURE 4   Examples of images obtained using functional magnetic resonance imaging.

Source: M.R.W.HH / Wikimedia Commons / Public domain.

Note: Cognitive Psychology and Neurobiology

Although the brain does not work like a computer, we can use a computer analogy to understand the difference between the approach proposed by cognitive psychology and that offered by neurobiology when it comes to studying the processes of learning.

Imagine we want to figure out how a computer program works when there is no instruction manual or tutorial to show us how to use it. The approach of cognitive psychology would involve pressing buttons and trying different combinations to observe what happens, that is, how the program responds. In contrast, neurobiology would open the computer, study its circuits, and analyze what happens within them when the program is running.

Although this analogy may seem somewhat forced, it effectively illustrates which of the two approaches is closer to guiding us on what to do in the classroom to promote learning—essentially, how to get the most out of the metaphorical computer program.

Cognitive psychology, in fact, provides valuable data and models for the field known as *educational psychology*—a multidisciplinary specialty that relies on cognitive psychology and related disciplines, such as developmental psychology and evolutionary psychology, to study learning and teaching processes in real contexts. It is the discipline closest to the classroom, and its main strength lies in directly bringing research into classrooms. When educational psychology focuses on teaching and learning specific knowledge areas, it branches into various "didactics," such as mathematics didactics, language didactics, or science didactics.

Of course, many other disciplines contribute to the study of teaching and learning processes, from sociology to computer science. Still, I have chosen to concentrate on those that predominate in the approach covered in this book.

With that said, I believe it is necessary to clarify where the field known as educational neuroscience fits into this landscape. Strictly speaking, the term *neuroscience* has always referred to research on the structure and functioning of the nervous system from a physiological perspective, and consequently, it is equivalent to the neurobiological discipline. That is why initially the concept *of educational neuroscience* pertained only to neurological studies on brain function related to learning and memory. However, in recent years, as scientific evidence on how the brain learns that is most relevant to educational practice has come primarily from cognitive psychology and related disciplines, the term *educational neuroscience* has been increasingly used in a broader sense than its original meaning, encompassing these disciplines under the same umbrella. In other words, in nonspecialist circles the term has evolved into a synonym for any discipline that employs the scientific method to analyze how we learn (Anderson & Della Sala, 2012).

Experiments in the Classroom

Educational research conducted directly in the classroom usually adopts two types of approaches: descriptive or experimental. In the first case, the aim is to gather data, whether numerical or qualitative, that objectively describe how things are. This type of research allows for the detection of correlations; that is, the coincidence of two or more variables, such as observing that children with higher self-esteem tend to coincide with those who achieve better academic results. On the other hand, experimental research aims to analyze the relationship between different variables and identify cause-and-effect relationships. For example, does higher self-esteem cause students to get better grades? The way to conduct such research would involve acting on the variable we assume to be the cause (self-esteem) and observing if, by modifying it, the variable we presume to be the effect (academic results) also changes. The rest of the variables that could affect academic results should be controlled during the experiment.

Thus, to conduct the experiment that addresses the previous question, we could set up two groups of students who are very similar in their average characteristics, such as the ratio of boys to girls, socioeconomic status, group's average grade, and so forth (this is better achieved by distributing the students in each group randomly). From here, one group could be exposed to a self-esteem enhancement program (assuming we already know it works), while the other group would receive sessions on any other topic (e.g., neuroscience). After the interventions, we could collect new data on their academic grades and measure the improvement in each group compared to their grades before the experiment. Then we would compare the academic improvements of each group to see if that of the group that received the self-esteem intervention is different from that of the group that did not receive it. If it were, we could conclude that our experiment would have provided evidence of the presumed effect of self-esteem on academic results.

This is essentially how research on how people learn in the school context works. It is important to highlight that a control group is always required for an experiment to be rigorous. Ideally, such a control group should only differ from the experimental group by not being subjected to the condition we want to analyze. It is also crucial to understand that experiments neither prove nor disprove anything. Research can only provide evidence of whether a variable can influence learning. Nonetheless, research results are quite often negative, which means that there is no evidence of a presumed effect. Therefore, when we scientists say there is no evidence for something, we are not saying that no one has investigated it. In reality, most of the time we mean that it has indeed been studied but no evidence of its presumed effect has been found. Obviously, this is not to say that it cannot be found in the future, but we cannot give it credence until it is. To assert something scientifically, one must provide evidence; arguing that if something has not been proven, then it must be true (*ad ignorantiam* fallacy) does not hold.

A Phenomenon Dependent on Many Variables

Some believe that studying our students' learning in the school context cannot be approached scientifically. Indeed, it is not easy to study it because it depends on multiple variables at once—perhaps even more so than those involved in the physiological processes studied in medicine, which are also quite numerous. In education, a variable is any characteristic inherent to our students (internal variables) or to their learning environment, including their experiences (external variables). Therefore, the teaching methods we use or the activities we do in class are all variables in the educational process. Among the countless variables at play, only some have an impact on learning, and among those, some have a greater effect than others.

When a phenomenon depending on many variables is studied, statistics is one of the most useful tools there are. First, because drawing conclusions based on a single case or a handful of cases will not simply do. In each case, such as with each student, the effects of various variables combine and interact to produce a result. The challenge then is to determine whether a specific variable truly caused a particular outcome or if it was another variable or a combination of several that was responsible. Therefore, a single observation (or a few) will not be enough to establish whether a variable caused the effect; a considerable number of cases need to be analyzed to determine the average result.

Second, statistical techniques allow us to determine whether a difference in the average results of two groups of students (which could be the same group in two different situations, such as before and after an activity) can be explained without attributing it to chance. When scientists claim that a difference between two groups is statistically significant, they are precisely addressing this aspect. In statistics, the term *significant* does not mean that the difference is necessarily important or large, but rather that this difference is unlikely to be due to chance. The most likely explanation is that there is some distinct factor between the groups that is causing this difference in their results.

For example, imagine I have a coin and I tell you that it has a defect that always makes it land on heads when flipped. To prove it, I toss the coin once, and indeed, it comes up heads. Would you believe me? Probably not. The outcome could have been simply a product of chance, resulting from the combination of all the variables we cannot control involved in tossing and landing a coin. What if I toss it twice and it lands on heads both times? You would still likely doubt the alleged effect of the defect. How many times should I toss the coin and get the same outcome for you to stop thinking that it could be due to chance? Ten times? A hundred? A thousand? Note that in any of these cases, it would not be impossible for chance to make it land on heads every time, even if the coin were not rigged. What we do know is that the more times we toss the coin, the less likely it is that heads would come up every time unless there was something causing it (Table 1).

Thus, when scientists statistically analyze the outcomes of an experiment and say that they are *significant*, what they mean is that the relationship between two variables (e.g., the defect and the heads outcome) could not be explained by chance, at least in a high percentage of cases—usually ranging from 95% to 99% of the time. In other words, the probability of it happening by chance is 5% or 1%, respectively. If an outcome can hardly be explained by chance, it is then assumed that there is a relationship or effect. On the other hand, given that it is relatively easy to accept that 10 consecutive heads are coincidental but much harder to believe that 100 are, using a large sample size will improve our ability to distinguish between an outcome due to chance and a real effect.

When tossing a regular coin, the probability of getting heads is 50%. If we expect some factor, such as a defect, to positively influence this outcome, we should anticipate the percentage to increase. Tossing the coin 100 times and having it land on heads 65 times (65% of the time) might lead us to believe that something is affecting

Table 1 **Probability that a coin will always come up heads when tossing it several times.**

Number of Coin Tosses	Probability That It Lands on Heads Every Time
1	0.5 (50%)
2	0.25 (25%)
3	0.125 (12.5%)
4	0.0625 (6.25%)
5	0.03125 (3.125%)
6	0.015625 (1.5625%)
7	0.0078125 (0.78125%)

how the coin lands. This observation also prompts us to note that, for example, it is not the same to have the defect increasing the probability of getting heads 65% of the time than 95% of the time. In other words, the influence of a variable—the coin's defect—on an outcome (getting heads) can vary in intensity. In statistics, the effect is the value that determines how important the influence of a variable is on the measured outcome. Thus, while a result may be statistically significant, indicating that an effect exists, this effect can vary in size from small to medium to large.

If we draw an analogy between the previous example of the coin and a study in the educational domain, the coin's defect corresponds to the variable we want to investigate (a characteristic of the students, a pedagogical intervention, a change in classroom organization, etc.) and the outcome of each coin toss represents the effect we aim to measure in each student, such as student performance. Therefore, in this analogy, the number of students analyzed is equivalent to the number of coin tosses.

However, the fact that the effects of a variable can only become evident through statistical analysis has an important consequence: the result will be observed at a group level, rather than at the individual level. When tossing our rigged coin, sometimes it will land on tails because, apart from the defect, there are other variables influencing how it lands. When interpreting a scientific result, we must always consider the effects at the group level and not rely on specific cases (individual students).

Correlation Does Not Imply Causation

With these considerations in mind, how do we know that it is indeed the coin's defect that consistently causes heads to come up? It is essential to distinguish between correlation and causation. Just because two things tend to occur together (correlation) does not imply that one causes the other. There may be a third variable that influences both occurrences. For example, there is a positive correlation between the ice cream consumed each month and the number of crimes committed (Salkind, 2016). Does eating ice cream fuel this criminal trend? Not at all. It is, in fact, the warmer weather that leads to increased ice cream consumption, which coincides with the months when more crimes occur for various reasons, especially the influence of heat on behavior and the proliferation of opportunities for criminal activities during vacation periods (Field, 1992; Anderson et al., 2000).

Sometimes, correlations may even be a result of pure chance. There is a website that shows all kinds of absurd correlations, such as the one linking the number of divorces in the state of Maine to the per capita consumption of margarine (Figure 5).

Clearly, these variables are not related, which illustrates the danger of assuming that correlation implies causation. While causation implies correlation, the reverse is not necessarily true.

Furthermore, even if a cause-and-effect relationship indeed exists between two phenomena, correlation alone cannot inform us about the direction of this relationship—it cannot tell us which is the cause and which is the effect. For example, in the 1970s and 1980s many studies were conducted that showed that students

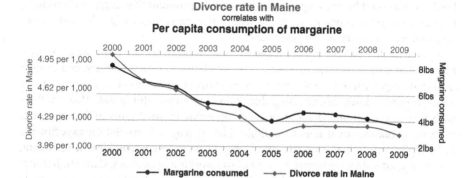

FIGURE 5 Graph showing the curious correlation between the divorce rate in Maine and margarine consumption between 2000 and 2009.

Source: Tyler Vigen / CC BY 4.0.

with higher self-esteem typically achieved better academic results. Building upon this observation, the government of California launched a multimillion-dollar program aimed at boosting students' self-esteem to promote better academic performance. The result was a failure (Baumeister et al., 2003). No one thought that perhaps it was good academic results that actually fostered high self-esteem. Furthermore, it turns out that self-esteem and academic results are simultaneously influenced by third variables, such as students' self-regulation skills—as discussed in this book—and the existence of a supportive family environment, as well as socioeconomic variables.

The preceding example of the unsuccessful implementation of an educational measure highlights the importance of not only consulting educational research but also interpreting it correctly when making decisions. This is particularly important given the number of variables that can influence student success. This vast number of variables often makes research conducted in the classroom—for example, to assess the effectiveness of a pedagogical method—challenging to compare. Thus, when a study contends that the use of digital devices (laptops or tablets) in the classroom has a negative effect on academic results, it is evident that other variables need to be considered: What educational level was the research conducted at? How were the devices used for educational purposes? What educational resources and infrastructure were available for their use? What training did the teachers receive on this matter? How motivated were the teachers to use these devices in the classroom? When so many variables come into play, the devil is in the details.

Moreover, it is imperative to be cautious about what we choose to read, because not all published studies meet the criteria of high quality. Some scientific journals employ more rigorous review processes than others, systems that assess the quality of studies based on whether the scientific method was applied correctly. Conversely, many publications lack any form of review process. In fact, books are a significant source of pseudoscience because most publishing companies prioritize their business interests over scientific rigor (which is completely understandable). To sell books, what could be more appealing than offering content that aligns with readers' cognitive biases? Ultimately, all of this means that we cannot assign the same scientific validity to everything we get to read.

On top of that, scientists are people too, and as such, we have our own cognitive biases. *Expectation bias*, for instance, is the tendency to believe, certify, and express data that align with one's own expectations or hypotheses regarding the outcome of an experiment, while disbelieving, discarding, or undervaluing data that conflicts with those expectations (Jeng, 2006). The scientific method aims to free scientists from these biases, but it is not infallible. That is why it is crucial for experiments to be replicated. Other scientists should repeat them to confirm similar results or, conversely, provide no evidence in favor of the working hypothesis. Only studies that have been successfully replicated, ideally multiple times, should earn the complete trust of those who want to base their decisions on them to implement changes in their classrooms.

Evidence-Informed Teaching

In the scientific literature within our field, it is quite common to come across disparate results—studies that demonstrate the effectiveness of a method and others that do not or even reflect quite the opposite (Clark & Mayer, 2016). In the introduction of this book, I pointed out that comparing educational methods is often futile because it all depends on the details, namely the multiple variables at play in each method. However, we tend to classify teaching methods based on one of their variables, and typically, it is not this variable that determines their effectiveness. For example, in project-based learning students ultimately create a product or organize an event that addresses a need, but this is not precisely what can make this method effective. The devil lies in the details, and these details must consider the students' characteristics, the purpose (learning goals), and the context. Thus, there is no one-size-fits-all recipe that is always effective. This is why, when we turn to educational research, we must differentiate between studies that inform us about the presumed effectiveness of one method compared to another and research that directly seeks to determine the common factors among methods that prove effective. Many of these factors have to do with how the brain learns.

In any case, the fact that there are no foolproof recipes for everything means that the teacher will always have the final say when it comes to adjusting methods to achieve the best results. And for this, it is crucial to be familiar with evidence-backed principles of learning. These are the "ingredients" that should never be missing from our "teaching recipes." In this sense, rather than talking about evidence-based teaching, we should discuss evidence-informed teaching. It is not about strictly applying specific methods that science has analyzed (in specific situations), but rather planning and adapting methods based on the particularities of the situation, with the guidance of what science can tell us about the factors that lead to better learning outcomes. Teaching will never cease to be an art, but it can be an art that grounds much of its practice in scientific knowledge.

Pseudoscientific Myths

To conclude, I would like to caution against the danger of confusing science with pseudoscience. Since scientific advances on how the brain develops and learns have reached the general public, multiple pseudoscientific myths have infiltrated education. They are called pseudoscientific myths because they are widely held ideas that seem to be supported by science but have arisen from the distortion or misinterpretation of scientific findings (Geake, 2008).

For example, the myth that attention spans only last for 30 minutes likely stems from an unfortunate interpretation of studies on vigilance—the kind of intense attention required from professionals like lifeguards, or airport security agents closely examining the contents of suitcases passing through X-ray machines. In fact, the concept of *attention* in scientific terms is quite different from the everyday meaning we assign to it.

Pseudoscientific myths are problematic because they can confuse us and lead us to make decisions and expend effort on practices that lack any evidence, even though we believe otherwise. They generally come with an opportunity cost, as we waste valuable time that could have been spent on more effective activities. They can also lead to financial losses and, at worst, have a negative impact on learning. The latter is the case with some methods of teaching reading, which are not only ineffective but also leave behind those children with fewer opportunities to learn to read behind (Castles et al., 2018).

Throughout this book, some of these pseudoscientific myths will appear in context. In addition, I have included an appendix at the end that reviews some of the most widely spread myths among the education community. I apologize in advance for any cognitive dissonance that this book may cause.

THE COGNITIVE PROCESSES OF LEARNING

Cognitive psychology emerged in the mid-20th century, inspired by the analogy that computational and information sciences suggested about the functioning of the brain. Motivated by the possibility of modeling the brain as an organ capable of encoding, manipulating, and preserving information, cognitive psychologists took the first steps to scientifically understand how human memory works.

If a computer could store words and images as ones and zeros, what kind of symbols would the brain use to represent the information it receives? If computers employed algorithms to manipulate information, what processes would the human mind undertake? Although today the computer analogy has been abandoned due to the significant differences revealed between the functioning of the brain and that of a computer, there is no doubt that memory uses mechanisms common to all human beings that can be deciphered and modeled.

The cognitive processes of learning are precisely the mechanisms involved in the processing of information reaching the brain through the senses, especially those related to how this information is encoded, stored, and subsequently retrieved. In this module, therefore, we will delve into how human memory works and what implications this has in the educational context. Thus, in addition to the foundations that cognitive psychology provides (and neurobiology, upon which it relies), the following chapters will also draw from research in developmental psychology, evolutionary psychology, and, of course, educational psychology.

Components of Memory

Multiple Memories

Although we commonly use the term "memorize" to refer to a very specific type of learning (one without understanding), the truth is that everything we learn, we learn through memory. Indeed, all our sensory experiences, perceptions, and actions reshape our brain, determining what we will later be able to perceive, remember, understand, think, and do. This property of our brain is called *memory*.

Memory is, therefore, the faculty that enables us to learn. However, we do not learn everything in the same way. There are several types of learning associated with different types of learning objects. For example, we do not learn how to ride a bike in the same way we learn about the causes of the French Revolution. Nor is it the same to retain information for a lifetime as it is to keep it in mind for just a few seconds to use it at that precise moment. In line with this, research has revealed that we have distinct types of memory that enable different types of learning and different uses of information. Indeed, memory is not a single skill but a set of skills dependent on distinct neural processes and structures. There is not just one memory but several memory systems (Squire, 2004). To begin with, evidence allows us to distinguish between sensory memory, short-term memory, and long-term memory.

Sensory memory acts as the gateway to the mind for all external stimuli we perceive through our senses (Cowan, 2008). Automatically and continuously, sensory memory encodes all incoming information and holds it for just a brief period—from fractions of a second to a few seconds—in a part of the mind separate from conscious perception. This process enables the brain to collect as much information as our senses can capture, to analyze it and decide what is worth processing consciously and what can be discarded. Thus, sensory memory reduces the operational cost associated with being aware of everything happening around us. It is important to note that, as we will see, everything that enters conscious awareness leaves traces in long-term memory, so it would be pointless to waste resources collecting irrelevant stimuli.

In essence, our senses are constantly receiving a wealth of information and sending it to the brain, even though we perceive only a small part of it. At this moment, you might not be aware of the force exerted by the ground or the seat you are sitting on against your feet or buttocks, counteracting gravity. Well, now you are. Sensory receptors have been picking up these stimuli while you were reading and have been recording them in sensory memory. By directing attention to them, you have transferred this information from sensory memory to short-term memory, which, as we will see later, is where the first fully conscious processing occurs.

Therefore, an important function of sensory memory is to enable our brain to analyze as much external information as possible, seeking outstanding stimuli that require an immediate response and demand our attention for our own benefit. This makes it possible, even when fully absorbed in reading this fascinating book, that if someone suddenly shouted "Fire!" our brain would capture it and compel us to focus on that stimulus, part of which we would still be able to hear because it would be available in our sensory memory. You have probably experienced a situation in which someone talked to you while you were focused on something else, and yet, one or two seconds later, you were able to recall what had been said and respond.

Another situation highlighting the role of sensory memory occurs when we move a lit sparkler around in the dark and perceive a fleeting trail of light tracing its path. Thanks to sensory memory, we can watch movies without noticing the empty space between each frame or generate a brief image of a dark room when it is instantly illuminated by lightning.

It should be noted that sensory memory is not a single entity; rather, we have sensory memory systems for each of our senses. The most extensively studied ones are those related to vision (iconic memory) and hearing (echoic memory).

Despite these interesting aspects, and while acknowledging its role as a precursor to conscious memory, sensory memory does not receive much attention from educational research. Hence, I will not dwell on it further. For our purposes, short-term memory and long-term memory are much more relevant.

Short-Term Memory and Long-Term Memory

Contrary to what we might think at first, short-term memory is not a repository for memories that are soon forgotten, such as what we had for breakfast this morning. Short-term memory, better known today as *working memory*, is the mental process by which we maintain and manipulate the information we are currently paying attention to (Gathercole, 2008). Although formally viewed as a process, it is useful to imagine it as a mental space where we place the information we are consciously aware of and work with it. To give you an idea, when someone asks us, "What are you thinking about?" or "What are you paying attention to?" they are technically asking, "What information is in your working memory right now?"

Working memory is critical for learning because it is the precursor to long-term memory: all the information we consciously learn must pass through it. Moreover, when we retrieve a memory or piece of knowledge from our long-term memory, we are precisely bringing it back into working memory. If I ask you to think of a giraffe, those images of a giraffe that were stored somewhere in your unconscious mind—in your long-term memory—have entered working memory and thus become conscious. Working memory is, therefore, the mental space where we place information we are thinking about, whether it comes from the environment, our memories and knowledge, or both at the same time.

If information from the environment leaves our working memory because we start paying attention to something else, but later we can still remember it without checking it again, that is because it "entered" long-term memory. In fact, almost everything we experience consciously leaves traces in long-term memory, which is why we perceive continuity in our lives even if we do not intend to remember everything that we do.

Long-term memory, therefore, allows us to retrieve information that we perceived previously and which we stopped paying attention to (Baddeley et al., 2015). It does not matter how long the information remains available, whether it is for years, days, or just minutes; long-term memory manifests whenever information can be retrieved from our mind after we stopped thinking about it—that is, after it left working memory. For example, we are likely to remember what we did this morning now, but in a few days we will probably forget it. Although these memories are only available for a few hours, the ability to retain them for that amount of time is due to long-term memory. After all, this is the type of memory we commonly refer to as *memory*.

Indeed, when we say things like "I have a very good memory" or "My memory fails me," we usually refer to long-term memory: the ability to store information about the events of our lives, as well as facts and ideas about the world around us, for varying lengths of time, or even for life.

Strictly speaking, the term *long-term memory* does not only refer to our ability to store memories and knowledge of what we consciously experience; it also includes our ability to learn motor skills (such as walking, tying shoelaces, or riding a bike) and cognitive procedures (such as reading or solving equations), as well as the ability to unconsciously form associations between objects and events or even to increase or decrease our sensitivity to environmental stimuli.

Indeed, long-term memory comprises various distinct systems, each consisting of various subsystems. There is not just one long-term memory (Squire, 2004).

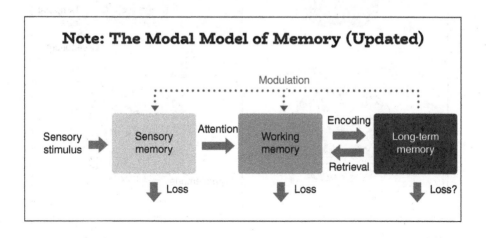

Note: The Modal Model of Memory (Updated)

The modal model is a way to represent the flow and processing of information through the various components of memory. While some aspects of this model, originally proposed by Atkinson and Shiffrin in 1968, have been challenged over time, its basic architecture with some modifications (as shown in the figure) continues to be influential and useful for understanding the processes of learning in the educational context. Therefore, this architecture is the foundation for our discussion in this book. It is worth noting that there are other equally valid models of memory.

Long-Term Memory Systems

In 1953, 27-year-old Henry Molaison underwent experimental surgery in the hope of alleviating the severe and continuous epileptic seizures he had suffered from since childhood. The surgeon removed a sizable portion of the temporal lobes of his brain (see Figure 1) because these regions seemed to be related to the origin of his seizures. The operation was a success, and Henry's epileptic seizures decreased significantly. Despite the aggressiveness of the procedure, he did not appear to have suffered any

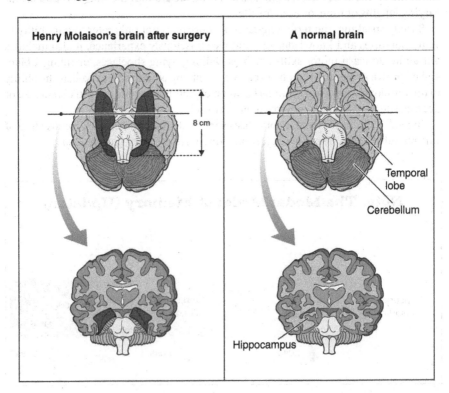

FIGURE 1   Extent of Henry Molaison's surgery compared to a complete, healthy brain.

alterations in his cognitive or motor functions: he spoke correctly and coherently, retained his knowledge, and had normal motor coordination. Everything seemed fine, except for one small detail—Henry could no longer form any new memories (Scoville & Milner, 1957).

Brenda Milner was a researcher who worked with Henry for many years after his surgery (Squire, 2009). Despite treating him almost daily, every time she left his room, even if only for a few minutes, Dr. Milner had to reintroduce herself and explain why she was there. Henry was trapped in the present. In technical terms, this is known as *anterograde amnesia.*

Henry retained many memories from the past, although he had mostly forgotten what had happened in the two years leading up to the surgery. That is, he also suffered from retrograde amnesia, but it was partial. On the other hand, he retained his knowledge about the world, and his vocabulary did not seem affected. Moreover, he could use his working memory normally. The problem was that as soon as he stopped paying attention to something, he just forgot it. Apparently, nothing was being recorded in his long-term memory, or he was unable to retrieve it from there. In essence, Henry could not generate new memories.

Nevertheless, studies by Milner and other researchers revealed that Henry could still learn certain things. For instance, he could learn new motor skills.

For days, Henry trained on a task that involved tracing a star with a pencil while looking at his drawing hand and the paper in a mirror (see Figure 2). This is not a straightforward task, as it can be quite puzzling initially. However, with practice,

FIGURE 2   Mirror tracing task.

one can improve this skill, and Henry responded to training like anyone his age. The catch was that every time he began a new practice session, he had no recollection of ever having done anything like it before (Corkin, 1968).

The fact that Henry could not create new memories yet could learn new skills supports the existence of at least two types of memory that depend on different anatomical structures. And Henry's case is not unique. In fact, several studies have shed light on the existence of different types of long-term memory, conducted in collaboration with individuals who, like Henry, suffered injuries to specific areas of their brains (Squire, 2004). Additionally, over the past 30 years, access to neuroimaging techniques, which allow us to visualize the relative activation of different brain regions in healthy individuals based on the tasks they perform, has also contributed to this knowledge (Poldrack, 2012).

Thus, cognitive psychologists today primarily distinguish between two types of long-term memory: the memory that enables us to store consciously perceived information through our senses, concerning the characteristics of our environment and the events in our lives, and the memory that changes our way of responding to stimuli. The former is a memory system that allows the explicit storage of information, while the latter consists of multiple systems derived from the ability to modulate, through experience, the neural circuits that control our responses.

These two types of memory are known as *explicit memory* and *implicit memory*, respectively. I will now delve a little deeper into them.

Explicit Memory

Explicit memory is responsible for creating and preserving representations of the world around us in the form of memories and knowledge (Roediger et al., 2008). It is a memory that is consciously generated, based on the information that enters our working memory through our senses. This is important because this type of memory cannot exist without us paying attention to the incoming sensory information. (The practice of putting on headphones and listening to a lesson while we sleep is not effective for learning.) Furthermore, the way to confirm that we have retained what we learned is by bringing it back into working memory (as illustrated earlier when I asked you to think of a giraffe).

Various pieces of evidence allow us to distinguish between two subtypes of explicit memory (Squire & Zola, 1998; Tulving, 2002): *episodic memory* and *semantic memory*. Episodic memory, also referred to as *autobiographical memory*, records memories of our daily life—that is, information linked to our experiences, whether they are as mundane as what, where, and with whom we had breakfast this morning, or more significant memories of life events. This type of memory always includes contextual references; memories are always linked to the places and moments when we experienced those events, and they come with a sense of "having been there." In contrast, semantic memory stores our knowledge about how the world is and how it works. This information does not typically include references to when or where we acquired it. For example, we may know what DNA is, but we may not necessarily remember when or where we learned it.

Both episodic and semantic memory contain associations of specific events and sensory information, especially images, sounds, smells, and the like. But semantic memory also contains information in the form of meanings. Indeed, when asked, "What is music?" we immediately know the answer, without needing to verbalize it in any way. In fact, it can be difficult to put it into words, yet we know what it is. Much of what we store in our semantic memory is in the form of meanings. In other words, ideas and concepts belong to semantic memory and result from how information is organized in memory. (I will explore this in more depth in the next chapter.)

The division between episodic memory and semantic memory is not as clear-cut as the division between explicit memory and implicit memory. In fact, one can hardly operate without the other (Greenberg & Verfaellie, 2010). Episodic memories are loaded with semantic information, and semantic information had to come from episodic information in the first place. Nevertheless, there is evidence that, from a functional perspective, episodic memory and semantic memory are not exactly the same. For example, individuals who, because of brain injury, suffer from retrograde amnesia (forgetting things prior to the injury) tend to have their episodic memory more affected than their semantic memory (Bayley et al., 2006; Manns et al., 2003). On the other hand, there are also descriptions of individuals with the opposite condition, that is, with reasonably intact episodic memory but severe losses of conceptual knowledge, known as *semantic dementia* (Hodges & Patterson, 2007).

Implicit Memory

From an evolutionary perspective, learning is an extraordinary skill. It enables us to adapt our behavior to diverse and changing environments, make predictions to guide our decisions, develop skills beneficial to us, and come up with creative solutions to interact with our surroundings. The ability to learn provides clear advantages to individuals who possess it. It is no wonder that all animals exhibit some form of learning capability. There is even evidence that unicellular organisms like amoebas can associate stimuli (De la Fuente et al., 2019). Undoubtedly, humans have developed a unique capability for learning, distinguished by the exceptional nature of our explicit memory. But we also have other memory systems of more primitive origin. These memory systems fall under what we call *implicit memory* and include all forms of learning that we can acquire through experience without needing to be consciously aware of it. This means that implicit memory does not follow the modal model because, unlike explicit memory, it does not require conscious recollection.

In this regard, implicit memory systems are the ones that enable us to modulate our automatic responses to stimuli. While explicit memory requires voluntary cognitive effort for retrieval, implicit memory operates independently of our will when triggered by the appropriate stimuli. In other words, when these memory systems learn something, we can hardly avoid acting or reacting as they have learned.

Among the implicit memory systems we know, the one most relevant to the goals and perspective of this book is procedural memory. Classical conditioning and emotional conditioning are also of interest. I will discuss them next.

Procedural Memory

Procedural memory refers to our ability to learn all sorts of skills (Foerde & Poldrack, 2009). It is a type of implicit memory because, as Henry Molaison and other patients who could not form new memories have taught us, it operates even when no conscious recollection of the experiences that lead to its development exists. Nor does it require making a conscious effort to retrieve it. When we ride a bike or tie our shoelaces, we do not really need to explicitly remember what to do—we simply do it. In fact, it would be quite challenging to explain how we get to coordinate our muscle movements for all the actions these skills require. The best way to teach them is by showing how it is done, and the best way to learn them is through practice.

Hitting a tennis ball that is coming at you with a racket involves a multitude of calculations that we clearly are not consciously aware of when we play tennis. Our brain takes care of those calculations, and through practice, it fine-tunes its precision. Of course, this does not mean that improving our skills through conscious strategies is impossible. In fact, we often start with explicit instructions that we apply consciously to develop certain skills (like when we learn to drive). However, these conscious strategies are insufficient without our implicit learning capability, which progressively makes them automatic and unconscious. Indeed, conscious strategies can be counterproductive; sometimes it is better not to think about how we do what we do.

Skills learning is also implicit in the sense that we cannot be sure we retain them until we put them into practice. If it has been a while since you have practiced something (like riding a bike), how can you be sure you will still do it well? The only way is to do it. This is because this type of knowledge manifests itself through changes in our performance and behavior. And, as noted earlier, it can show up even when we do not intend it to, provided the right stimulus is present in the environment. For example, try looking at the following word without reading it:

IMPOSSIBLE

Indeed, reading is procedural knowledge, and as such, it is impossible to avoid doing it when we see words (if we are expert readers).

The previous example also illustrates that procedural memory is not limited to learning motor skills like riding a bike, dancing, or playing tennis; it also includes cognitive skills such as reading or playing chess. Both types of skills are often, to some extent, simultaneously necessary to perform any action.

One significant difference between procedural memory and explicit memory is that the latter can generate learning immediately, while the former is usually slow and gradual (Ullman, 2016). Developing a skill requires a substantial amount of practice sessions, while learning new explicit information often occurs after just one exposure.

Classical Conditioning and Emotional Conditioning

Another type of implicit memory system that is of interest is classical conditioning. You have likely heard about Pavlov's dogs. In his famous—and rather cruel—experiments, Ivan Pavlov (1927) demonstrated that a stimulus initially devoid of meaning to an individual (the sound of a bell) can elicit the same response as another stimulus with inherent significance (a plate of food) when both stimuli are presented simultaneously on various occasions. For example, if we ring a bell just before feeding a dog and repeat this process several times, the dog will eventually associate the bell with mealtime and salivate as soon as it hears it, as if it had already seen the food.

Humans also exhibit this type of learning, and we know that it is independent of conscious recollection because it happens even when we cannot remember why a particular stimulus triggers a particular reaction. In fact, emotional conditioning is a form of classical conditioning, in which a stimulus is associated with an emotional response (often fear) because it was part of an experience that evoked those emotions (Phelps, 2006). Unlike classical conditioning, in this case the link between stimulus and response can be established through a single experience if the experienced emotion is very intense. Conversely, erasing this association requires a slow and gradual process, as is often the case when overcoming the fear of driving after a car accident, for example (Hofmann, 2008).

Since the early 20th century, we have known that learning by conditioning operates independently of explicit learning, although they interact under normal conditions. Specifically, the first evidence comes from a small, somewhat cruel experiment (unthinkable today) reported by Swiss neurologist Édouard Claparède in 1911. Claparède worked with a patient who had anterograde amnesia, much like Henry Molaison. This means she retained her knowledge and most of her memories but was unable to form new memories. Thus, Claparède had to introduce himself every time he visited her, which he always did by shaking her hand. On one occasion, the neurologist concealed a pin in his hand and, upon greeting her, pricked her. The next day, Claparède visited her again, and even though she did not recognize him, when the doctor offered his hand, the patient hesitated for the first time. When asked about her reluctance, the patient could not exactly explain why she was wary of shaking his hand, but she sensed it would hurt.

More elaborate—and ethical—studies involving participants have confirmed that our brains have mechanisms dedicated to learning which stimuli should elicit emotional responses when we encounter them again (e.g., Bechara et al., 1995). These mechanisms operate independently of conscious recollection, although in healthy individuals they work in coordination. In fact, we now know that emotional conditioning learning allows our brain to activate physiological and motor responses tenths of a second before we consciously perceive the stimulus that triggered them. This is a crucial self-preservation mechanism in situations that threaten our well-being and require a rapid response (LeDoux, 2000).

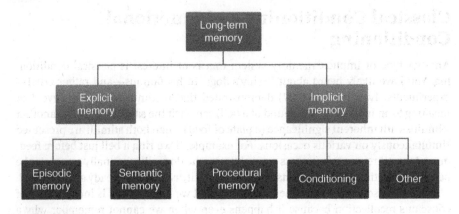

FIGURE 3   Types of long-term memory.

   While there are other systems of implicit memory, the most relevant ones for the objectives of this book have already been presented. Therefore, this chapter concludes here. From this point onward, I will examine the memory components that are of greater interest to us as teachers.

   The next four chapters describe how semantic memory is organized and the processes involved in learning the type of knowledge it contains. Chapter 6 discusses working memory, as it is a key process for learning. Finally, the last chapter of this section focuses on skills learning, especially cognitive skills targeted by education, such as problem-solving, critical analysis, or creativity. The remainder of the book continues to address topics regarding the types of memory outlined here (Figure 3). That is why I introduced them before inviting you to delve into the fascinating intricacies of learning, which follow.

Organization
of Memory

2.2

Analogies of Human Memory

Back in ancient Greece, Plato described memory as a wax tablet upon which our experiences leave marks inscribed to varying depths. In the centuries that followed, memory was likened to various data storage systems, from a vast library to the computer hard drives that emerged in the mid-20th century. Throughout history, various analogies have been proposed to explain how our memory functions. However, all of them diverge significantly from what we now know about how memory truly works.

To begin with, our memory is nothing like the empty shelves of a library that can be filled with new books. If we use this analogy, imagine the shelves are made up of the books themselves—the knowledge we already possess constitutes the base on which we can place new knowledge.

Indeed, evidence suggests that memory is organized in such a way that our memories and knowledge form networks where each element connects to those with which it shares semantic meaning. To incorporate new information, we must connect it to existing knowledge structures with which it shares a semantic relationship.

A Memory Model

This theoretical model of how long-term memory is organized is supported by a wealth of evidence from research in cognitive and developmental psychology, as well as neurobiology (Carpenter, 2001). Indeed, it is a way of understanding memory that proves especially useful for making sense of phenomena related to learning.

However, this idea is not new. As early as the beginning of the 20th century, the Russian psychologist Lev Vygotsky (1896–1934) suggested that people connect what they learn to what they already know, interpreting new information through the lens of their prior knowledge. In similar fashion, the Swiss psychologist Jean Piaget (1896–1980) developed his constructivist theory of learning in the mid-20th century, which posited that people rely on their prior knowledge to acquire new knowledge and, in doing so, adapt the incoming information to the structures formed by preexisting knowledge.

In 1932, the British psychologist Frederic Bartlett (1886–1969) published a famous experimental work in his book *Remembering*, where he described how people's prior knowledge determines the way in which they remember the new things they learn. Specifically, he analyzed how a group of English students (Bartlett was a professor at the University of Cambridge) remembered a story from Native American folklore after reading and attempting to memorize it. Rather than remembering the story as it was, the study participants reconstructed the story to fit their cultural assumptions and omitted aspects that did not align with their knowledge. As a result of this and many other studies, Bartlett developed his theory of *schemas*—mental structures that organize our knowledge by connecting it through relationships of meaning and determine the assimilation of new knowledge. In summary, Bartlett hypothesized that our schemas form the base on which we incorporate new information, distorting it to better fit these structures.

Prior Knowledge

It is easy to see how our prior knowledge influences our capability to learn. For example, read the following list of cities once. Then close your eyes and try to remember as many as you can, regardless of the order:

Paris, Rome, Berlin, London, Madrid, Amsterdam, Brussels

Now, do the same with these other cities:

Honiara, Yamoussoukro, Naypyidaw, Vientiane, Lilongwe, Melekeok, Bloemfontein

Your prior knowledge about the first cities will have allowed you to remember them easily. You may have even made connections of meaning between them, such as the fact that they are all capitals of Western European countries. In contrast, the second list of cities would have been much harder to remember, even though they are also capitals of countries worldwide. Their names may be entirely new to you, and you may not even know their geographic locations. If you do not know anything about them, it will be more challenging to remember them—not being able to relate new information to prior knowledge makes it very difficult to remember. In fact, you may have tried to link the unfamiliar name of some city to a more familiar word in the hope of remembering it better. This is because most mnemonic strategies (memorization strategies) involve connecting new information to prior knowledge. These strategies are based precisely on the model we use to explain how our memory is organized and constructed.

Moreover, a particularly important consequence of this model of learning—based on linking new information to existing knowledge—quickly comes to light: each element we incorporate into a network or schema becomes a new base for connecting more elements related to that schema. In other words, the more meaningful the knowledge (connected by relationships of meaning) we have about something, the more new information we can acquire related to it, and the more new ideas we can build by connecting the pieces of knowledge we have. The more we know, the more we can learn. This is why one of the most significant differences among students lies in the knowledge they bring to the classroom.

Multiple studies have provided evidence of how individuals with extensive knowledge in a particular area can remember many more new things related to that field after a given study time. For example, expert chess players can recall all the positions of the pieces on a chessboard that they have seen for five seconds, while novice players can typically recall only about eight pieces (Chase & Simon, 1973). Likewise, expert technicians can recall the components in electronic circuit diagrams better than nonexperts at a glance (Egan & Schwartz, 1979), and baseball experts can recall more information about an informative text about this sport than people with little knowledge of it (Spilich et al., 1979).

Making Connections

We learn by connecting new information to our prior knowledge, and the connections we can make are of a semantic nature—relationships of meaning that arise from experience. These connections occur when we realize that the learning object shares properties, contexts, or cause-and-effect relationships, among others, with our prior knowledge. Therefore, if I tell you that Bloemfontein, one of the cities in the second list from the previous exercise, is one of South Africa's capitals (that's right, South Africa has three capitals), renowned for its rose festival, and the hometown of J.R.R. Tolkien, author of *The Lord of the Rings*, the likelihood of remembering it next time is much higher. Of course, you may need to find connections between the city's name and other words you know if you not only want to recognize it in a list but also want to be able to retrieve its name.

Since prior knowledge constitutes the base on which we learn new things, trying to learn something without first having learned its fundamentals proves futile. When someone explains something to us that we do not understand, it is because we cannot locate the related prior knowledge to connect with that information. Sometimes we simply do not have it; at other times, however, we may have it but do not find it because we fail to identify its relationship with the information we are receiving. For example, read the following passage once, close your eyes, and try to remember as many details as possible:

> First, we will arrange it into two groups. We will proceed with one and then the other to avoid irreversible problems. The products to use will vary depending on the group. It is also important that the temperature is the right one. The time used will determine the results. It is essential to remove it immediately when finished because if it is left sitting, we will have to start over.
>
> (adapted from Bransford & Johnson, 1972)

You may have found it difficult to recall the details of the passage. But what if I told you that the title of this paragraph is "Doing the Laundry"? Now you can likely remember many more things about it because you can use your prior knowledge, connect it to the passage through relationships of meaning, and recall it better. As you can see, the problem you had in remembering the passage when you did not know the title was not that you lacked prior knowledge about it; the problem was that you had not activated it because you did not see what relationship it bore to the text. Activating relevant prior knowledge is crucial for creating the connections that lead to learning.

Indeed, learning occurs when we activate relevant prior knowledge and connect it to the learning object. The more connections we make, the more robust the learning will be, and it will be easier to retrieve when needed because more diverse contexts will activate it.

Therefore, a new question arises: How can we promote connections between prior knowledge and new information?

Levels of Processing Theory

In 1973, Thomas Hyde and James Jenkins examined whether the explicit intention to remember something had any effect on our ability to recall it—that is, whether the wish to remember something, without consciously using memorization strategies, would lead our brain to remember it better. To study this, a list of words was played to two groups of participants. One group was informed that after hearing the words, they would take a test to see how many they could recall; the other group was not informed, so the test would be a surprise. However, to prevent the group that had been informed about the subsequent test from employing memorization strategies, the researchers asked all participants to engage in various mental tasks with the words as they heard them: either to detect the occurrence of certain letters in the words or to rate the degree of pleasantness or unpleasantness of their meanings.

The results of the study showed that there were no significant differences between the group that knew their memory would be evaluated and the group that did not. Both groups recalled the same number of words on average. However, the researchers noticed something very interesting: in both groups, participants remembered many more words from the set they had processed in terms of meaning (those that had been rated as to their pleasantness or unpleasantness) than from the set they had analyzed trying to detect whether certain letters occurred, without thinking about their meaning.

What happened in that experiment was not exceptional; it had been observed by other researchers previously and has since been replicated in countless experiments (in fact, it is very easy to replicate in informal situations). This remarkable phenomenon led Fergus Craik and Robert Lockhart to propose their *levels of processing* model

(Craik & Lockhart, 1972), which can be summarized as follows: the more deeply we process information in terms of meaning, the more firmly it is rooted in our memory. In other words, we learn what we think about in terms of meaning. Or, as Daniel Willingham (2009) puts it more poetically, "Memory is the residue of thought."

In essence, Craik and Lockhart's idea is closely related to the model of memory and learning discussed earlier: thinking about something in terms of its meaning involves associating new information to our prior knowledge. After all, making sense of something involves connecting it to the knowledge we already have. Indeed, ideas only make sense to us in light of our prior knowledge. The more relationships we establish with our prior knowledge while reflecting on the learning object, the more solid its assimilation will be.

Note: Learning by Thinking

The following exercise is an illustrative example of what it means to think about the learning object to enhance its assimilation:

Draw a $1 bill from memory.

Most people have seen a $1 bill many times, but if asked to reproduce it from memory, they can only draw two or three details correctly. They would likely say, "I've seen it hundreds of times, but I've never really paid attention." By "paying attention" they mean that they have never really thought about its appearance or looked for relationships between the elements on it and between these elements and their prior knowledge. Naturally, they have not done so because to use these banknotes, they only need to recognize its overall aspect, which is quite different from being able to reproduce it.

In any case, this illustrates how seeing or hearing something, even if many times, does not guarantee that we will remember it well, whereas thinking and reflecting on it improves our ability to remember it.

Another good example is when we want to remember a phone number. What we often do is repeat it many times in our mind, but no matter how much we repeat it, once we have used it, we usually forget it. Mere repetition is not enough. If we want the number to remain in our memory, even after we have stopped paying attention to it, then we must actively think about the number and look for patterns that are familiar to us or establish connections between the digits.

The kind of information processing that leads to better learning can even be observed in our brain in real time using functional magnetic resonance imaging (fMRI) techniques. These techniques show the specific parts of the brain that are activated over a threshold during a particular mental activity. In this case, it has been observed that when words are processed in terms of meaning (as in the earlier experiment), the frontal region of the brain is highly activated. In contrast, when words are processed superficially, such as counting how many letters they contain, the activation is much lower (Buckner & Koutstaal, 1998). In fact, it is possible to predict the likelihood that a stimulus will be remembered later based on the degree of activation in the frontal region of the brain (Brewer et al., 1998).

Active Learning

The simple yet powerful idea that emphasizes the importance of students actively seeking meaning in what they are learning, trying to relate it to their prior knowledge, reflecting on its implications for what they already know, and ultimately, thinking about it forms the basis of what is known as *active learning*.

Active learning is often confused with educational practices in which the student "does things"—or what is known as *learning by doing*. But active learning could be better defined as *learning by thinking*. It encompasses any learning experience in which the student actively thinks about the learning object, seeking meaning and comparing it with their prior knowledge (Prince, 2004).

In this regard, giving students a lecture or something to read can be a method of active learning provided that they actively think about what is being explained or read. However, since these instructional methods do not guarantee that this will happen (as it often depends almost exclusively on the student), they are not formally viewed as active learning methods. Similarly, activities where students "do things," such as conducting experiments in the laboratory, may not be active learning if students can get away without thinking about what they are doing (such as when they simply follow a set of instructions without needing to understand what they are doing). In that case, they will hardly learn anything.

Therefore, any active learning practice initiated by the teacher must include activities that ensure that students will be thinking about what they are learning. This is an important distinction between teaching and helping to learn.

The superiority of active learning methods is well documented in educational research, and the best results are obtained when the teacher guides the experiences (which can certainly include explicit or demonstrative explanations) and directs the reasoning and reflection of the students. When this reasoning occurs in a group setting, where students are given the opportunity to share, compare, and discuss their ideas with their peers and the teacher in a relaxed environment, the positive effects on learning are also significant.

In short, to learn more and better, we must engage in activities that lead us to relate what we are learning to our prior knowledge.

Note: Constructivism

Constructivism is not a teaching and learning methodology; instead, it is a psychological (and previously philosophical) theory about how people learn. The theory posits that learning involves building upon our prior knowledge, and this process determines how we acquire new knowledge. A large body of scientific evidence in support of constructivism has accumulated over the last few decades, and it now constitutes a basic model of cognitive psychology on how we learn. Nonetheless, constructivism does not aim to define teaching methods; it only explains how our minds behave in response to an experience, whatever it may be, from which we ultimately gain learning.

Thus, constructivism as a theory of learning should not be confused with so-called *constructivist teaching methodologies* that claim that students should construct knowledge through discovery rather than explicit teaching (Mayer, 2009). This has nothing to do with constructivism as a theory of learning, which merely informs us about the processes occurring in the student's mind for learning to take place—a connection between prior knowledge and new information, fostered by the effort to make it meaningful.

Nevertheless, understanding the constructivist nature of learning can guide our teaching practices to enhance their effectiveness. To begin with, we should assume that our students are not blank slates but come to our classes with knowledge about what they will learn, and at best, they will use it to make sense of new information. That is precisely what we should promote to be consistent with the nature of learning: students relating what they are learning to the knowledge they already have and that is relevant to the learning object. When students can connect what they are learning with what they already know, they learn more effectively (Bransford & Johnson, 1972).

Activating Prior Knowledge

For students to relate what they are learning to what they already know, they need to activate their prior knowledge, specifically those pieces of knowledge that are most relevant to the learning task at hand. However, despite some students doing this spontaneously in response to any type of activity, even in a purely expository class, most of them tend not to bring their prior knowledge to the learning task if the appropriate conditions are not in place. That is why it is critical to engage in activities that explicitly aim to help them activate their prior knowledge so that they can build new knowledge upon it (Gick & Holyoak, 1980).

For instance, posing questions that mobilize their prior knowledge helps students use their existing knowledge to enhance their learning (Martin & Pressley, 1991).

However, starting the class with one or two questions about what they know about the topic may not be sufficient. It is worth going one step further and presenting them with a familiar situation in which the learning object is at play, even if they are not yet aware of it. This situation can be used to ask them, through questions or problems, to express their ideas and, ideally, share and discuss them with their peers. It is important that the questions asked are not just factual but force students to use and apply their ideas to answer them.

Devoting an entire class session to an exercise like this may seem like a waste of time, but evidence suggests that investing time in activating prior knowledge promotes the acquisition of new knowledge much more effectively than not doing so (Peeck et al., 1982). We can choose to use our time in class to teach students as much as possible, or we may use it to help them learn as much as possible.

Assessment of Prior Knowledge

Given that prior knowledge forms the foundation upon which students will build new knowledge, it is clear that assessing what knowledge they possess when starting a unit is critical for achieving meaningful learning. This is related to what we often call "adapting the lesson to the students' level." However, as we will see in later chapters, it is much more relevant than it seems at first sight.

Checking whether students have the required knowledge to begin a teaching unit is not the same as mobilizing their prior knowledge about what they will learn. Activating their ideas related to what they are going to learn to facilitate the connection with new ideas is one thing; ensuring that students possess the knowledge we assume they have is another. For example, if we are about to start a physics unit on the concept of *density*, we will likely use the concept of *matter* repeatedly, assuming it is known. However, many students may not consider gases as matter and may have difficulty understanding that gases can have mass or density (Séré, 1986). Similarly, students have serious difficulties in understanding and remembering the mechanism of photosynthesis correctly because their immaterial conception of gases makes it challenging to grasp the critical role of carbon dioxide as a substrate for sugar production by plants (Simpson & Arnold, 1982).

Therefore, it is highly beneficial to make an initial analysis of the learning goals and the planned activities to identify the knowledge that will be taken for granted and which will be crucial for constructing new learning. Once identified, we can run diagnostic tests to assess whether our students already possess this knowledge, and if not, engage them in preliminary activities to address it or, at the very least, be sufficiently ready to tackle the unit.

Learning with Understanding

When students lack the necessary prior knowledge or when they are not given time to activate or relate it to the learning object, their most natural reaction to the inevitable test at the end of the unit is to memorize it without giving it much meaning—that is, without making connections. Since, in general, students pass traditional exams by mechanically memorizing definitions or procedures described in the textbook, they also develop a culture of rote learning and get accustomed to memorizing facts or algorithms with a very low level of understanding. Because this knowledge barely connects with the students' prior knowledge and only associates with elements of the school context and the teaching unit (or the exam), it becomes "inert" knowledge. This type of knowledge cannot be activated in other contexts and is ultimately destined to be forgotten. Whether it disappears from long-term memory or simply gets lost there forever due to a lack of strong connections with other existing knowledge remains unclear. In any case, the student is unlikely to use it again, even in situations where it would be relevant.

Therefore, it is essential to devote time to delve into the learning object. Please note that here delving does not mean providing more and more details about the learning object. Delving means increasing depth, not breadth. That is, spending more time reasoning about the same concept in different contexts and giving the student the opportunity to transition from the concrete to the abstract, from a specific fact to multiple situations where the learning object is at play or applicable. It means connecting it to numerous prior knowledge schemas. The more prior knowledge is connected to the learning object, the stronger it roots in memory, and the easier it will be to retrieve it in the future because it will be activated by more different contexts.

Obviously, doing this requires more time than we usually dedicate to each of the topics covered in class, whether due to curriculum pressures, administrative demands, or other reasons. However, it is worth reflecting on this, especially in light of studies such as the one published by Schwartz and colleagues in 2008. In this study, which involved more than 8,000 sampled students, the group that had studied fewer topics but in greater depth (rather than breadth) in their high school science classes achieved better academic results in their first year of college science courses. The foundations that prior knowledge provides for building new knowledge are more robust when prior knowledge is well connected. Not surprisingly, in their conclusions, the authors of this study recommend that teachers use their judgment to reduce curriculum coverage in favor of a deeper mastery of certain topics.

Design of Activities

If we learn better what we think about, then there is something we must consider when designing learning activities: What will our students think about the most when they perform them? Often, we design activities without taking this into consideration. In my early years as a biology teacher, I once suggested to my students that they create PowerPoint presentations to explain the existence of blood groups, their biological basis, and their implications in blood donations to the rest of the class. I realized too late that my students had spent only a few minutes searching and copying information from the Internet, while they had dedicated hours to designing their presentations—searching for impactful images, and adding effects, animations, transitions, and various embellishments to each slide. Not surprisingly, they learned a lot about PowerPoint and very little about blood groups, as became evident when I asked them questions during their presentations. If my goal had been for them to learn how to use PowerPoint, I would have been pleased, but that was not the case.

When designing a lesson or activity, it is advisable to start by clearly defining the learning objectives—what we want students to have learned by the end of it. Next, we should determine how to check whether the students have achieved these objectives, that is, how we will assess their learning. With all of this in mind, we can then create the lesson or activity that will enable students to reach these goals. The design of the activity should ensure that students spend more time thinking about the learning goals—similar to how we will later ask them during assessment—and not get lost in superfluous details that only aim to provide context or structure to the activity. Being clear about this can make the difference between carrying out an activity successfully or failing in the attempt. The best activities are those that, during their development, lead students to think about the learning object, either because they must use it, analyze it, compare it, interpret it, discuss it, explain it in their own words, or perform any other action that requires giving it meaning. Moreover, these activities should help us teachers see that reasoning is happening. In other words, they should make students' thinking visible.

In the next chapter, I will outline other types of actions that should be promoted to help students learn in a way that makes learning more durable and transferable to new situations.

Memory Processes

2.3

A Virtually Infinite Warehouse

The distinguished Russian psychologist Alexander Luria described in 1968 the case of Solomon Shereshevsky, a man with a prodigious memory whom Luria studied for 30 years. Shereshevsky could literally remember everything he experienced, and in great detail. In his studies, Luria tested him using random lists of over 70 words, numbers, meaningless syllables, or sounds, among others. Shereshevsky would listen to them just once and effortlessly repeat them. Furthermore, if Luria asked him to recite them days, months, or even years later, he did so without difficulty. In Luria's words, his memory seemed to have no limits, neither in terms of space nor time.

The capacity of our long-term memory is practically infinite; it is likely prepared to retain the memories of all our life experiences. If this does not seem to be the case for most people, it is probably due to a matter of biological efficiency. We do not need to remember everything to survive, so evolution may have selected individuals with, let's say, sufficient memory. It is worth noting that Shereshevsky suffered from various cognitive issues due to his condition.

However, while the ability to accumulate a lot of information may seem like a great advantage, it also has a downside: the more information we store, the more difficult it can be to find a specific detail and retrieve it when needed. Practically speaking, we cannot claim to have learned something if we do not have the ability to retrieve it from memory.

Retrieving What Has Been Learned

The ease with which a memory can be retrieved from our mind allows us to gauge various "levels of remembering" for a piece of information.

- The lowest level of remembering is likely to be that which occurs in situations of *familiarity*, when we say that something "sounds familiar." We believe we have seen it before, but we do not know when or where. We have no memories of the event where we first encountered it.

FIGURE 1   The three key processes of memory.

- At a higher level, there is *recognition*, which occurs when we are aware that we know something but are unable to recall it spontaneously. For example, when we cannot remember an actor's name but can confirm it when someone else mentions it.

- The next level up is *cued recall*, which occurs when we can retrieve a memory if given the appropriate clues to help us find it in our memory. For example, when shown the picture of an actor, all it takes for a person to remember their name is being given the first letter of their first and last names.

- Finally, the most difficult level of retrieval is *free recall*, where we can retrieve information based on a single cue, such as when that person is only shown the picture of the actor.

While this gradation may not apply in all cases, it allows us to appreciate the difference between having something in memory and being able to retrieve it.

Interestingly, it is possible for a memory to be well consolidated in our memory, allowing us to retrieve it even many years after it was generated, and yet still be quite challenging to call it to mind. The opposite may also be true, meaning that we can easily retrieve a memory even if it is not firmly consolidated—which usually occurs, for example, right after it has been generated (Björk & Björk, 1992). This means that consolidation and retrieval are distinct processes. In fact, consolidation continues for minutes or hours after we have stopped paying attention to the stimulus that generated the memory. In contrast, retrieval is a conscious act that usually requires voluntary effort, although, as explained later, it can be facilitated (and even automated) through practice.

In summary, when we talk about learning, it is critical to understand that learning must involve three processes (Figure 1): getting information into the memory system (encoding), retaining it (consolidation and storage), and being able to call it to mind later (retrieval).

In fact, what we assess in school is the students' ability to retrieve and demonstrate what they have learned—how else could we evaluate learning? And yet, we hardly devote time to this process in the classroom. Most of the time is spent on encoding—that is, getting students to acquire information.

Retrieval Practice

It is obvious to us all that to learn to ride a bike, you must practice riding a bike. The same is true for most procedural knowledge; learning requires practice. However, when it comes to learning facts and concepts, what should we practice? The common belief is that by simply paying attention to the information that is being provided, we will assimilate it and be able to retrieve it later. Big mistake. What we ask students to demonstrate in the exam is not that they can encode information but that they can retrieve it from their long-term memory—an aspect that is often overlooked in practice.

Interestingly, cognitive and educational research has provided substantial evidence suggesting that practicing the retrieval of learned information makes us learn it better (Karpicke & Roediger, 2008). At the very least, it improves our ability to retrieve it again later, allowing us to demonstrate that we know it.

Several studies indicate that after a study session, better results are achieved in a subsequent test when a retrieval session follows, as opposed to dedicating the second session to restudying the material (Rowland, 2014). That is, engaging in a study session followed by retrieval is more beneficial for memory than engaging in a study session followed by restudying. Figure 2 shows the results obtained in the two types of learning sessions, serving as just one example from numerous studies that have replicated this phenomenon.

However, few students engage in spontaneous retrieval practice, and even fewer believe that it enhances their learning. Most students use it as a means to "check if they know it." Unfortunately, surveys indicate that the majority of students do not use this strategy (Karpicke et al., 2009), and it is understandable that they do not.

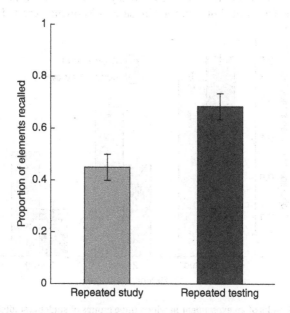

FIGURE 2   Results of a test consisting of inferential questions conducted one week after the learning sessions. In these sessions, one group studied the material once and then was repeatedly tested, while the other group restudied the material repeatedly (Adapted from Butler, 2010).

The first reason for this is that no one has taught them that this practice is more effective—generally, no one teaches students how to study. Therefore, students who have spontaneously developed this practice have a huge advantage without realizing it.

Second, practicing retrieval requires much more effort than simply rereading lesson materials; cognitively, explaining what has been learned is much more challenging than reading it again. It is not so much a matter of time as it is of mental effort.

Third, when practicing retrieval, especially the first few times, students may experience frustration, quickly realizing how little they know. Conversely, rereading the lesson gives them a pleasant feeling of knowing it (Karpicke, 2012), although this is merely an illusion—it is a sense of familiarity with the content, or, at best, recognition. These are perhaps the lowest levels of conscious knowledge that can exist. However, the leap from there to being able to retrieve the learned information to respond to exam questions is substantial. It is no wonder that many students, upon completing an exam or receiving their grades, do not understand why they did so poorly "if they knew it." The feeling of knowing something is quite different from being able to explain it or put it into practice.

Finally, in line with the points above, the practice of studying and restudying proves quite effective in the very short term. When we check what students have learned immediately after a study session, those who engaged in studying and restudying achieve even better results than those who studied and retrieved what they had learned. But if we do the check only two days or a week later, the results reverse (Figure 3). This fact contributes to the "illusion of knowing" created by restudying

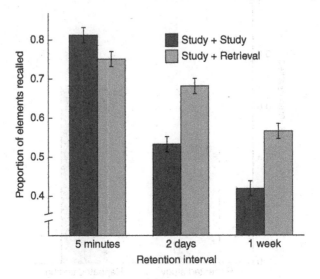

FIGURE 3   Results of an experiment in which three groups of students studied a text for seven minutes and then either restudied it or took a recall test to retrieve it. Each group took a final retention test on the material studied five minutes, two days, or one week after the learning activity, respectively (Roediger & Karpicke, 2006 / with permission of Sage Publications).

compared to practicing retrieval because the former seems more effective in the short term. Nevertheless, being able to remember something right after studying it does not necessarily guarantee that we can remember it later. Engaging in retrieval practice increases the likelihood that this will be the case.

Desirable Difficulties

Retrieval practice is more mentally demanding (and frustrating) than simply reread-ing the material, but the truth is that the more effort we put into trying to remem-ber what we have learned, the stronger the impact of this practice on our long-term memory (Björk, 1994). On the other hand, methods such as rereading, underlining, or copying deceive us because, in the short term, they leave us with a satisfying feel-ing of having learned something (Karpicke, 2012). However, the problem is precisely that it is short-term learning. Retrieval is a challenging learning practice, but it leads to durable learning. In contrast, less demanding strategies such as rereading typically lead to short-term learning.

This principle is related to what prominent researchers in memory and learning Robert and Elizabeth Björk called *desirable difficulties*. In short, when we put what we have learned into practice, facing a series of specific circumstances that make it cognitively more challenging—though not impossible—will lead to better long-term learning (Björk & Björk, 2011). In this sense, retrieval poses cognitive challenges that we do not encounter if we simply "restudy." Moreover, when the effort we put into retrieving is greater, its effect on learning is also greater. It is as if the brain notices that what we are trying to remember is genuinely important (because we are putting in a lot of effort to retrieve it) and, therefore, reinforces our ability to retrieve it more quickly and with less effort next time.

Let's take a moment to think about learning a new language. People with a mod-erate level of proficiency often find it much easier to read and listen to a language than to write or speak it. The fluency developed while reading can create a false sense of overall fluency, which can turn into frustration when trying to express oneself verbally. However, just as the best way to solidify learning is not by repeating its assimilation but by trying to retrieve it, the most effective way to learn a language is unlikely to be through reading or listening. Naturally, we need to start there to learn, but when we can begin generating the language, whether by writing or speaking it, considerable progress occurs. Practicing writing, and especially speaking, is more demanding and can be frustrating, but this generative practice is highly effective in improving various aspects of learning a new language (Ullman & Lovelett, 2016).

What Happens When We Retrieve a Memory or Knowledge?

While the analogy of a library or a computer's hard drive is often used to explain how memory works, these analogies have their limitations. Among other things, human memory does not store or reproduce memories with the fidelity that books or computers do. Our memory only retains some details and then uses everything it has already linked to them, drawn from many other memories, to reconstruct complete memories. Indeed, memory is not reproductive but reconstructive.

Take a moment after reading this sentence and picture a white sports car in your mind. Now, imagine the same car in different colors (e.g., red, black, yellow, green). It's easy, right? Our memory can combine various elements to create a single image in our mind. Not only can we do it voluntarily through what is called *imagination*, but we also do it involuntarily all the time with our memories.

To make the memory–library analogy more accurate, we should think of its books not as complete memories but rather as documents, each with a single piece of information. Therefore, to retrieve a complete memory, we need to consult several books at once and reconstruct it using all the data. The pattern of connections between these books is what truly constitutes the memory.

But the set of books that make up a memory are not all shelved together in the same part of the library. They are scattered in different sections based on the type of data they contain (visual, auditory, etc.). Not only do they maintain connections among themselves, but rather, as noted earlier, new data must be linked to previous knowledge or memories. Therefore, each book is connected to many other books involved in other memories whose content is related.

According to our model, retrieving a memory requires activating only a set of fragments scattered throughout memory and connected by relationships of meaning to other fragments from previous or subsequent experiences. This has a natural consequence: the set of data that can be activated when retrieving a memory at various times may spontaneously change, causing our memory to vary without us realizing it. Thus, every time we retrieve a memory, it may come with new elements from other memories and lose some of the fragments that composed it.

Indeed, every time we activate a memory, all the other data in memory linked to it by relationships of meaning can also be activated and lead to a different reconstruction. These new elements of the memory can also be reinforced by simply being retrieved together and become a firmly established part of the memory. This is what typically happens with any of our memories and knowledge. That is why it is critical for retrieval practice to always seek feedback from a more reliable source than our memory: students should ensure (with the aid of the teacher, a book, or their notes, among other resources) that what they retrieve is faithful to the original learning. In fact, receiving this kind of feedback enhances the positive effect of retrieval practice (Roediger & Butler, 2011).

Retrieval Does Not Only Improve Factual Learning

One of the most fascinating aspects of retrieval practice is that it does not just improve factual learning (facts and data), as one might expect. Naturally, if what is practiced is the retrieval of knowledge of that type, such as the capitals of European countries or the parts of a cell, that learning will be enhanced. But retrieval practice can go much further.

Retrieving what has been learned encompasses a wide variety of practices, from reciting a poem to using a new concept or idea to solve a problem in a new context. In this sense, retrieval practice can promote learning with understanding and the ability to transfer knowledge—that is, the ability to use what has been learned in a new situation (Karpicke, 2012; Karpicke & Blunt, 2011; Butler, 2010; Carpenter 2012). This is because when students have to retrieve what they have learned by explaining it in their own words (not just repeating it word for word) or using it to solve problems, they are forced to give it structure and meaning, which means connecting it to other knowledge. In each retrieval episode of this kind, there is a new opportunity to integrate what has been learned into our meaningful knowledge schemes.

Retrieval practice also comes with other advantages, such as helping the student become aware of their learning weaknesses. And, of course, it also helps the teacher identify areas for improvement.

Methods for Practicing Retrieval

Several ways of practicing retrieval have been scientifically analyzed, and all of them have shown beneficial results. The general rule is that the more cognitive effort retrieval requires, the greater its impact on learning. This means that, typically, retrieval based on free recall has a greater impact than retrieval based on recognition (Carpenter & DeLosh, 2006). The more a student has to mobilize their knowledge to find an answer, the greater the benefit. Nonetheless, recognition-based practice, such as multiple-choice questions, is sufficient in providing significant and nonnegligible improvements (Smith & Karpicke, 2014).

Briefly reviewing what has been learned at the end of each lesson is a simple practice that has a significant impact, especially if it is done at the beginning of the next lesson. Although it may seem counterintuitive, retrieval practice is more effective when we have started to forget what we learned. When that happens, retrieval becomes more challenging, and as noted earlier, the greater the challenge, the more effective it typically becomes.

If the goal is to improve understanding and transfer, retrieval practice can involve activities in which students basically try to apply what was learned in new situations. In this scenario, the role of the teacher as a guide is critically important, since they can provide hints to help students see the connections between what they know and the new situation at hand. In general, applying what was learned is one of the most effective practices for consolidating learning, especially if it can be done in multiple different contexts. In the case of conceptual and procedural learning, this method significantly promotes understanding and transfer (Markant et al., 2016; Perkins & Salomon, 1992).

One of the most effective practices for reinforcing learning, which we often use but almost never to that end, is the assessment test (Roediger & Karpicke, 2006).

We typically assign two functions to assessment tests: a summative function (judging and certifying the degree of achievement of learning objectives by students) and a formative function (obtaining information about the student's situation regarding learning goals to make subsequent decisions to help them improve). The first is the function we assign most often, although it barely contributes to learning. The second, on the other hand, plays a critical role in learning because it allows teachers to provide feedback to students (or students to make decisions about their next steps). In addition, assessment tests have another direct function on learning that is often overlooked: they facilitate learning because they are based on retrieval. Thus, if properly designed, assessment tests may become very useful tools for learning.

Before taking this last statement literally, it should be noted that certain factors of assessment tests can undermine their potential as promoters of learning. First, if assessment tests have a significant weight in students' academic grades, they may be a source of anxiety for students and overshadow the didactic benefits the test might have. It is also true that if students have nothing at stake, their level of attention and involvement (or effort) may not be optimal. Therefore, it may be advisable to do more assessment tests (and more diverse) so that they become routine learning practices that cumulatively incorporate what has been taught in class and address the weaknesses of previous tests. Since there are many of them, each will have a relatively low weight in school grades (they will be low-stake tests). The idea is that students take these tests seriously enough—as they contribute to their final grade—but that the tests do not cause high levels of anxiety or solely focus students' attention on the grade.

In this regard, it is important that these tests be used to help students see where they need improvement. This is why feedback should focus on how to avoid making the same mistakes in the next test. One important consequence of this is that students must be aware that the assessment tests are cumulative, meaning that the same learning goals—especially those that are most challenging—will be assessed in multiple tests. Therefore, it is worth paying attention to feedback on mistakes to avoid repeating them the next time. (I delve further into these aspects in the chapters on feedback and assessment.)

Spaced Retrieval

Let me state this once again: the greater the cognitive difficulty of retrieving what was learned previously, the greater its effect on memory. This means that our ability to retrieve it the next time will be better. The degree of difficulty in retrieval practice can be modulated according to whether it is based on free recall, cued recall, or recognition. But there are also other factors that affect the level of difficulty associated with retrieval.

For example, I mentioned earlier that retrieval becomes more challenging when we have partially forgotten what we learned. In this sense, when retrieval practice is spread out over a period of time, the benefits for long-term learning are significant

(Karpicke & Roediger, 2007). In fact, spacing out learning sessions, whether devoted to retrieval or restudy, has positive effects in and of itself. Interestingly, the greater the interval between each successful retrieval attempt of the same material, the more effective it is in the long term. Figure 4 shows the results of a study in which three groups of subjects completed six learning sessions (with a test at the beginning of each one) and took an exam one month after the last session. The difference between each group was the delay between each learning session: less than a day, 1 day, or 30 days.

Other studies, such as the one by Budé et al. (2011), report that the same number and type of classes spaced out over time (distributed practice) produce better results in learning. Figure 5 shows the scores obtained by two groups of students in a statistics course that only differed in the intervals of time in between the classes: spread out over a time span of six months or massed over eight weeks.

Although spaced practice has a beneficial effect on its own, research also shows that if spaced practice sessions involve retrieval, its impact on learning is much greater than if they are dedicated to restudying (Carpenter et al., 2009).

Spaced practice obviously benefits from the repetition it entails, but its effect is related to the fact that spacing out study or practice sessions is much more effective than cramming them together. For example, studying for one hour each day for five days is preferable to studying for five consecutive hours. In other words, having shorter but more regular sessions is more effective than massing the practice in one

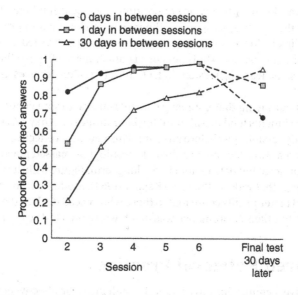

FIGURE 4 Proportion of questions answered correctly in the tests before each learning session (six sessions) and in the final exam conducted 30 days after the last session of each group. The learning sessions were spaced 0, 1, or 30 days apart (Adapted from Bahrick, 1979).

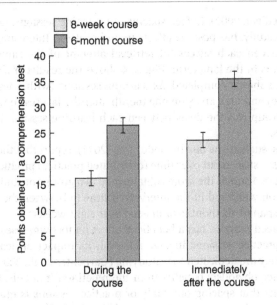

FIGURE 5   Points obtained in a comprehension test at the end of a statistics course spread over six months or eight weeks. The number of classes and type of activities conducted were the same (Adapted from Budé et al., 2011).

or a few sessions. Even with only one opportunity to review, it is better to leave some time between the learning session and the review session than to proceed with the review immediately. Moreover, trying to retrieve what was learned at the beginning of the next class (or the next study session) is much more effective than doing it at the end of the same learning session. In fact, the latter often deceives us (Soderstrom & Björk, 2015).

It goes without saying that not many students choose to spread out their practice sessions. Most students tend to wait until the last minute (i.e., they procrastinate) and mass their study sessions just before an exam. This may be an effective way of passing exams, but the learning does not last. Just like restudying, massed practice is effective in the very short term but detrimental in the long term. Figure 6 illustrates the results of an experiment that reflects this fact (Keppel, 1964). Students who crammed their study obtained better results compared to those who spaced it when the test occurred 24 hours later, but their performance was much worse on a test several days later.

Interleaved Retrieval Practice

Another relatively counterintuitive factor that enhances the effectiveness of retrieval practice, according to a solid body of evidence, is *interleaved practice* (Kang, 2016). It may seem strange, but to learn different things—which may cause confusion when they are related—it is better to combine them rather than focusing on mastering

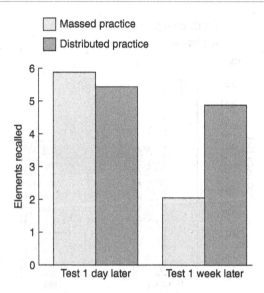

FIGURE 6 Number of elements recalled after a massed or spaced study session, in a test conducted one day or one week after the study session (Adapted from Keppel, 1964).

one before moving on to the next. Obviously, this is only possible when learning one thing does not depend on having previously learned the other—that is, when this learning can be done independently and in parallel.

For example, when students are learning to solve mathematical problems, it is better for them to mix various types of problems (involving different procedures) than concentrating on each type of problem before moving to the next. Again, interleaved practice may seem counterintuitive because it appears that we are learning less in the short term. Indeed, a student engaging in interleaved practice throughout a study session will feel like they have learned less than someone who mass practices each learning goal. However, research has clearly shown that this is an illusion: interleaved practice produces more durable and flexible learning. In other words, it provides much better outcomes in the medium to long term than concentrated (blocked) practice.

For example, in a study by Rohrer and Taylor (2007), students learned to calculate the volume of four geometric solids. For each solid, the activity included a tutorial on how to find its volume and four practice problems. One group of students worked on the figures one by one, first reading the corresponding tutorial and then solving the problems. The other group watched all four tutorials in a row and then randomly solved the 16 problems. One week later, the students took an exam on what they had learned. Figure 7 shows the students' performance with the exercises solved during the learning sessions and the results of the final test.

As shown in Figure 7, massed practice leads to higher short-term performance but results in poor long-term performance.

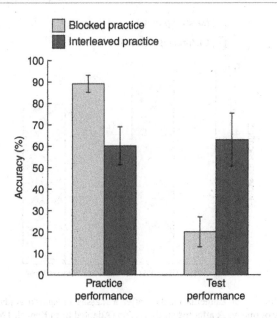

FIGURE 7 Results from the exercises completed during the learning sessions and in the final test of two groups of students whose learning was based on interleaved practice or blocked practice (Adapted from Rohrer & Taylor, 2007).

In this case, the beneficial effect of interleaved practice could be related to the degree of flexibility that this strategy provides to learning. This means that it facilitates abstraction and reduces reliance on what is learned to a single context. With interleaved retrieval, the benefit may come from not allowing the student to rely on irrelevant contexts when retrieving what was learned. In other words, when a student repeatedly practices exercises of the same type, they do not need to consider which strategy or knowledge to use. But if the exercises are mixed, they must contemplate which strategy or knowledge is appropriate. In fact, as explained in the previous chapter, reasoning about what we learn also contributes to solidifying learning (Willingham, 2008).

On the other hand, interleaved practice adds complexity to the learning task but in a beneficial way, thus increasing the cognitive effort needed to carry it out. This can improve learning in the long term according to the theoretical framework of "desirable difficulties." So, once again, interleaving makes learning more challenging in a way that it becomes more durable.

Both the effectiveness of spaced practice and interleaved practice may seem rather counterintuitive because, in the short term, it may appear that we are not learning as much as if we massed study. But again, this is an illusion; massed practice does indeed produce better short-term results, but only in the short term. In the long term, learning achieved through concentrated practice fades. In contrast, while spaced practice and interleaved practice may be frustrating at first, they produce much more robust and durable learning in the long term.

All of this leads us to realize what happens when academic performance is measured by exams that take place at a given time in the school year and represent the end of a specific learning process. Students tend to prepare for them by studying intensely in the hours leading up to the exam, and indeed, their performance can be good. But by studying this way, what is learned is quickly forgotten.

Repetition

I mentioned earlier that spaced practice benefits from the implicit repetition it involves. Surely you agree that one way to consolidate learning and make it last is through repetition. This is something intuitive, but is it really the case? Does repetition lead to more durable learning? The short answer to this question is: it depends. As we saw in the previous chapter, just because we have seen a $10 bill many times does not mean we will remember what it looks like.

First, talking about repetition by itself does not make much sense. The question is, repeating what? Repeating actions that strengthen our learning has additional effects on memory. But then, what are these actions?

As always, it depends on what we want to learn. If it is procedural learning (i.e., learning motor or cognitive skills), then we must practice it once we have been taught how to do it (and preferably receive feedback). This is obvious. But if we are to acquire factual knowledge (data, facts) and conceptual knowledge (ideas, concepts), the repetitive action that strengthens them in memory is not the restudy of them but their retrieval from memory once learned. Moreover, it is not only more effective to retrieve them but also to "use" them.

What does this mean? As you may recall, based on what we know about how learning occurs, learning involves making connections between prior knowledge and new information through relationships of meaning. The practical way to do this is by thinking about what we are learning. After all, thinking is interpreting new information in light of our prior knowledge.

In this respect, we think about what we are learning when we suggest examples from our own experiences, imagine the consequences of what we have learned on other facts or ideas, or compare it to other concepts or objects, analyzing their similarities and differences. We also think about what we are learning when we consider possible applications or try to solve problems based on this new knowledge and, of course, when we look for patterns and ultimately try to give meaning to what we have learned.

The action of thinking about what we are learning in terms of meaning is known in academia as *elaboration* (Cornford, 2002). Therefore, retrieval and elaboration are more effective for learning than repeated exposure or study—and, needless to say, repeated retrieval and elaboration are even more effective.

Nonetheless, it is not useful to overdo retrieval or elaboration—research indicates that repeating these actions during the same study session after having successfully performed them does not strengthen memory further. For example, in a study by Rohrer & Taylor (2006), 216 students learned a mathematical concept. Then, half of them solved three problems, and the other half solved those three and six more.

In both groups, 90% of the students demonstrated that they could solve that type of problem after doing the third one. Therefore, those who did six more problems in the same study session "overstudied."

A week later, all students took a test based on problems of the same type and no significant differences were found between the group that practiced with only three exercises and the one that practiced with nine. Four weeks later, they took another test and the same thing happened. In short, doing six additional exercises on the same concept during the same study session without interruption was a waste of time. Massed repetition is not very effective, especially when it has already been shown that the material has been learned.

In contrast, repetition is effective when it is spread out over time (spaced practice). If we let what we learned be forgotten a bit and then practice it again, learning will become more durable. Partly for a similar reason, practice done during the same session is also more effective when interleaved—that is, alternating the learning objects instead of focusing on each one persistently before moving on to the next.

In short, it is evident that repetition is essential for improving learning. However, not just any repetition will do, nor is it advisable to mass the repetitions since it is better to space them out and interleave them. Furthermore, we must remember that while repetition is effective for learning, it can be detrimental to motivation (Willingham, 2014).

Forgetting: Loss of Information or Inability to Retrieve it?

Our brain learns all the time from all our experiences and actions, whether we intended to learn or not. That is why, even if we did not mean to remember it, we can recall what we had for breakfast this morning. However, most of our experiences are irrelevant to our survival or goals and end up being forgotten sooner or later (do you remember what you had for dinner four days ago?).

Forgetting is a genuine problem in the school context. This is because it not only affects things we do not care to forget but also those we would like to retain for the rest of our lives, or at least for a few years.

But what about everything we forget? In other words, why do we forget? Surely, we can all agree that forgetting is not always a foregone conclusion. Sometimes we struggle to remember some information, but after a while it suddenly pops into our head. In this sense, one question we can ask is this: Does forgetting occur because the information we learned is no longer in our memory, or is it actually because we cannot find it in there and retrieve it? This question has been at the center of some of the most intense debates in the scientific community about the process of forgetting.

Indeed, there are researchers who believe that all our experiences leave traces in our memory that last forever, but that most of these traces are so weak that retrieving them spontaneously is too difficult. This would mean that everything we once learned, even if we think we have forgotten it, is lurking somewhere (or in several places) in our memory.

The first person to scientifically investigate memory and forgetting was German psychologist Hermann Ebbinghaus in the late 19th century. He observed that as soon as we learn something, we begin to forget it, especially during the first hours and then at a slower rate. But he also found that, in many cases, what seems completely forgotten must leave some kind of mark in memory because relearning it is significantly easier than not having learned it before. In other words, something that seems completely new to us because we have forgotten it is learned more quickly than if we had never learned it in the first place.

These results, which have been successfully replicated several times since, are more relevant when what was learned was part of a schema that gave it meaning—when learning was accompanied by understanding and linked to many other pieces of knowledge or memories (Arzi et al., 1986).

At a neurobiological level, there is evidence that the neuronal connections (synapses) formed during a learning process may be preserved even if they are no longer in use (Hofer et al., 2009), which could explain the greater ease of relearning something previously learned.

The current consensus on forgetting is that, in practice, we cannot determine if everything that has been in our memory is still there. It is assumed that some things can be forgotten through interference with other learning, by forming alternative connections that are stronger and have a greater retrieving power. Of course, it is also believed that disuse weakens the ability to retrieve what has been learned, ultimately leading to the inability to retrieve it. Whether disuse can even lead to complete erasure of what was learned is a more questionable matter, at least from the perspective of cognitive psychology.

Finally, in school settings, learning may be fragile, and this often depends on the fact that students tend to link what they learn to very few schemas—that is, very few contexts. Outside of these contexts, students cannot access their knowledge because the cues they receive do not relate to the ones they possess; they fail to see the connection between what they know and what is being asked or the context in which it is asked. Moreover, the strategies they usually use for studying (rereading, massing, etc.) make learning more prone to being forgotten.

Memory Is Not Like a Muscle

I would not like to conclude this chapter without addressing a widely held belief about how memory works. It involves comparing memory to a muscle—if we use it, it becomes stronger. This highly intuitive concept of memory has implications in educational practice, often used to justify the need to assess students through exams that require memorizing a lot of data (even if they may never need it again) or through activities like memorizing a poem. However, although there seems to be nothing wrong with this idea, it is inaccurate; memory does not work this way.

Indeed, memory is not a general skill that improves simply through training. As discussed in the previous chapter, memory becomes more effective as we acquire more knowledge—the more we know, the more we can learn. This knowledge needs to be imbued with meaning; it must be connected to previous ideas and become transferable. Memorizing without understanding or relying solely on *ad hoc* mnemonic connections does not strengthen memory as effectively. Such knowledge will not serve as a base for new knowledge and, in fact, might be quickly forgotten.

But gaining meaningful knowledge does not strengthen memory in general, either. For example, learning a lot of biology does not give me an advantage in learning geography. Memory is not like a single muscle that becomes stronger simply by acquiring meaningful knowledge about anything. A more accurate analogy is to envision memory as consisting of millions of muscles, each strengthened by acquiring specific knowledge connected through meaningful relationships. It is as if studying biology strengthens the muscles of the big toe in your left foot, and studying geography strengthens the neck muscles.

For example, it would seem logical, at first glance, that someone who has practiced enough to be able to remember any series of more than 70 random numbers after hearing them once should have a well-developed "memory muscle." In the early 1980s, the Swedish psychologist Anders Ericsson and colleagues trained a college student until he acquired this skill (Ericsson et al., 1980). Presented with lists of random numbers of up to 79 digits, the student was able to recall them after the sessions. However, if sequences of letters were used instead of numbers (even if only 10 different letters were used), he could only remember between 7 or 8 letters, like most people. So, the strength of memory is determined by the learning object itself.

Therefore, studying a lot and learning many things about biology with understanding makes us better at learning more biology (and, by extension, medicine, and anything we can connect through relationships of meaning with biology). However, we should not then expect to be better at, for example, learning constitutional law.

There is nothing wrong with wanting students to strengthen their ability to memorize in general. In fact, wanting our students to become better learners is commendable. What is wrong is believing they will improve their memory in general simply because we ask them to memorize facts.

If we genuinely want them to enhance their skills as learners in general, we need to explicitly teach them to be better learners—to use their ability to learn more effectively. Just as throwing a child into a pool does not guarantee they will learn to swim—and certainly not to swim effectively—students will not strengthen their ability to learn just because we force them to do so. Nevertheless, we can boost their effectiveness by teaching them study strategies and habits that apply to any subject. Some of these strategies have been discussed in this chapter, such as retrieval practice, spaced practice, and interleaving.

In conclusion, when we justify memorization as a means for students to become better learners, we should consider teaching study strategies and promoting certain habits. Instead of waiting for students to develop them spontaneously when faced with exams, those who learn these strategies and habits are more likely to succeed. Research indicates that a major difference between successful and less successful students is their self-regulatory learning strategies, which I address in the penultimate section of the book.

Reorganization of Memory

2.4

The Persistence of Ideas

A popular documentary on education from the late 1980s (Schneps & Sadler, 1988) begins by showing a graduation ceremony at Harvard, one of the world's most prestigious universities (Figure 1). It is a well-known fact that students who are admitted to this university and graduate from it are generally those who achieved excellent academic results during their school years. The documentary continues by randomly selecting 23 of these recently graduated students, who are then asked a simple question: Why do the seasons exist? In other words, why is it hot in summer and cold in winter?

This scientific question can be explained through an astronomical model that these students likely studied up to three times during their time in school

FIGURE 1 Frame from the documentary *A Private Universe* (Schneps & Sadler, 1988).

(in primary, middle, and high school), as summarized in Box 1. Given that these students were admitted to Harvard, it is highly likely that they excelled in school exams on basic astronomy. And yet 21 out of the 23 students interviewed in the documentary provided an incorrect answer that involved Earth's distance from the Sun:

> *"Earth's orbit is elliptical, and, therefore, it's summer when Earth is closer to the Sun and winter when it's further away."*

In short, these students gave the same intuitive explanation that they probably had before learning the scientific model of the seasons for the first time in school.

While the previous case is merely an anecdote, it serves as a paradigmatic example that illustrates how persistent the ideas people develop are when they genuinely try to make sense of what they learn, even if they are mistaken. It also reflects how, all too often, the way students approach knowledge in school does not result in meaningful learning that transforms their preconceptions. Indeed, students may learn to pass exams successfully but soon forget much of what they supposedly learned and revert to their initial conceptions (which, by the way, they had never abandoned). When these conceptions do not align with the formal knowledge of a discipline, we refer to them as *misconceptions* or *alternative* conceptions.

BOX 1   The scientific model of the seasons of the year.

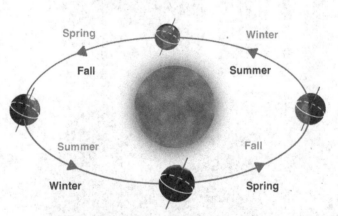

■ Northern Hemisphere
■ Southern Hemisphere

Earth's rotational axis is tilted relative to the planet's orbital plane around the Sun. This means that at one end of the orbit, the Northern Hemisphere is facing the Sun, receiving a greater amount of solar energy per unit of surface. At the opposite end of the orbit, the Southern Hemisphere gets more sunlight due to its orientation. In the intermediate points, both hemispheres receive the same amount of sunlight, experiencing spring and fall, respectively.

Learning Facts and Learning Concepts

As noted in the previous chapters, students come to the classroom with prior knowledge about what they will learn. Ideally, they will use this knowledge to make sense of new information and experiences. If this happens, they will connect new information with their prior knowledge—or some pieces of their prior knowledge in novel ways—and thus expand their *schemata*, that is, the networks of interconnected knowledge that shape concepts and memories. In short, they will have learned.

However, expanding schemata with new data (facts, contexts, emotions, etc.) is one thing, and reorganizing the set of relationships between these elements to give them a new meaning is quite another. This is what happens when students' ideas about a topic (such as the cause of the seasons) differ from the ideas we intend for them to learn. Changing these ideas is not as simple as adding new connections; it requires altering existing connections, and that is a slow and costly process. This is especially true when students' schemata are solid because there exist many connections between their elements derived from multiple experiences that have reinforced them. For example, the incorrect model of the cause of the seasons is strengthened by the numerous experiences students have regarding the effects of getting closer to or farther from a heat source, their perception of the Sun as the primary natural heat source on the planet, and the observation of solar system diagrams with exaggeratedly elliptical orbits in some textbooks, which imply that Earth is much farther from the Sun at one end of its orbit than at the other end. All these ideas connect to form a very solid and consistent conception of the model of the seasons that resists changing in the face of a new explanation.

Ultimately, when students' ideas clash with the formal explanations or procedures we try to teach them, what hinders learning is not so much what they do not yet know but what they already know.

Learning New Concepts

We saw in earlier chapters that, for learning to occur, new information from learning experiences must be connected to our prior knowledge through associative relationships based on meaning or context. Learning, in many cases, may involve accumulating new data and facts and expanding our conceptual networks. This information reaches the learner's mind "by transmission," and to retain it, they must connect it to their networks of prior knowledge through semantic relationships. In this way, concepts are expanded with more data, strengthening and making them flexible. This is typically the most usual form of learning.

But often, we do not want students to learn new facts or new data about a concept they already understand well. Instead, we want to directly teach them a new concept. Here it is important to assume that teaching concepts "by transmission" is not possible. Concepts are constructed in the learners' mind based on the knowledge available in their long-term memory. Through our efforts, we can only aspire to promote changes in how learners establish relationships between their knowledge and perhaps provide some new connectors (new data) to guide them in building the concepts. However, as noted earlier, this "rewiring" is not straightforward; it requires time, multiple opportunities, and student motivation.

Researchers in cognitive and developmental psychology refer to the transformation of mental schemata leading to the learning of new concepts as *conceptual change*. While there is no absolute consensus on its nature and development, it is clearly a slow and complex process. There is also some consensus on the teaching strategies that promote conceptual change and those that are less effective.

Types of Conceptual Change

There are many forms of conceptual change, varying in depth and difficulty of occurrence (Carey, 1991). In fact, an ongoing debate among researchers in this field revolves around how best to classify the various forms of conceptual change that can occur during learning.

Most experts distinguish between changes that can happen relatively easily and changes that are more difficult to occur, depending on whether they involve a deep restructuring of learners' original conceptions or are only superficial. Some researchers also suggest that more complex changes can also be differentiated based on the degree of reorganization required and the extent to which they challenge learners' most fundamental ontological beliefs—their most basic ideas about how the world around them is and how it works.

The different learning goals we pursue in school may require different types of conceptual change, varying in complexity and, therefore, in the most appropriate way to approach them. Unfortunately, we teachers are often not aware of this and, as a result, may not adapt our teaching methods accordingly.

The most basic form of conceptual change—and also the simplest—involves expanding a concept by adding new properties without having to undo any of the properties it already had. This is such a subtle form of conceptual change that some researchers do not even consider it a proper conceptual change. For example, learning about new types of animals usually does not require a change in the student's concept of an *animal*. The student already knows that animals vary in size, shape, habitat, and diet, among other things. Therefore, if they observe new types of animals with different combinations of these features, it may help them broaden their understanding of animal diversity without questioning the basic principles on which their concept of what an animal is are based. However, the new animal specimens must have the features the student uses to define this concept. Otherwise, this represents a more profound case of conceptual change, involving a reorganization of the student's network of concepts (which is what might happen when presenting sea sponges as animals).

When a conceptual change requiring a significant reorganization occurs, the existing concepts involved cease to be valid. They change not because they expand but because they change their meaning. This happens, for instance, when an original idea is replaced by two or more distinct concepts, and none of them aligns with the original concept. For example, children initially combine the concepts of *dead*, *not real*, and *inanimate* into an undifferentiated concept of *nonliving*, which they later distinguish as three different concepts describing essentially different types of objects (Carey, 1985; 1999).

In other cases of conceptual restructuring, the new idea combines concepts previously viewed as fundamentally different types. For example, initially students see solids and liquids as different from gases (Stavy, 1991; Smith et al., 1997), but introducing the concept of *matter* can lead them to appreciate that all are different forms in which matter can exist.

Another typical form of conceptual change occurs when the features thought to be central or peripheral to defining concepts are modified. For example, to develop a biological concept of a *living organism*, which includes plants, fungi, microorganisms, and animals, students must abandon the idea that being active and moving without external intervention is a basic requirement to define a living organism and instead focus on other characteristics such as having a life cycle—involving reproduction, growth, and death—and carrying out essential life-sustaining processes, such as feeding and interacting with the environment. In turn, these changes require other simultaneous changes in conceptions related to reproduction, growth, death, nutrition, and interaction with the environment since they must gain a wider meaning that can then be applied to organisms as different as animals, plants, fungi, and microorganisms (Duschl et al., 2007).

In summary, learning with understanding requires students to modify their initial concepts to describe objects, events, or explanatory models, especially when they do not align with the concepts we expect them to learn. The more solid their initial concepts are and the more they differ from the concepts to be learned, the more challenging conceptual change—and therefore learning—becomes.

At this point, I would like to revisit a phenomenon discussed in the first chapter concerning the advantages of using the scientific method to explain how the world works—confirmation bias. This bias arises when we experience cognitive dissonance because we receive information that does not fit with our prior ideas. In this situation, confirmation bias prompts us to protect our ideas at all costs—for example, reinterpreting the information to make it fit, ignoring it, forgetting it, and seeking evidence that supports our ideas and allows us to dismiss the new information. Indeed, confirmation bias is a phenomenon that illustrates our tendency to maintain our prior conceptual schemata and reflects how challenging it is to provoke conceptual change.

Conceptual Change and Lectures

We often associate the ability to teach in the classroom with the ability to provide structured and clear explanations, especially if they include plenty of examples and can spark the interest and attention of students. Of course, this is a crucial aspect of effective teaching (as will be covered in the chapter on instruction). But several studies provide evidence that a good explanation is usually not sufficient to bring about certain types of conceptual change.

For example, Stella Vosniadou and William Brewer (1992) interviewed 60 first-, third-, and fifth graders to learn about their ideas about the shape of Earth. When asked directly, most students across all ages responded that Earth was round, as they had learned in school. But when the researchers delved deeper into their ideas through indirect questions or by asking them to produce drawings, the diversity of conceptions that emerged was vast, often reflecting many aspects that could only be explained by the idea that Earth was flat, with people, animals, and houses placed on top (see Figure 2).

This observation, among others, led Vosniadou to describe synthetic models—explanatory models that emerge when the learner tries to integrate the new data they receive into their previous ideas and models. In their study, students found it very difficult to let go of the idea that there is an "up" and a "down," and to envisage a round Earth no matter how much their teachers and other adults asserted otherwise.

Dunbar et al. (2007) provide another example that illustrates the difficulty of inducing profound conceptual changes through explanations. In a study with

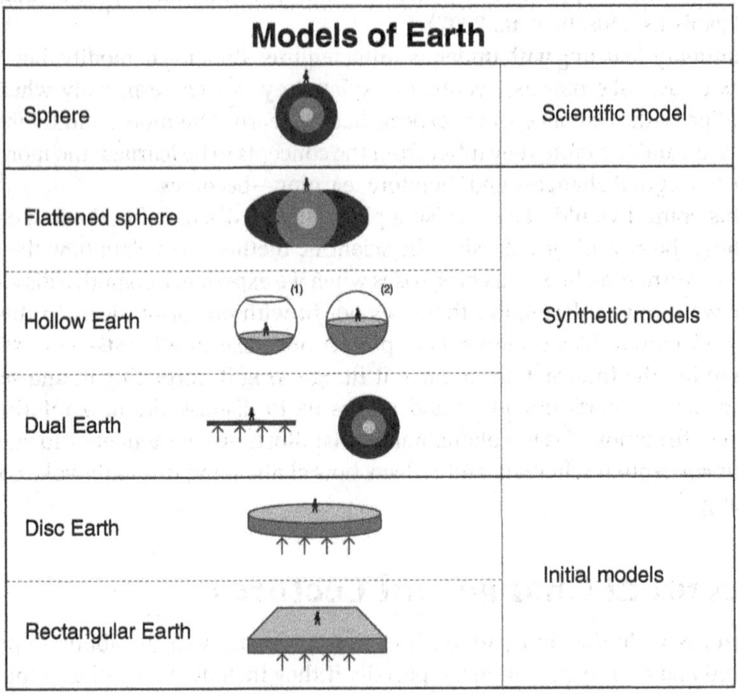

FIGURE 2   Some Earth models that the students drew for the Vosniadou and Brewer (1992) study.

50 university students, they first found that only three of them correctly used the scientific model to explain the phenomenon of seasons. Most other students gave the same explanation as the Harvard students in the documentary mentioned earlier in this chapter—the distance of Earth from the Sun—or said that Earth's axis of rotation was tilted and that summer occurred in the hemisphere that happened to be closer to the Sun. But the most surprising thing was that after showing them a highly informative video by NASA explaining the scientific model of the seasons in the most graphic way possible, only one of them changed their explanation to the scientifically accurate one. Among the other students, however, there was an increased reference to the tilt of Earth's axis and the explanation related to the relative distance of each Earth hemisphere to the Sun: "It's summer in the hemisphere closer to the Sun."

The researchers also used functional magnetic resonance imaging to observe what happens in the brains of students when they are exposed to observations that either fit or clash with their prior knowledge (Fugelsang & Dunbar, 2005). Specifically, they noted that when participants were provided with data consistent with their conceptions, some brain areas involved in learning—the caudate nucleus and the parahippocampal gyrus—showed activation levels above the baseline. But when they were presented with data inconsistent with their conceptions, the areas showing high activation were the anterior cingulate cortex, the precuneus, and the dorsolateral prefrontal cortex (see Figure 3). The anterior cingulate cortex is believed to be a brain region associated with error detection and response inhibition, while the dorsolateral prefrontal cortex is one of the key regions involved in working memory. These results indicate that when students receive information consistent with their prior knowledge, it can be relatively easy to incorporate it into existing concept networks. On the other hand, this experiment also provides evidence for one of the reasons why conceptual change can be so challenging—when people receive information inconsistent with their prior ideas, learning does not occur easily.

Promoting Conceptual Change in the Classroom

We saw that conceptual change is not just about building on preexisting ideas with more information, which can be effectively achieved through lectures. Conceptual change involves reconstructing ideas upon which the student bases their understanding of the world (and the new ideas they receive). These ideas typically form part of larger conceptual structures with internal coherence. Changing an idea that aligns with many others and explains numerous phenomena is not something that can be easily accomplished through lectures alone. It is not that it is impossible—in fact, some students can spontaneously achieve it. But it is not a very effective method by itself, especially if the teacher is not aware of the difficulty of the conceptual change in question. Unfortunately, conceptual change cannot be easily and immediately induced through other teaching methods, although there is evidence that some strategies are more effective than others (Brown & Clement, 1989; Smith et al., 1997; Stewart et al., 2005).

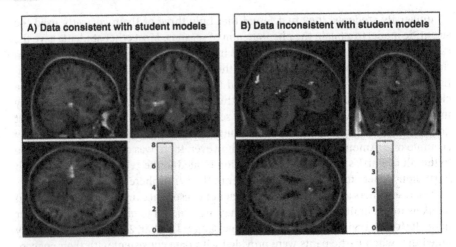

FIGURE 3 Functional magnetic resonance images showing brain regions activated above baseline when participants were presented with data consistent or inconsistent with their prior ideas (Fugelsang et al., 2005 / with permission of ELSEVIER). A) Consistent data: caudate nucleus and parahippocampal gyrus. B) Inconsistent data: anterior cingulate cortex, precuneus, and dorsolateral prefrontal cortex.

To promote conceptual change, it is first recommended that the student explicitly realizes that their prior ideas have weaknesses or simply cannot provide satisfactory explanations in all situations. In the case of the seasons, the most common explanation students provide—that it is hotter in summer because Earth is closer to the Sun—is called into question when they are told that the seasons do not occur simultaneously across the entire planet. When it is summer in the Northern Hemisphere, it is winter in the Southern Hemisphere, and vice versa. This "discrepant" event may be the starting point to encourage students to seek a new explanation; however, the process they follow to find it is likely to be all the more important, given the students' cognitive tendency to develop synthetic models. For example, to incorporate the fact that the two Earth hemispheres do not experience the same season simultaneously and the key information about Earth's axial tilt into their model, students tend to adopt, as noted earlier, a synthetic model that situates one hemisphere as "closer to the Sun" than the other.

For a learner to adopt a new explanation, it must meet certain criteria—among other things, it must succeed in explaining both the situations previously explained by the original model and those it could not explain. In other words, the new explanation must be satisfactory in all cases. Also, it is essential that the new model is understandable and coherent to the student, fitting with their prior knowledge, and has predictive power, successfully explaining new situations not previously considered (Posner et al., 1982).

Furthermore, we must remember that for conceptual change to occur, the student must be motivated for it to happen, as this process requires time and effort (Pintrich et al., 1993).

Guiding Students Toward Conceptual Change

The development of a new explanatory model requires teachers to provide guidance, who can benefit from understanding the most common preconceptions around each concept and the usual derivations in the form of synthetic models. The teacher's role is not just to impart new knowledge and experiences but also to guide students in their conceptual reconstruction and establish the underlying conditions to achieve it. To do this, the teacher can use empirically supported strategies, such as pedagogical conversation within a framework of guided inquiry.

Thus, providing students with experiences in meaningful contexts that allow them to externalize, share, and discuss their ideas on specific topics, while asking them to justify their reasoning, is an instructional strategy that facilitates conceptual change. This is all the more effective when the analysis of new situations to be studied is organized progressively, allowing students to start from their existing models and gradually build new models on the foundations of their ideas through a structured sequence of new experiences.

For example, the concept of *normal force*—the force exerted by any surface on an object resting on it in the opposite direction to gravity—is difficult for many students to grasp. Indeed, it is not very intuitive to accept that when an object is at rest on a table, the table exerts a force on the object that counters gravity and prevents it from moving toward the center of Earth. Yet we can help students conceptualize this situation by starting from another scenario where, instead of a table, they hold the object in their hand. The more objects they hold, the more force they need to exert. We can then transition from their hand to an inanimate support that students agree "exerts a force," such as a spring.

Finally, experimenting with both springs and the table will help students understand that the table, indeed, acts like a spring exerting a force on the objects placed on it. To make this sequence effective, it is essential to promote reflection and discussion at each step with the class group, allowing students to share their ideas, argue them, debate them, and put them to the test. Ultimately, inviting students to explicitly apply the new model to explain new situations in new contexts or to solve real problems will help consolidate conceptual change (Brown & Clement, 1989).

To promote conceptual change, there is likely nothing as effective as providing students with opportunities to use a new explanation in multiple instances and contexts (Markant et al., 2016; Perkins & Salomon, 1992). You may recall that each time a memory (or knowledge) is retrieved, it undergoes a process of reconstruction that increases the chances of it being altered by the inclusion of new details related to it and the loss of others it previously contained. In other words, retrieval practice is a process in which the pattern of connections between the elements that make up a schema, a concept, or a memory may be altered. Thus, the retrieval of a new concept or model may significantly promote conceptual change (Karpicke, 2012).

Self-Explanations

One method for practicing retrieval that contributes to conceptual learning is self-explanation, the practice in which the student tries to explain what they have learned to themselves, in their own words (Chi et al., 1994). Of course, explaining what they have learned to a third party would also have this effect (hence, one of the best ways to learn is by teaching a third party). In any case, what is important is that the act of forcing themselves to explain what they have learned compels the student to structure and make sense of their knowledge. In doing so, it promotes the connection between prior knowledge and new information, compelling the learner to accommodate the latter into their existing schemas, making adjustments to these schemas as necessary. In other words, self-explanation reveals conceptual conflicts and provides the student with the opportunity to resolve them (Chi, 2000).

Self-explanation was initially studied in the context of problem-solving learning. It was found that when students are prompted to explain, step by step, how they solve or have solved a problem, their learning is more robust and transferable to new problems (Berry, 1983). Later, it was shown that self-explanation also contributes to the acquisition of conceptual knowledge, improves understanding, and makes it more transferable (Chi et al., 1994). In this regard, it is worth noting that self-explanation is more robust when the learner explicitly tries to connect what they are learning to what they already know—for example, when they try to provide examples related to what they have learned, compare it to other similar ideas, or reflect on its plausibility, among other possibilities. This aligns with what was introduced in the previous chapter as *elaboration*.

Remarkably, evidence shows that students who perform well tend to use self-explanation spontaneously when they study (Chi et al., 1989). Also, when students are prompted to engage in this practice during learning sessions, their results improve (Bielaczyc et al., 1995). In this sense, we can teach them to do it on their own when they study, or we can create situations that prompt them to do so. For example, we can teach them to pause at regular intervals while reading to explain what they have read or provide them with questions they must answer after reading. As is covered later in the section on learning regulation, while it is very positive for us teachers to create situations that lead to effective learning, it is better in the long run to have students develop the habit of creating these situations themselves.

Transfer of Learning

2.5

Learning and Transferring

To begin this chapter, I will ask you to solve a classic problem, which appears in one of the most famous research studies on the topic we will discuss here (Gick & Holyoak, 1980). The problem goes as follows:

> A general wishes to capture a fortress, and he needs his entire army to do so. All the roads leading to the fortress are laden with mines, which only explode if a large group of people passes over them. Assuming the mines cannot be deactivated, how can the general lead his army to the fortress walls?

Indeed, the most obvious solution is to divide his army into small groups, send each group to a different road, and have the group converge on the fortress.

But what does this problem have to do with education? Obviously, we have no interest in teaching military strategies in school or anything of the sort. However, we often use teaching contexts that are quite different from the contexts where learning will be applied. Let me explain. In the previous problem, the specific situation is that of a general besieging a fortress, but the actual goal of the activity is to learn that, when facing certain problems, the solution is to divide forces and approach the objective from different angles—the "pincer movement" tactic, as is known in military terms. Therefore, my goal as a teacher is not for my students to learn how to besiege fortresses, but to be able to apply the principles underlying the solution to that problem to solve other similar problems in vastly different contexts.

We would surely agree that every teacher aspires to have what they teach their students in the classroom be useful to them outside of it (or in other classes). Formal education aims, among other things, to provide students with knowledge and skills they can use in the future to face various situations in life, whether personal, social, academic, or professional.

This noble purpose assumes that what students learn in a context like the classroom, through specific activities, will have implications for their performance in related but often significantly different contexts. In other words, it involves trusting that the learning they acquire will be transferable.

Indeed, transfer of learning occurs when learners can apply the knowledge or skills acquired in a specific context or through specific activities to accomplish new goals in other contexts, such as solving new problems, answering new questions, or learning new concepts or skills (Perkins & Salomon, 1992). Therefore, formal education operates under the assumption of transfer.

Unfortunately, the problem is that, based on more than a century of research, we have found that the transfer of learning does not happen as spontaneously as one might believe. On the contrary, transferring learning from one context to another is genuinely challenging and, therefore, infrequent.

The Doctrine of Formal Discipline

In the early 20th century, it was widely assumed that some school subjects, such as Latin or Greek, were essential for education because they helped "discipline the mind"—that is, they allegedly enhanced the development of general cognitive skills (such as attention, reasoning, or memory) that had a positive impact on students' performance in any other subject. This idea was known as the *doctrine of formal discipline* and had been around for quite some time. In fact, it had already been proposed by Plato many centuries earlier when he wrote about the need to study certain subjects, such as arithmetic or astronomy, to develop speculative reasoning (rather than for their practical value). Throughout history, education continued to embrace this notion, assuming that transfer was a given, as John Locke put it back in the 17th century:

> Would you have a man reason well, you must exercise . . . his mind. . . . Nothing does this better than mathematics, which therefore I think should be taught to all those who have the time and opportunity.

For some reason, the idea that certain subjects contribute generally to the development of cognitive skills applicable to any context is highly intuitive—some might say "common sense." But is this intuition correct?

During the first quarter of the 20th century, Edward Thorndike and colleagues investigated the validity of the assumptions underlying the doctrine of formal discipline (Thorndike & Woodworth, 1901). To address this, they conducted a series of scientific studies that soon questioned these assumptions. In their early experiments, they found that transfer of learning between relatively similar activities was rare. Also, when comparing the performance in other subjects of students who had studied Latin—a subject to which transferable benefits to other disciplines were attributed—with those who had not studied it, they found no significant differences (Thorndike, 1923). These studies were replicated multiple times over the years by other researchers, highlighting how weak the common assumptions about the transfer of learning were.

As a result, Thorndike became extremely pessimistic regarding the possibility of learning acquired in one context and around specific knowledge being transferred to other contexts. He believed transfer depended on the existence of "identical elements" between the learning activity and the application activity; that is, the transferability of learning depended on how similar the learning and application contexts were. He differentiated between *near transfer*, which occurred between identical or very similar activities or contexts, and *far transfer*, which occurred between seemingly different contexts or activities. While the former was not too rare, the latter was extremely infrequent.

Thorndike and colleagues initiated a line of research that has produced hundreds of studies on transfer of learning to date. Although these studies, collectively, allow us to be somewhat more optimistic than Thorndike, they still underscore that far transfer is truly exceptional (Barnett & Ceci, 2002).

Nevertheless, some remnants of the doctrine of formal discipline are still relevant today, such as the argument that learning computer programming contributes to improving students' problem-solving abilities in general (Wing, 2006). While the ability to program can nonetheless be particularly useful in a world where computers are ubiquitous—similar to being proficient in typing—studies have not found compelling evidence that learning programming enhances the ability to solve problems in any other context (Grover & Pea, 2013).

Although I will add some nuances to this statement later, the evidence suggests that learning to program contributes to developing skills associated with programming. For instance, learning to program in a specific programming language helps with learning to program in other programming languages—although, at times, initially, it can hinder learning, which is known as *negative transfer*.

What is not as obvious, in light of the evidence, is that learning programming improves our problem-solving ability in any context (Perkins & Salomon, 1992). The evidence supports that the ability to solve problems—like other cognitive skills—is not so much a general skill that can be applied to any context but largely depends on the context and the related knowledge. In fact, general problem-solving strategies that are transferable across disciplines are known as *soft methods*, while discipline-specific strategies are referred to as *hard methods*. These terms refer to their contribution to problem-solving ability (Mayer & Wittrock, 1996).

In any case, you may be thinking that when the problems we need to solve have the same deep structure as other problems we learned to solve—that is, they are based on the same principles, even if they seem different—then perhaps transfer should occur. While this is indeed the case, it is not easy to achieve. For instance, a classic study by Nunes-Carraher and colleagues (1985) describes how Brazilian children who worked selling items on the street had a great ability to perform mathematical calculations related to the monetary transactions they dealt with daily. However, they found it much more challenging to solve the same mathematical problems, with the same numbers and operations, when presented in an abstract form or through problems in imaginary contexts. For example, a child could easily calculate how many cruzeiros (the Brazilian currency at that time) they should charge a buyer who wanted 6 kg of watermelon at 50 cruzeiros per kg, but they struggled to solve the operation written as "6 × 50" or to solve a problem that required the same operation in a different context—namely, "A fisherman caught 50 fish. Another fisherman caught 6 times as many. How many fish did the second fisherman catch?"

Another classic experiment that demonstrates how challenging transfer between contexts is when solving problems was conducted by Gick and Holyoak in 1980. The researchers presented a problem to a group of university students, which can be summarized as follows:

> Suppose you are a doctor who must treat a patient with a malignant tumor in his stomach. It is impossible to operate on the patient, but there is a type of ray that can be used to destroy the tumor if applied with sufficiently high intensity. The problem is that it will also destroy all the healthy tissue it passes through. What solution could be provided to treat the patient's tumor?

Only a few students were able to solve this second problem. Could you solve it? What if I tell you that the solution is analogous to the story of the general and the fortress earlier in this chapter? The students in Gick and Holyoak's study had just read that same story about the general and the fortress a few minutes before facing the tumor problem, and yet they did not realize that both problems were related. Both could be solved using the same principle—dividing forces and attacking the problem from various angles, concentrating all the force on the target. With the tumor, if low-intensity rays are emitted from different positions and made to converge on the tumor, it can be reduced without affecting the surrounding tissues too much. This is actually how radiotherapy is often applied in some cases.

These and many other studies reflect the fact that our brains have a strong tendency to learn from the concrete and associate learning with the specific contexts in which they were acquired. Primarily, we learn from the concrete. After all, providing examples when explaining a concept is crucial for facilitating understanding; our brain evolved to learn from anecdotes (Willingham, 2002). As Thorndike already pointed out back in 1901,

> The mind is . . . a machine for making particular reactions to particular situations. It works in great detail, adapting itself to the special data of which it has had experience. . . . Improvement in any single mental function rarely brings about equal involvement in any other function, no matter how similar, for the working of every mental function-group is conditioned by the nature of the data in each particular case.

According to current models of cognitive psychology, this phenomenon may be a consequence of how learning operates; when we learn, we tie new information to a set of previous knowledge with which we have semantically related it. As you may recall, these sets of knowledge linked by relationships of meaning are called *schemas*, so we could say that the new information is linked to specific schemas. To retrieve what was learned in the future, some stimulus must activate the schemas to which the new information was associated. If the association was made based on the superficial features of the example used (e.g., military tactics), this knowledge is unlikely to be activated in a situation where knowledge associated with other schemas is being retrieved (e.g., medical treatments). In summary, the ability to transfer knowledge to a new context depends on whether the schemas to which that knowledge was linked during learning are activated when it is appropriate to apply them (Morris et al., 1977).

A drawback of memory operating in this way is that it makes it very difficult for us to realize the possibility of applying knowledge acquired in one context to other different contexts. Thus, even when two situations are analogous and can be solved using the same knowledge, realizing this is unlikely if they look different on the surface.

Nevertheless, the good news is that far transfer is not impossible. In fact, if a hint is provided that two seemingly different problems are related, transfer becomes more likely. In the experiment by Gick and Holyoak (1980), when the researchers informed the participants that the second problem was related to the story of the fortress, 90% of them could solve it (perhaps you have just experienced the same thing). Therefore, despite our tendency to learn by associating what we have learned with very specific contexts, this does not mean that we should give up on far transfer; it is simply more challenging than we usually think. In this respect, far transfer becomes more likely if certain conditions that we can promote are met. Let's explore them below.

Factors Facilitating Transfer

I explained earlier why the transfer of learning is so challenging. What we learn is connected to pieces of our prior knowledge through relationships of meaning, and that specific knowledge determines the context in which learning will be activated in future situations. If I connected what I learned to schemas related to military feats, I would hardly recall it in a medical context. The problem, therefore, could be resolved by also connecting this learning to other contexts.

Indeed, knowledge becomes more transferable when we connect it to multiple contexts during learning (Gick & Holyoak, 1983; Bransford et al., 1990). However, this inevitably requires time and opportunities. In each learning opportunity, we can only connect what we learn to a few pieces of prior knowledge—those we can hold simultaneously in working memory. The bottleneck that represents limited working memory capacity makes it impossible to develop flexible and highly transferable knowledge unless we provide the time needed to work with what has been learned in multiple contexts (preferably spaced out over time). When learners are challenged to identify or use the same ideas or procedures in different contexts, they are more likely to spontaneously abstract their underlying principles and make them less dependent on the superficial context in which they were learned.

Furthermore, when the use of concrete examples in different contexts is combined with the explicit presentation of the abstract principles that these examples share—with the aim of guiding and promoting abstraction explicitly—transferability is further enhanced (Schwartz et al., 1999). Exercises designed to identify the common deep structure of seemingly different cases through comparison are also quite effective (Gentner et al., 2004). So, for example, when teaching students about historical events, it is advisable to help them extract and recognize the basic principles that characterize them and relate them to events from different times or places, including the present. If we are teaching students to measure the area of rectangular objects (tables, soccer fields, screens, walls, etc.), although it may seem obvious, it is still a good idea to explicitly state the abstract principle that all these cases have in common—they are rectangular shapes. In short, it is not a matter of choosing between teaching with concrete examples or teaching through abstraction, but rather combining both approaches (Schwartz et al., 1999).

As far as we know, learning through concrete examples or contexts can be beneficial for the early stages of learning (Bransford et al., 1990). However, from this point onward, it is appropriate to enrich learning experiences with other cases that prevent *overcontextualization* of what is learned—where learning becomes too tied to a single context, making it virtually impossible to transfer. In this sense, methods such as project-based learning, case-based learning, or problem-based learning should address this issue derived from the nature of learning and include "remedial" activities. For example, by posing challenges that involve developing solutions for a wide range of problems rather than focusing on a specific problem; including "what if. . ." activities that require students to think about the consequences of changing certain problem variables; expanding the possible perspectives from which to approach the challenge; or simply extending the activity to apply what was learned in new situations (Bransford et al., 2000).

Note: Formal Discipline and the Expert's Blind Spot

The doctrine of formal discipline claims that certain subjects, such as computer programming or Latin, enable the development of general skills that students can transfer to very different contexts. This notion may seem intuitive, but when put to the test it is not entirely accurate.

One of the reasons the premises of formal discipline seem correct to us is the fact that experts in a subject can use their knowledge in a way that transcends their discipline. But this is only possible because experts have very deep knowledge in their specialty, rich in connections and linked to countless application contexts. This allows them to perceive and abstract familiar patterns in situations quite different from those of the context of their own subject. In contrast, a student will hardly achieve this capability without developing similarly deep learning. In other words, adding a subject to the curriculum under the premise of formal discipline will not necessarily help achieve the general transfer goals it aims for.

In the chapter on deep learning, I discuss the *expert's blind spot* (also known as the *curse of knowledge*), which points out that experts tend not to be aware of the difficulty involved in doing what they do. They do not realize all the knowledge they had to acquire to achieve it. This phenomenon helps validate the formal discipline doctrine in situations where students will not reach the level of deep knowledge required for the expected transfer capacity.

In conclusion, distant transfer is more likely to occur when learning is deep, that is, when it connects to multiple schemas and, as a result, involves a certain level of abstraction—when learning occurs with understanding. Therefore, as attested by numerous experiments, when we teach for understanding—and not just for the reproduction of facts or procedures—we promote transferability.

One of the earliest experiments was conducted by Schoklow and Judd in the early 20th century (Judd, 1908). These researchers had two groups of students practice dart throwing to hit a target located a few inches underwater. One of the groups also received a lesson on the refraction effect of light as it passes from water to air, which causes light rays to bend. Both groups practiced until they achieved an acceptable performance for a situation where the target was 12 inches below the water surface. However, when their accuracy was tested for a target 4 inches deep, the group that understood the refraction effect performed much better.

Teachers might find the work of Wertheimer (1959) more interesting. He studied how teaching certain procedures to determine the areas of geometric figures could influence the subsequent ability to transfer that knowledge. He compared a computational (reproductive) teaching method and a conceptual one (with understanding). Specifically, he worked with students who knew the formula for calculating the area of a rectangle and taught them how to calculate the area of other parallelograms. One group was taught to apply the formula of multiplying the base by the height, with the height being the length of a line perpendicular to the base, extending from the base to the upper side of the polygon (Figure 1).

In contrast, the other group learned that a nonrectangular parallelogram could be rearranged to show that its area is actually equivalent to that of a rectangle with the same base and height (Figure 2).

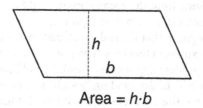

$$\text{Area} = h \cdot b$$

FIGURE 1

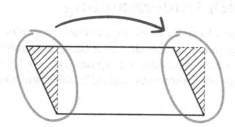

FIGURE 2

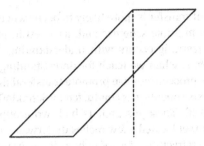

FIGURE 3

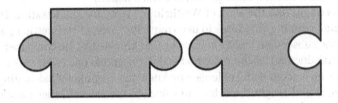

FIGURE 4

The students then took an assessment test to evaluate their knowledge. While both groups performed similarly when solving typical parallelogram area problems, only the second group could solve cases like those in Figure 3.

Moreover, only students from the second group could distinguish between solvable and unsolvable problems, as shown in Figure 4.

Some students in the group that learned to calculate areas without understanding the formula's rationale expressed that they "had not yet studied this type of problem."

Therefore, the way a student approaches learning (and how the teacher promotes it) influences the degree of understanding, which in turn affects its potential for transfer (Mayer, 2002). For this very reason, I will now discuss the types of activities that promote learning with understanding.

Learning with Understanding

The previous example of two different ways to teach how to measure the area of a parallelogram clearly illustrates the difference between learning with understanding and learning for purely reproductive purposes (i.e., rote learning). If learning is defined as the acquisition of knowledge and skills, this distinction between different types of learning shows that learning is necessarily more than that. Indeed, while reproductive learning only allows us to remember what was previously learned, learning with understanding enables us to use it in new situations. We could say that the former generates knowledge that looks to the past, while the latter focuses on the future (Mayer, 2002). For example, the former allows us to describe what an ecosystem is, and the latter enables us to propose an explanation of the consequences that the disappearance of a particular species would have on a specific ecosystem. Thus, only the latter allows for transfer, as transferring learning requires making sense of what is learned and being able to use it (Bransford et al., 2000).

Ultimately, learning with understanding, essentially equivalent to what I referred to earlier as *meaningful learning*, allows us to perform a range of cognitive activities that go beyond mere retrieval of what was learned. In this sense, you may be familiar with Bloom's taxonomy (1956)—a classification of learning goals defined by the type of cognitive activities we can perform with what was learned. Bloom's taxonomy has become popular as a hierarchical classification, with the ability to recall (that is, to reproduce a piece of information) at its base, supporting the possibility of carrying out other actions, all associated with deeper learning that comes with understanding. Without delving into the debate of whether these higher categories should be interpreted hierarchically or not (the original taxonomy is not hierarchical), they provide a particularly useful framework for classifying the types of activities associated with meaningful learning. When it comes to promoting transfer, these are the kinds of activities we should aim for in learning.

To give you a more concrete idea of the different categories the various learning goals are included in, Table 1 is an updated version of Bloom's taxonomy that a multidisciplinary team of researchers (cognitive psychologists, teaching and learning experts, and assessment specialists) published in 2001, based on advances in the science of teaching and learning. It details the various cognitive processes associated with each category (note that this revised version is also not hierarchical).

It is evident that the cognitive processes included in categories other than "remembering" are intimately related; the differences between them are sometimes a matter of nuance. In any case, what is important is that any activity involving any of these processes will prompt the student to make sense of what they are learning, thus promoting the development of meaningful and transferable learning. Moreover, this type of activity will also provide opportunities to assess learning in terms of transferability; that is, it will be useful for both promoting and assessing transferable learning. In summary, the type of activities that allow us to develop transfer is the same that allow us to put it to the test.

In this sense, it is worth noting that two learning activities may seem equally effective when we only assess the students' ability to reproduce knowledge or skills. However, they can turn out quite different when we assess the students' ability to transfer what they learned (Bransford & Schwartz, 1999).

Table 1 Cognitive processes that can be performed with acquired knowledge, based on the flexibility they have achieved (Adapted from Anderson et al., 2001).

Categories and Cognitive Processes	Alternative Names	Definitions
1. Remember — Retrieve relevant information from long-term memory.		
1.1 Recognizing	Identifying	Confirm that the information that is explicitly presented is already in long-term memory.
1.2 Recalling	Reproducing	Extract information from long-term memory given some stimulus.
2. Understand — Give meaning to the information being processed.		
2.1 Interpreting	Clarifying; paraphrasing; representing; translating	Switch from one form of representation (e.g., verbal) to another (e.g., numerical).
2.2 Exemplifying	Illustrating	Provide examples that illustrate an idea or principle.
2.3 Classifying	Categorizing; grouping	Determine that something belongs to a category (a concept or principle).
2.4 Summarizing	Abstracting; generalizing	Extract the main ideas or data from information.
2.5 Inferring	Concluding; extrapolating; interpolating; predicting	Draw conclusions from the information presented.
2.6 Comparing	Contrasting; mapping; relating	Detect correspondences between two ideas, objects, or events.
2.7 Explaining	Modeling	Build cause-effect models.
3. Apply — Use a procedure in a given situation.		
3.1 Executing	Carrying out	Apply a procedure to a task that is familiar.
3.2 Implementing	Using	Apply a procedure to a task that is unfamiliar.
4. Analyze — Break the learning object into its constituent parts and determine how the parts relate to one another and to the whole.		
4.1 Differentiating	Discriminating; distinguishing; selecting; focusing	Distinguish relevant elements from irrelevant ones.
4.2 Organizing	Integrating; structuring; schematizing; dissecting	Determine how elements fit or function in a structure.

(Continued)

Table 1   (Continued)

Categories and Cognitive Processes	Alternative Names	Definitions
4.3 Attributing	Deconstructing	Determine the perspective, bias, or double entendre of the information.

4. Evaluate — Make judgments based on criteria or standards.

5.1 Checking	Coordinating; detecting; monitoring; testing	Detect internal inconsistencies or fallacies in a process or product; determine the effectiveness of a process.
5.2 Critiquing	Judging	Detect inconsistencies in a process or product in relation to external criteria; determine the convenience of a procedure to solve a given problem.

5. Create — Put elements together to form a coherent or functional whole; reorganize elements into a new pattern or structure.

6.1 Generating	Hypothesizing	Generate alternative hypotheses based on a criterion.
6.2 Planning	Designing	Conceive a process or object that fulfills some function.
6.3 Producing	Constructing	Elaborate a product.

Note: Physical Context and Transfer

The knowledge we connect to what we have learned also depends on the physical context in which we find ourselves. Indeed, we associate what we are learning with information related to where, when, how, or with whom we are learning it.

In this respect, experiments have compared the performance of a group of students in an exam when the test was conducted in the same classroom where they had learned or in a different one (Smith et al., 1978). As expected, those in the first group performed better than those in the second, in line with the fact that transfer is easier when the learning and assessment contexts are more similar, even when the context is determined by the physical environment we find ourselves in.

In another experiment, one group of students had several study sessions in different classrooms, while another group had all the sessions in the same classroom. Both groups were evaluated in a new classroom, and those from the first group performed better (Smith, 1982). This may be related to the fact that combining different learning contexts helps develop more flexible knowledge. In this case, it helps not to associate what we learn with irrelevant knowledge from the learning situation, such as the place where we study or the textbook chapter we are reading. Thus, combining contexts allows us to abstract significant principles from what we learn.

However, even though these studies are quite striking, the effects of the physical context on transferability are generally small and, in many cases, undetectable (Smith & Vela, 2001). Therefore, instead of considering major measures that would disrupt the organization of the educational institution to provide diverse learning environments, it is much more productive to focus on providing diverse examples or application contexts to relate what is being learned.

Learning Is Transferring

To end this chapter, I would like to highlight an interesting fact implicit in the relationship between learning and transfer. Indeed, one of the consequences of the cognitive model of learning is that when we learn, we transfer. This is because the act of learning involves the activation of prior knowledge that is related to what is being learned, with a view to making connections. Learning requires applying what we already know to the new learning activity.

In fact, one of the most important pieces of evidence for transfer is the ease of learning something new. Transfer not only occurs when we use what we know to answer new questions or solve new problems; it also occurs when what we already know helps us learn new things. Paradoxically, it also occurs when what we know hinders new learning, such as when knowledge of one language interferes with learning a second language—for example, mastery of English grammar interfering with the correct construction of sentences in Spanish or experiencing difficulty in remembering the meanings of words that are very similar in both languages but have different meanings (for example, the Spanish word *sensible* means "sensitive"). In these cases, as noted earlier, this is known as negative transfer, which often occurs in the early stages of learning.

In any case, the main takeaway is that learning is the act of transferring what we previously learned.

Working Memory

2.6

Beyond Short-Term Memory

The amount of information we can store in our long-term memory is virtually unlimited. However, we cannot be aware of everything we know because we can only simultaneously retrieve a few details. When we retrieve some of our knowledge or memories, we place them in what is called *working memory*. Furthermore, when we pay attention to information from our environment and temporarily store it for use or manipulation—for example, when we keep a telephone number in mind before writing it down—we also place it in our working memory.

In psychology, the term *working memory* is used to describe our capacity to consciously maintain and mentally manipulate a limited amount of information over short periods of time (Baddeley & Hitch, 1974).

The term replaces and goes beyond the classic concept of *short-term memory* because it highlights the fact that this capacity not only allows us to retain information for a brief period of time but also to manipulate it and combine it with information from our long-term memory.

For example, we can hold the word *dinosaur* in our working memory, but we can also rearrange some of its letters in our mind to form new words, such as *radio* or *sound*, which we know exist because they are in our long-term memory. The following box lists other examples of everyday situations in which we use working memory.

In short, working memory allows us to retain valuable information while consciously processing it. In other words, it is the cognitive function that operates on the information we are paying attention to at any given moment, whether it comes from the external world or our long-term memory. Although technically considered a cognitive process, for our purposes it is helpful to think of it as a mental workspace—the mental space where we consciously perceive reality, remember, reason, and imagine.

Limitations of Working Memory

In this chapter, we will see how working memory is a critical function for learning. Unfortunately, it has several limitations and can readily let us down when we need it most.

BOX 1   Examples of activities we perform with working memory.

Manipulating the letters of a word like *dinosaur* is just one of the activities we can perform with our working memory. We do many other things with it, such as:

- Remembering a question we were asked while answering it
- Imagining how our living room would look if we rearranged the furniture
- Calculating how to split the bill for a group gift
- Keeping a phone number, an email address, or a car license plate in memory while looking for a pen and paper to jot them down
- Solving a problem using logical principles with the resources at our disposal
- Analyzing and interpreting data from a chart in a newspaper
- Following a sequence of instructions given verbally, such as "Tip the flour into a bowl, drizzle in two tablespoons of water, and mix to form a thick batter."
- Remembering the beginning of a sentence or paragraph we are finishing reading

First, to keep information in working memory, we cannot stop paying attention to it and must avoid distractions. A spontaneous thought that crosses our mind, someone speaking to us, a fire alarm, or a ringing phone can be enough to divert our attention, causing the information we were holding in working memory to be lost suddenly.

In fact, our attentional system compels us to divert our attention to any salient stimulus in the environment, no matter how focused we are, such as when we hear a loud noise in the classroom next door. This is an ancestral adaptive feature of our brain. Similarly, it is difficult for us to ignore what someone suddenly says to us, like "Dinner's ready!"—indeed, teenagers can hear us despite pretending not to sometimes. The classic joke of reciting random numbers aloud when someone is trying to remember a phone number is based on this fact.

However, perhaps the cruelest limitation of our working memory is its strict capacity constraint (Miller, 1956). It turns out that the amount of information we can hold in working memory is limited. For example, most of us could calculate 43 times 5 without a calculator or pen and paper relatively easily, but multiplying the numbers 494 and 927 would likely be challenging because the amount of information that needs to be held in working memory while performing this calculation exceeds the capacity of most people. When we try to hold too much information, working memory overflows, resulting in the loss of information.

Moreover, activities demanding high mental processing, like using multiplication algorithms during mental calculations, decrease the amount of mental space available in working memory to hold information. This reduction can lead to the loss of the data that was initially held, which might happen if, while applying the multiplication process to two large numbers, we forget which numbers we were multiplying. To get it right, we would have to start over.

Finally, controlling what occupies the limited mental space in our working memory is not always easy. We noted earlier the impossibility of avoiding distractions from salient stimuli, such as when someone suddenly shouts "Fire!" or when someone recites random numbers while you try to remember an important telephone number. In addition, working memory is highly sensitive to stress and anxiety, emotional states that flood it with thoughts unrelated to the task at hand—whether it is learning something new or answering an exam question—making it almost impossible to perform. We are also too familiar with the peculiar *earworm*, the phenomenon of having music "stuck" in the head that makes us sing a tune that we know (or that we have heard recently) over and over, even when we do not want to keep singing it and would do anything for it to leave our working memory.

Note: Attention and Working Memory

The concepts of *attention* and *working memory* are closely related. From a cognitive perspective, attention could be defined as the process that allows us to select the information that enters and is maintained in working memory. Therefore, when we say that we can only pay attention to a limited amount of information at any given moment, we are alluding to the limited capacity of working memory, which can only accommodate a reduced amount of information.

Attention is a dynamic process that continually shifts its focus, whether we want it to or not. As noted earlier, the attentional system has evolved to prioritize any salient stimulus; it is a matter of survival. Even in the absence of a salient stimulus, attention continues to shift back and forth. Therefore, in the context of a classroom, it does not make much sense to talk about the duration of attention, except in tasks that require a lot of concentration. The duration of attention in the classroom is not as relevant as motivation, which is what truly leads us to redirect our attention repeatedly toward learning activities (and, in practice, knows no limits, except for physical fatigue).

Of course, this is not to say that having an attention deficit disorder is not a disadvantage. The ability to maintain attention on a specific task and avoid distractions (inhibitory control), coupled with the ability to quickly shift the focus of attention (cognitive flexibility), are two higher cognitive processes that, along with working memory, constitute the so-called *executive functions* (Diamond, 2013). These functions are related to human skills such as planning, self-control, and problem-solving, among others. As will be seen several times throughout this book, executive functions are crucial for the learning process.

The Components of Working Memory

As already noted earlier, working memory can be filled with information from two possible sources: our senses or long-term memory. Thus, we can fill working memory with the information we are currently seeing or hearing—such as what you are reading now—or we can fill it with information retrieved from our long-term memory, like when I ask you to visualize a panda bear. The image of the panda bear that is now in your working memory comes from your long-term memory.

You may have noticed that you can visualize a panda bear and still continue reading, right? Although working memory has limitations and does not allow us to hold much information at once, it actually comprises different, relatively independent "compartments" for different types of information (Baddeley & Hitch, 1974). Specifically, working memory includes a component that processes visual information—like the image of a panda bear—and another that handles auditory information—such as the inner voice reading these words. Interestingly, working memory can process these two types of information simultaneously with minimal interference between them. In contrast, attempting to perform two or more mental tasks with the same type of information quickly overloads its capacity.

An implication of this feature of working memory is evident: we can optimize learning by employing both visual and auditory compartments simultaneously whenever possible (Mousavi et al., 1995). This phenomenon is related to the so-called *dual-coding theory*, which has significant implications for learning (Paivio, 1971, 1991). In summary, when verbal (oral or textual) explanations are combined with visual resources or when students are encouraged to connect what they learn with images, their learning is significantly enhanced. This is not only due to a more efficient use of working memory but also to dual encoding in long-term memory, which also favors images.

Another consequence of the dual nature of working memory is that it is a bad idea to deliver slide presentations that display more than one line of text on the screen while the speaker reads it aloud or simply continues with their speech. Although written texts enter our minds visually, expert readers automatically convert them into auditory information, which appears as such in our working memory (that voice seemingly reading aloud inside us). Therefore, we cannot read and listen to someone speaking at the same time; working memory becomes overwhelmed, making it difficult to understand what the text and the speaker are trying to convey. In slide presentations, it is advisable to limit text to very short words or phrases and use the visual resources they provide to enrich oral explanations with appropriate images, graphics, or animations.

Cognitive Load Theory

Taking into account the limitations of working memory is fundamental when it comes to promoting learning. Indeed, working memory serves as a bottleneck that dictates our capacity to learn; everything we consciously learn must pass through it. In fact, it is the "place" where we can connect our prior knowledge with new experiences and information to construct fresh insights. Therefore, one could say it is the cognitive function that allows the types of learning relevant to school to occur.

In this sense, one of the theories about how we learn with the most empirical evidence and practical application in the classroom is Cognitive Load Theory (Sweller, 1988, 1994). This theory acknowledges the critical role of working memory in learning and recognizes its limitations. In essence, it contends that for effective learning to occur, it is critical not to overload working memory.

The proponents of this idea state that there are three types of cognitive load (Table 1) that occupy mental space in our working memory and that may contribute to cognitive overload (Sweller et al., 1998). The first is intrinsic cognitive load, which is related to the learning object itself. The more complex and the more new components the learning object contains for the learner, the higher the cognitive load it places on working memory. The best way to reduce it is to break down the learning object into smaller pieces and sequence learning progressively, minimizing the number of new components the learner must consider simultaneously to reach the learning goal.

The second type is extraneous cognitive load, resulting from the intrusion into working memory of information that is superfluous for reaching the learning goal. These elements occupy some mental space that cannot be used to support and manipulate truly essential information. Thus, extraneous cognitive load should be avoided as much as possible.

The third type of cognitive load, germane cognitive load, is described as that generated by the process of relating new information to our prior knowledge and identifying relationships between new knowledge. Therefore, it is a desirable cognitive load for achieving learning.

Cognitive Load Theory posits that these three types of load can occur simultaneously, and their effects are cumulative in terms of occupying mental "space" in working memory. If the cognitive load produced collectively exceeds the working memory capacity of the learner, learning is compromised. In fact, when working memory is overwhelmed, it leads to a feeling of frustration, prompting an immediate reaction to abandon the task at hand.

Table 1 Types of cognitive load.

Intrinsic	It is the load that occurs when the information specific to the learning object is held in working memory.
Extraneous	It is the load that occurs when superfluous information intrudes into working memory and interferes with the learning object.
Germane	It is the load due to manipulating information necessary to give it meaning, connect it to prior knowledge, and ultimately, to facilitate learning.

Working Memory Capacity as a Learner Attribute

I emphasized earlier the significance of working memory in the learning process. Not surprisingly, there is a significant correlation between students' working memory capacity and their academic performance. Some studies indicate that approximately 70% of children with reading difficulties score very low on working memory tests (Daneman & Carpenter, 1980). In fact, working memory capacity may be a better predictor of academic success than IQ (Alloway & Alloway, 2010).

Indeed, the limits of working memory, especially in terms of capacity, vary from one individual to another; each person has a relatively fixed capacity that falls within a certain spectrum. Therefore, a particular activity may be within the working memory capacity of one person but exceed that of another.

Moreover, working memory capacity is not constant throughout life but increases significantly with age during childhood (and then gradually declines throughout adulthood). Consequently, young children typically start with very small capacities, which increase gradually—more rapidly at the outset—until well into adolescence. It is at this point that they reach working memory capacities typical of adults, usually more than twice those of four-year-old children (Gathercole et al., 2004). This development seems to be related to the fact that the prefrontal cortex areas of the brain, which support working memory (among other higher cognitive functions), mature last (Sowell et al., 2003). Figure 1 illustrates the growth curves for an individual with an average working memory capacity and one with low capacity for their age.

Differences in working memory capacity among same-age children can be significant. For example, according to some studies, in a typical class of 30 seven- to eight-year-old children, at least 3 of them are expected to have the working memory capacity of four-year-old children, and another 3 may have the capacity of eleven-year-olds, which is quite close to adult levels (Alloway & Alloway, 2014).

As can be seen in the graph in Figure 1, children with low working memory capacity typically do not catch up with their peers as they mature. While their working memory capacities increase with age, they do not do so at a rate that allows them to catch up. In fact, it is common for the differences between them to become even more pronounced (Gathercole et al., 2004; Gathercole & Alloway, 2007).

The causes for individual differences in working memory capacity are still not fully understood. Despite what one might think, research suggests that working memory capacity is not strongly influenced by environmental factors, such as social or intellectual stimulation at home or the quality of preschool education. Instead, it is likely that the genes involved in the development and functioning of the frontal brain areas that support working memory play a predominant role (Ando et al., 2001). Nonetheless, environmental factors that can alter the maturation processes of these areas, such as chronic stress or active or passive drug use, should not be ruled out. After all, the brain regions that support cognitive processes related to working memory and other executive functions mature progressively throughout childhood and adolescence (Gathercole et al., 2004).

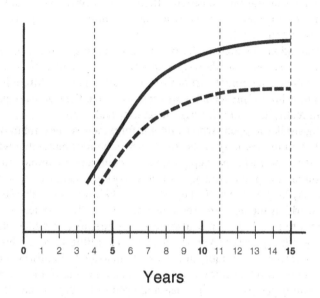

Years

FIGURE 1 Changes in the working memory capacity of an average child are shown as a solid line. Scores of a child with low working memory capacity are represented by the dashed line (Gathercole & Alloway, 2007 / with permission of Sage Publications Ltd.).

On the other hand, there is no evidence to suggest that working memory capacity can be expanded in general through mental training. However, it is possible to optimize its functioning and overcome its limitations in a specific knowledge domain through learning (Hambrick & Engle, 2002). The more we learn about something, the more effective our working memory becomes in that domain (provided the learning is meaningful, that is, with understanding). I will examine this further in the next chapter.

Working Memory and Learning in School

I noted earlier that working memory is the mental space where learning occurs. But not all learning tasks require the same cognitive resources; some tasks are light, while others impose considerable loads on working memory.

School learning activities often require the student to hold a certain amount of information in their working memory—such as a problem statement—while they engage in a mental challenge—like applying algorithms they have learned to solve the problem. When activities demand a high level of cognitive resources, students with low working memory struggle to complete them. Often, they cannot complete them correctly because they fail to retain the necessary information to guide their actions, thus missing out on the benefits their peers receive. As already mentioned earlier, when working memory is overwhelmed, the immediate response is to give up what we are trying to do with it.

A typical situation in which students with low working memory have difficulties is when they have to follow a relatively long series of instructions to complete a task. In these cases, they often forget part of the information halfway through the task, so they do not know how to proceed. It may seem to us that they were not paying attention when, in reality, they simply forgot what they had to do.

Something similar happens when students forget where they are in the task process. Indeed, working memory is also necessary to help us remember where we are in the task as we perform the steps needed to complete a complex mental activity. For example, imagine a student with low working memory capacity trying to solve a relatively long mathematical operation in their notebook. The student needs to bring to working memory the sequence of actions that the learned algorithm instructs them to follow, but they also need to remember at which step they are and likely use other pieces of knowledge, such as multiplication tables. This can overwhelm their working memory and cause them to get lost halfway through. Suddenly, the student who had started well gets stuck and does not know how to continue. They simply get lost in the process and need to start again, and this no doubt affects their motivation.

BOX 2   Characteristics of children with reduced working memory.

Children with reduced working memory capacity typically exhibit the following characteristics (Alloway, 2006; Gathercole & Alloway, 2007):

They have difficulty remembering all the instructions in a statement or the goals of an activity.

They behave as if they were not paying attention; for example, by forgetting part or all of the instructions.

They often get lost during complicated tasks and eventually abandon them.

They appear to have low attention spans and are easily distracted.

They rarely volunteer to answer questions and sometimes do not respond to direct questions.

They prefer group activities.

They show poor academic progress, especially in reading and mathematics.

They do not necessarily have social integration problems.

Note: a child displaying some or all of these characteristics does not necessarily have reduced working memory; it could be due to other factors.

Measuring Working Memory

We argued that there is a significant correlation between academic performance and students' working memory capacity (Alloway & Alloway, 2010). Therefore, you are probably wondering what methods can be used to measure the working memory capacity of individuals.

There are many methods that allow us to infer different levels of working memory capacity in individuals. Generally, they involve having the person try to store and manipulate as much information in their mind as they can for brief periods of time.

The simplest methods involve reciting or displaying increasingly longer sequences of numbers, letters, or objects, and asking the person to recite them back in the same or reverse order. The individual's ability to recall a longer sequence indicates a higher working memory capacity.

More complex methods involve reading out loud lists of sentences, such as "The dog fetched the largest ball"; asking a question after each sentence, such as "Who fetched the largest ball?" (which the person must answer correctly); and instructing individuals to remember the last word of each sentence at the end of the sequence of sentences. The higher the number of words remembered in order of occurrence, the greater their working memory capacity.

As performance in these tests can be influenced by environmental or emotional variables, it is always advisable to repeat them several times at different intervals and combine the use of different tests for a more accurate diagnosis.

Working Memory and Learning Difficulties

Students with reduced working memory capacity may have difficulties with learning tasks that do not pose significant challenges for other students. However, not all academically challenged students have working memory problems. These difficulties may be due to other factors, such as emotional and behavioral disorders.

In any case, working memory is a factor to consider in a significant number of cases of academic failure. As we have seen, working memory is important for learning because it provides a mental workspace where we can store information while manipulating and making sense of it, connecting it to our prior knowledge. Moreover, it is also important for using this information in creative, analytical, or problem-solving activities.

Students with low working memory capacity struggle in these activities simply because they cannot hold and manage the information necessary to complete the task. In such cases, their working memory is overwhelmed, causing them to lose crucial information needed to complete a task, such as the goals of the activity they are doing, the instructions they need to follow, or the elements that help them understand an explanation. Moreover, working memory overload leads to frustration and negatively affects motivation. Given that students with low working memory capacity struggle across many different types of activities, they are likely to show poor overall academic progress. To support such students, it may be helpful for the teacher to oversee their learning activities and make necessary modifications to ensure they operate within the limits of their working memory capacity. This proactive approach will assist students in successfully completing tasks, accumulating knowledge and skills over time, and reinforcing their capacity for future learning. In the next chapter, I will argue that acquiring meaningful knowledge helps us cope with the limitations of working memory. But before that, let me offer some guidance on managing cognitive load during learning tasks.

Managing Cognitive Load in the Classroom

The most significant advantage of understanding the role of working memory in learning for educational practice is the ability to manage cognitive load in classroom activities.

In brief, our knowledge of how working memory plays a role in the learning process and its limitations draws our attention to Cognitive Load Theory. The aim is to mitigate the disruptive consequences of excessive working memory loads on learning.

The following recommendations apply both to guiding the development of activities for students with working memory problems and enhancing the performance of all students in the classroom. The goal of these recommendations is to reduce the likelihood of students failing to achieve their learning goals due to an overload of their working memory.

Reduce Extraneous Cognitive Load

While some aspects of extraneous cognitive load—that which is unnecessary for achieving learning goals—can be challenging to control (such as those resulting from emotional situations the student may be going through), there are several measures that can be taken to minimize it. For example:

- Avoid providing additional information that is not directly related to the learning objective of the current activity.

- Avoid giving examples that divert students' attention to other topics irrelevant to the learning goals.

- Provide clear and structured outlines of what will be done or covered during the activity.

- Provide simple rubrics that focus students' attention on the aspects that will be emphasized when assessing an activity.

- Provide all the information students need to process simultaneously to achieve the learning goal in a situation of spatial and temporal proximity.

- Avoid cognitive redundancy that occurs when trying to process the same type of information from two different sources, such as reading and simultaneously listening to a third party who is also reading.

Regulate Intrinsic Cognitive Load

Activities that simultaneously introduce many new elements for the student place heavy demands on working memory. Similarly, procedures involving long sequences of instructions can easily overwhelm working memory capacity. To manage intrinsic cognitive load during an activity, we can:

- Minimize the number of learning objectives pursued simultaneously in an activity.

- Break down learning goals to reduce the total amount of new material the student must keep in their working memory; for example, the number of new elements that need to be considered to understand a concept.

- Structure activities into separate steps that allow the gradual acquisition of new knowledge.

- Repeat important information frequently.

- Simplify the linguistic structures of verbal material, for example, avoiding overly long and complex sentences.

- Promote the use of tools and strategies that act as external support for working memory, such as problem-solving guides, concept maps, or diagrams.

Optimize Relevant Cognitive Load

When assessing the cognitive demands of learning activities, it is important to consider that the processing demands also increase the demands on working memory. Although students may be able to store a specific amount of information in a situation, a demanding processing task will escalate the load on working memory, potentially resulting in a failure of this memory type. To optimize the relevant cognitive load, we can:

- Explicitly state the relationships between what is being learned and the students' prior knowledge.

- Use specific examples that allow the student to rely on known elements to recognize concepts or apply the procedures being learned.

- Provide explicit explanations with detailed examples of how to solve specific tasks.

- Whenever appropriate, present visual and auditory information simultaneously.

- Encourage the use of tools and strategies that free up some of the cognitive load, such as calculators, manipulative materials, or step-by-step problem-solving procedures with notebook use.

Deep Learning

2.7

Talent or Practice?

When he was just seven years old, Wolfgang Amadeus Mozart embarked on a concert tour of Europe with his father, marking the beginning of his legendary career. His mastery of the violin and other stringed instruments at such a young age was undoubtedly extraordinary. Among his many musical talents, Mozart possessed an exceptionally rare ability that only one in 10,000 people has: perfect pitch, the ability to identify any musical note after hearing it, without reference to other notes.

Mozart's unique musical gift may lead us to believe that his talents were innate. However, to the surprise of many, we now know that perfect pitch is not a skill reserved for those who have it in their genes. Almost any child between the ages of two and six can develop this skill with the right training (Sakakibara, 1999, 2014). As one of the leading researchers in the field of skill development (Ericsson et al., 1993) writes,

> People believe that because expert performance is qualitatively different from normal performance the expert performer must be endowed with characteristics qualitatively different from those of normal adults. . . . We agree that expert performance is qualitatively different from normal performance and even that expert performers have characteristics and abilities that are qualitatively different from or at least outside the range of those of normal adults. However, we deny that these differences are immutable, that is, due to innate talent. Only a few exceptions, most notably height, are genetically prescribed. Instead, we argue that the differences between expert performers and normal adults reflect a life-long period of deliberate effort to improve performance in a specific domain.

Mozart's innate gift for music was probably not as unique as it seems; much of his mastery can likely be attributed to his environment. From birth, Mozart's father, Leopold—an experienced composer and music teacher—dedicated himself exclusively to training his son, especially in the musical domain. According to biographers, while Leopold was a strict and demanding teacher, young Wolfgang was even more demanding of himself, pushing his practice beyond what his father required. Mozart's fascination with music from a very early age motivated him to learn and practice for long hours since childhood. While he may have been born with some musical talent and other qualities that contributed to his great skill, such as an excellent memory, it was the training his father subjected him to and his own dedication that led him to achieve the pinnacle of music composition and performance. In fact, Mozart did not begin to compose works worthy of an expert until 10 years after he began practicing intensively (Hayes, 1985).

Although there are cases of individuals with extraordinary innate talents, most people who achieve outstanding mastery in a specific field do not initially have an uncommon advantage. Even the best in some disciplines are ordinary individuals who simply make use of the ability to learn—a gift we all have (Ericsson et al., 1993). It is also important to note that innate talent leads to nothing without a strong dose of practice and training. While those who have it might have more of a head start compared to others, the goal is always further, and reaching it requires the ability to learn (Hayes, 1985). Indeed, in many disciplines, most individuals who achieve international prominence have been engaged in intensive practice before the age of six (Ericsson & Crutcher, 1990).

What Sets Experts Apart from Novices?

The qualities that distinguish experts from beginners and the process by which a beginner becomes an expert have received significant attention from the scientific community in the fields of psychology and the neuroscience of learning. This is, not surprisingly, a highly relevant research topic for education.

Expertise development has been studied in areas that demand a significant amount of motor skills (sports, dance, etc.) and in fields dominated by cognitive skills (mathematics, science, history, linguistics, chess, etc.). This chapter will primarily focus on the development of cognitive skills, as they are more prominent in the school context and are ultimately involved in all areas of learning, including physical education. Nevertheless, the development of both types of skills shares many commonalities.

Studies comparing the characteristics of experts and novices in various disciplines consistently highlight the fact that experts do not differ from novices because of extraordinary innate talents. On the contrary, experts stand out because they have an extensive body of knowledge about their discipline that is well structured and organized around overarching principles, providing meaning, coherence, and flexibility. This knowledge enables them to perceive, interpret, and process information differently, affecting their ability to learn, reason, and solve problems more efficiently. The expert not only has extensive knowledge but, more importantly, deep knowledge.

Even in disciplines where it may seem that knowledge is not important at first glance, such as chess—where many believe it is a matter of intelligence—there is ample evidence that what sets world-class chess players apart from amateur players is a vast amount of knowledge acquired after countless hours of practice. It is estimated that a master has knowledge of up to 50,000 possible board positions, which they rely on to choose the best move (Chase & Simon, 1973).

Perception

Deep or highly meaningful knowledge (i.e., knowledge imbued with meaning, well organized and interconnected, and associated with multiple contexts of applicability) provides experts with several cognitive advantages in their area of expertise. First, experts can detect patterns that novices cannot perceive. This is because experts have integrated data sets into larger units that have meaning for them. For example, someone with extensive chess knowledge can look at the board shown in Figure 1 and describe the position of the pieces as follows:

> While the whites have a clear spatial advantage, with only two minor pieces per side, the blacks are not in too much trouble. The white pieces are more active; they are better positioned than their black counterparts. It all depends on whether the black pieces can play c6-c5 under favorable conditions. If they did, the blacks would revive their pieces and compete for space.

In contrast, a novice player will barely notice half of these insights (Chase & Simon, 1973). Similarly, a Rubik's Cube expert, upon seeing the cube in Figure 2, will recognize the situation and think, "To solve it, I just need to perform half a corner twist algorithm, that is, R' D' R D R' D' R U." To a beginner, the cube might appear to be in a random state.

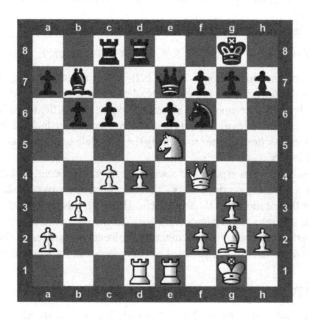

FIGURE 1

FIGURE 2 Rubik's Cube showing one of its more than 43 trillion possible configurations.

Now, let's consider an example in an area where everyone about to read this text is an expert. Please observe the following sequence of letters and try to read them:

N R A S O D U I – R E H P Y S I O R T – E Q A T K U R E A H

As an expert reader, you surely recognized the letters and were able to decode them, converting them into sounds in your working memory as you read them. But your ability to recognize patterns likely ended there, identifying each letter with its phoneme.

Now observe the same letters, presented in a different order:

D I N O S A U R – P R E H I S T O R Y – E A R T H Q U A K E

This time, you instantly recognized the pattern in the letter arrangement, which results in meaningful units for the expert reader—words. Deep knowledge of these words and their graphic composition allows the expert to identify them immediately, automatically, and effortlessly. In contrast, the novice reader lacks this ability and must decode words letter by letter to identify the complete word, just as you did with the first set of letters.

In similar fashion, when experts and novices are given five seconds to look at a chessboard in play, experts can reproduce the positions of almost all the pieces, whereas novices can remember the location of only about eight. However, this only happens when the board positions are from actual games. That is, when the pieces are placed randomly on the board, experts are no better at remembering the location of pieces on the board than novices (Chase & Simon, 1973). The expert can only recognize meaningful patterns.

Reasoning

The extensive and well-organized prior knowledge of experts also makes them more effective in reasoning about problems or situations related to their discipline.

Organizing their knowledge around significant concepts and ideas enables them to use their working memory more efficiently.

You may recall that working memory is the mental space where we consciously reason, and unfortunately, its capacity to manipulate information is limited to a few elements at a time. On average, working memory can hold about seven items (Miller, 1956). But what exactly is an item? An item is a unit with meaning. Thus, the letters *N R A S O D U I* can constitute eight items, which you could keep in your working memory with some effort after viewing them once. In contrast, the word *DINOSAUR* allows you to hold the same eight letters with very little effort because your knowledge of this word lets you combine them into a single meaningful unit.

The advantage of meaningful knowledge in reasoning is crucial. To understand its significance better, consider performing the following mental operation: 891×32. What I want you to notice is that you would probably find it much easier to solve the operation if you could use a notebook to write down the procedure and intermediate steps. Well, just as we can lighten the load on working memory by relying on external support, knowledge that we have well consolidated in our long-term memory also lightens the load on working memory (Sweller et al., 1998). That is, our knowledge allows our working memory to process much more information simultaneously than it could without that knowledge. But this knowledge must be meaningful; it should be part of solid schemas that include strong meaningful connections and conditions of applicability. When learning something new, what we already know about it and what needs to be brought into play for further learning will no longer occupy space in our working memory. On the contrary, everything we do not know—or rather, is not well consolidated in our long-term memory—will behave as "new information" that occupies space in working memory, limiting our capacity to learn.

In summary, the best way to optimize working memory capacity for a specific task is to acquire meaningful knowledge related to that task. As we will see at the end of this chapter, an extreme case occurs when we automate the cognitive processes involved in that task.

Problem-Solving

The broad and meaningful knowledge of experts also has implications for their ability to solve problems and generate solutions in various contexts.

When addressing problems related to their discipline, experts rely on their knowledge, organized around key concepts, to transcend the superficial aspect of the problem situation and identify the underlying fundamental principles. For example, Chi and colleagues (1981) asked students and physics teachers to classify a set of problems in this discipline based on their typology. While the teachers classified them based on the physical principles needed for their resolution (e.g., Newton's second law, the law of conservation of energy), the students classified them based on their superficial features (whether they involved inclined planes, free falls, and the like).

The ability to abstract the underlying principles of a problem situation also explains the greater ability of experts to transfer their knowledge to entirely new situations. It should be noted that expert knowledge includes information about its conditions of applicability, drawing from numerous cases and different contexts where the expert knows that this knowledge can be applied (Glaser, 1992).

Moreover, experts can fluently evoke and use their knowledge when needed, without significant cognitive load (Anderson, 1982). In many cases, experts employ their knowledge without having to generate any cognitive load—that is, without conscious effort or even awareness. For example, studies on chess mastery have revealed that when deciding on a move, both expert and novice players analyze all possible options and their consequences. However, experts immediately and spontaneously narrow down their analysis to high-quality moves (Chase & Simon, 1973).

Critical Thinking

While it is certainly possible to teach attitudes of critical thinking to students, it is challenging to put them into practice without the knowledge that allows us to verify the information we receive. Indeed, expert knowledge is also essential for developing critical analysis skills. For example, in a study by Paige and Simon (1966), experts and novices were asked to solve the following mathematical problem:

> We've cut a board into two pieces. The first piece is two-thirds the length of the original board, and the other is 122 cm longer than the first. What was the length of the board before it was cut?

Experts quickly recognized that the problem made no sense. Although some novices also noticed this, many others simply applied formulas and obtained a negative length.

An even more intriguing study, described by Reusser (1988), posed the following problem to first and second graders:

> There are 26 sheep and 10 goats on a ship. How old is the captain?

Surprisingly, three-quarters of the children attempted to solve the problem by performing operations with the numbers given in the problem. When aiming to solve a similar problem involving a shepherd instead of a captain, one student showed that their reasoning consisted of applying different arithmetic operations until the result provided a reasonable age.

Creativity

You only need to look at the work of John Hayes (1985) on the productivity of the great composers in history to appreciate that hardly any of them created masterworks with less than 10 years of intense preparation. Their production of creative works comes after this period of dedicated practice, following the development of a solid knowledge base on which to work (Figure 3).

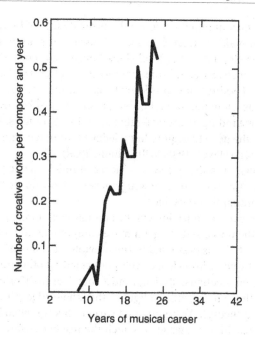

FIGURE 3 Number of masterworks created by composers based on the number of years of musical career (Adapted from Hayes, 1985).

Creativity is the ability to generate solutions that are new to the person developing them by combining their knowledge in a unique way. Of course, the ability to identify problems and opportunities is one of the most critical steps in the creative process.

Many inventions arise from the process of identifying everyday problems and turning them into opportunities to develop useful products or services.

For example, surgeon Henry Heimlich identified a significant problem when he read a report stating that choking was the sixth leading cause of accidental death. While many other doctors may have already detected this problem, Heimlich saw in this an opportunity for a creative solution. He soon realized that two of the recommended treatments for choking victims (removing the object with fingers and hitting the victim's back) would likely push the object farther down the victim's throat. Heimlich's experience as a thoracic surgeon helped him realize that there would probably be enough air in the victim's lungs to clear the airway if someone pressed on the diaphragm. His solution, the Heimlich maneuver, is now recognized as the best technique for saving the lives of choking victims and would not have been possible without his knowledge of thoracic anatomy.

How Is Expertise Achieved?

As noted earlier, the higher cognitive skills (typical of experts) highly valued today, such as reasoning, problem-solving, critical analysis, and creativity, necessarily rely on a broad base of meaningful knowledge. Thus the duality of knowledge and skills, as expressed when making statements like "Knowledge is not important" or "One should focus on developing higher-level skills," makes no sense. If such statements aim to criticize practices based on rote memorization of curricular content, the critique should instead address how this knowledge is acquired. For this knowledge to be relevant in the development of higher-level skills, it must be meaningful—that is, imbued with understanding and transferable to multiple contexts. However, we cannot underestimate the need to acquire knowledge because it is impossible to develop these skills without it (Hayes, 1985; Willingham, 2008).

In short, expertise in a discipline is achieved through the acquisition of meaningful knowledge. This raises the following question: How do we promote students' acquisition of meaningful knowledge?

The short answer to this question can be summarized in one phrase: by creating opportunities for them to use it. To get a more comprehensive and detailed answer, we need to revisit what was presented in the previous chapters of this section. First, meaningful knowledge is knowledge well connected to other related knowledge. To establish these connections, students must mobilize their prior knowledge and think about what they are learning in light of this knowledge (Craik and Lockhart's levels of processing theory). As highlighted earlier, this is related to *active learning*, encompassing all teaching strategies in which the teacher ensures that students try to make sense of what they are learning. You may recall how a one-way, expository class alone is not considered an active learning method as it does not guarantee that students are thinking about what they see and hear (even though some may do so spontaneously). Therefore, to promote meaningful learning, additional activities are necessary to motivate students to make sense of what they learn.

Furthermore, applying what was learned in multiple contexts also promotes the creation of new connections and encourages abstraction, resulting in better-organized and more transferable knowledge. Guiding students in identifying patterns and applying what they have learned in new situations, explicitly making visible the (abstract) principles underlying them, is a very effective way to promote meaningful learning (Willingham, 2008). This was extensively discussed in the chapter on transfer of learning.

Similarly, using knowledge involves retrieving it. As explored in the chapter on memory processes, retrieval strengthens learning and helps better organize the acquired knowledge by creating new connections with other related knowledge, enhancing its transferability.

In a broad sense, students develop meaningful knowledge when they use it to analyze and interpret situations, solve problems, and create all kinds of solutions. These situations and solutions range from a text to a large technological project.

In light of all this, practice is no doubt essential for developing meaningful knowledge that leads to mastery. However, this requirement demands a precious commodity often scarce in the school context: time. Thus, it is important to reflect on the scope of educational goals. In this regard, evidence consistently supports the choice of less extensive but deeper curricula, where fewer concepts and procedures are addressed, but a greater mastery of these is sought, over extensive but shallow curricula attempting to cover many topics without allowing for proper understanding—especially in cases where what is being taught contradicts the students' preexisting knowledge (Bransford et al., 2000). An important distinction between deep and superficial learning will be revealed in the students' ability to transfer their newly acquired knowledge (apply it in new contexts).

Practice Makes Perfect

As the saying goes, to master a discipline, you must practice. However, not all ways of practicing are equally effective. Swedish psychologist Anders Ericsson, one of the foremost authorities in the study of expertise development, emphasized this idea through the concept of *deliberate practice* (Ericsson et al., 1993).

One of Ericsson's major findings is that the skill one develops in a discipline has more to do with how it is practiced than with the simple repetition of that skill. According to Ericsson, deliberate practice is conscious and serves a purpose. The expert-to-be breaks down the skills needed to achieve mastery and focuses on improving each of these skills during practice sessions, often with the feedback from an expert teacher. Another important feature of deliberate practice is that it progressively increases in difficulty, reaching ever more challenging levels for the learner to master the desired skill.

While Ericsson developed his ideas on deliberate practice in the context of competitive disciplines (sports, dance, chess, music, etc.), many of his principles are equally valid in academic disciplines, as other researchers have noted (e.g., Anzai, 1991; Patel & Groen, 1991). To begin with, we could highlight the fact that breaking down, dosing, and timely sequencing the learning object facilitates its mastery.

Decomposing and Integrating

Any concept, model, procedure, or skill we wish to teach or learn can be broken down into multiple parts or components. Often, experts are unaware of all the components enabling them to understand or be proficient in something because they have integrated them so intimately into their long-term memory that they apply them automatically, without passing through working memory. For example, people who can read have forgotten everything their brain needs to do to carry out this extraordinary skill. All the processes shown in Box 1 are components that make up the skill of reading. Expert readers have integrated them so intimately into their long-term memory that they are no longer aware that they are applying them when they read, because they no longer need to pass through working memory. We call this "unconscious competence" the expert's *blind spot*, and if a teacher is to improve their effectiveness as an educator, it is essential that they are fully aware of it.

Therefore, to optimize learning, we can break down the object to be learned into its components and learn them one by one, gradually consolidating them in long-term memory. What is learned no longer occupies space in working memory, freeing up room for new information while also supporting its learning if the sequence is coherent. After mastering the components, they should gradually be integrated, and, finally, multiple opportunities should be provided to use them in an integrated manner. However, it is advisable not to lose sight of the final goal in the process.

An example from cinema that illustrates this idea is in the movie *The Karate Kid* (1984). Daniel LaRusso's karate master, Mr. Miyagi, has a rather unique teaching method. Instead of training his disciple in the art of karate from day one, he has him wax cars ("Wax on, wax off") and paint fences ("Side, side. Lock the wrist"). Once Daniel has mastered these techniques, Mr. Miyagi teaches him to integrate and apply them as defensive moves against his opponent's attacks and then continues with other karate components. This iconic line from the movie sums up Mr. Miyagi's teaching method well: "First learn stand, then learn fly."

There is substantial evidence that students learn more effectively when the components of the learning object are temporarily worked on in isolation and gradually combined (White & Frederiksen, 1990; Salden et al., 2006; Wightman & Lintern, 1985). Even a small amount of practice in one of the components of the learning object leads to a significant improvement in overall learning (Lovett, 2001).

It is true that breaking down learning goals into their components and learning them one at a time can have adverse effects on motivation. In *The Karate Kid*, Daniel LaRusso saw no use in waxing cars or painting fences, and this demotivated him at first. But when he started applying what he had learned, using the same moves to defend against the opponent's attacks, his motivation rocketed. The same happens when students start applying what they have learned to understand ideas that interest them or to solve relevant problems.

BOX 1 Reading skill components, in order of acquisition.

1. **Phonological awareness:** Recognizing that spoken language is composed of a finite set of sounds that combine
2. **Alphabetical principle:** Understanding that written language graphically represents each of the sounds of the language using letters or sets of letters
3. **Phonetic decoding of letters and syllables:** Identifying the sounds represented by letters and syllables
4. **Phonetic decoding of words:** Reading complete words following the logic of the relationship between graphemes and phonemes
5. **Semantic decoding of words:** Extracting the meaning of the words read
6. **Semantic decoding of texts:** Extracting the meaning of texts read based on grapheme-phoneme decoding
7. **Visual word recognition:** Visually recognizing complete words and phonetically decoding them as a reading unit
8. **Semantic decoding of complex texts:** Understanding complex texts, which depends directly on the reader's prior knowledge

Adapted from Willingham (2017).

Nonetheless, there is no need to wait for the integration of components to generate motivation for what is being learned. Often, it is possible to connect the components with contexts or purposes that give them meaning, whether directly related to the ultimate learning goal or to other peripheral or complementary goals. Mr. Miyagi could have explained to Daniel the utility of waxing cars and painting fences for karate practice, or he could have given them meaning by themselves, such as by asking him to paint the fences of a nursing home.

Properly dosing and sequencing learning is also a way to reduce intrinsic cognitive load (Sweller, 2010). You may recall that this is the cognitive load attributed to the complexity of the learning goal itself. As noted in earlier chapters, this type of cognitive load depends on the student's prior knowledge. That is why the small-dose strategy is very useful—what is learned with each "dose" facilitates the learning of the next one. Although students can regulate their own learning in small doses, the intervention on intrinsic cognitive load is particularly important from the teacher's perspective. As the designer of instructional units, the teacher can break down the learning object into its components, sequence them, and guide their integration properly. Clearly, the teacher (the expert) is crucial for guiding the learning process. However, as was mentioned, they must be careful with their expert blind spot.

Practice in the School Context

In the school context, practice should be understood in two ways. First, it is the opportunity to engage in multiple activities in which acquired knowledge is put into play, time and time again, but in different contexts to reinforce understanding and flexibility (i.e., its transferability). This applies to knowledge such as the concept of *density*, the meaning of *carpe diem*, or the use of rhetorical figures. Second, practice can be aimed at developing fluency in specific procedures within a discipline, such as decoding in reading, arithmetic calculations, or the use of the past simple tense in irregular English verbs.

In either case, practice aims to improve the fluency with which we use our knowledge, whether it is conceptual or procedural. Its greatest achievement is to lead us to a level of mastery where we can use this knowledge effortlessly. This highly desirable state is known as *automaticity*.

Automaticity is another quality of deep knowledge, especially in the development of cognitive and motor skills. As previously mentioned, it involves the ability to retrieve knowledge or perform procedures without the need for conscious thought when the environmental stimuli are appropriate. This means that automated tasks do not occupy space in working memory—we do not need to think about them continuously to perform them. Given the limited amount of information a person can attend to at any one time, automating certain aspects of a task gives individuals more capacity to focus on other aspects of that task or other tasks (Anderson, 1982).

Driving is a good example of how automaticity unfolds with practice. In the first driving lessons, beginners need to be mindful of everything they must do to operate the vehicle, follow traffic rules, and take all necessary precautions, so they cannot even hold a conversation. With experience, driving skills become automated to the point where they can drive with full attention on the road and not on the mechanisms to operate the car or the actions to perform in each maneuver. They can even hold a conversation or think about what they will do when they reach their destination (although I will always recommend keeping your eyes on the road).

Similarly, novice readers, whose ability to decode letters and words is not yet fluent, cannot focus on understanding what they are reading (LaBerge & Samuels, 1974). Expert readers have developed such a high level of automaticity that they cannot help but read a word as soon as they see it.

Psychology explains the development of automaticity based on the duality between explicit memory and procedural memory (Poldrack & Packard, 2003; Ullman, 2016). As you may recall, explicit memory contains all kinds of information of which we are aware and that we can use for reasoning and problem-solving. Procedural memory, on the other hand, exists without us being aware of it and allows us to perform actions without thinking about how to do them, such as driving a car or reading a text (knowing that we can do these things when we are not doing them is a feature of explicit memory). While explicit memory allows us to learn very quickly, even with a single exposure, procedural memory requires much more time and multiple exposures. Thus, our conscious memory predominates when we start learning a new skill, but with practice, procedural memory can take over, enabling us to achieve automaticity (Ullman, 2016).

Undoubtedly, automaticity is particularly desirable for a range of fundamental skills in the educational context. Perhaps one of the most important skills is related to reading decoding processes, but fluency in speaking a second language or basic arithmetic calculation are also good candidates. In any case, achieving automaticity is not easy and requires a lot of practice, which can be demotivating depending on how it is managed. Therefore, it is critical to decide which tasks should truly be automated and which can remain in the realm of explicit memory, so that students have the knowledge to perform them but need to consciously think about what they are doing.

SOCIAL AND EMOTIONAL FACTORS IN LEARNING

When psychology and neuroscience embarked on the exciting task of studying how we learn, the focus was on the cognitive processes of learning—how the brain acquires information from its environment and how it manipulates, stores, retrieves, and uses it (Lachman et al., 1979). In the 1950s and 1960s, the rise of computer science and the subsequent introduction of computers provided a model for cognitive sciences that inspired researchers for decades. This model excluded mechanisms related to emotion as they were considered unnecessary to understand how the brain processes information, relegating them to other fields of study.

However, the brain-computer model lost validity as research progressed. First, it became apparent that human memory does not handle, accumulate, or retrieve information in the same way as a computer or any other machine or instrument we have invented (as discussed in earlier chapters). Second, studies revealed the limited capability of our brain to make decisions or solve problems logically (Kahneman, 2011). Finally, in the late 20th and early 21st centuries, research in all areas of human cognition, both at the neurological and psychological levels, began to show that emotional mechanisms play a very relevant role whenever we engage in any information processing task, from perception to reasoning. These findings suggested that the classic division between the study of emotion and cognition was unrealistic, and that understanding cognitive processes—such as those related to learning and memory—required the consideration of emotion.

Furthermore, educational research has increasingly emphasized how the social nature of our species influences teaching and learning processes. Teaching, in fact, is a clear manifestation that we are a highly social species, and the way we learn has also evolved in this context.

This section explores the main social and emotional factors involved in the processes of learning and teaching. Since one of the most relevant factors is undoubtedly motivation, I dedicate two chapters to discuss it. I also shed light on what we really know about how emotions modulate our capability to learn.

The Role of Emotions in Learning

Learning and Emotions

Research on the impact of emotions on cognitive processes of learning and memory is quite recent (with the exception of research on exam anxiety). Consequently, there are still very few rigorous findings that we can apply to educational practice. Despite this, we often come across information reportedly backed by science about how emotions modulate learning and how we should use them in the classroom. One of the most repeated ideas is that "'we only learn through emotion" or "emotions make lesson content more memorable." But what does science really say about the relationship between emotion and learning? Combining reason and emotion has a clear ideological appeal, which can lead to confirmation bias. Hence, it is advisable to approach such claims with caution. So far, science has recognized that emotions influence even processes considered to be exclusively "rational" and has provided evidence of how they do so. But not everything stated in the media (or even in teacher training courses) has a scientific basis. In this chapter, I briefly outline the existing evidence of how emotions influence teaching and learning processes.

What Do We Mean When We Talk About Emotions in Education?

Perhaps one of the factors causing confusion and misunderstandings in discussions about emotions in education is the broad and diverse use of the term *emotion*. This can lead to individuals thinking about different things when discussing it. For example, what do we mean when we say we need to pay attention to emotions in the classroom? It is different to talk about emotions as a modulating factor of learning than to talk about emotional education. Discussing emotions as a modulating factor refers, for example, to whether educational activities should be "emotionally charged" for effective learning—whether we can use emotions to promote better memory of classroom experiences. It can also refer to the importance of creating learning environments that consider students' emotional dimension to contribute to their academic and personal development. On the other hand, the latter focuses on the significance of teaching students to recognize and manage their emotions.

Both aspects have an impact on learning, but emotional education goes further, aiming for holistic goals: equipping students with social and emotional skills that contribute to building their personal and social well-being. Since these aspects go beyond the role of emotions in learning (and this book is about how we learn), I will only address aspects related to how emotions influence the learning process. I also dedicate a chapter to emotional regulation in self-regulated learning in the next section of the book.

Now, with the focus on how emotions modulate our ability to learn, an important distinction must be made. Many times when we talk about emotion, we specifically refer to motivation. The role of motivation in learning is evident and highly relevant (I discuss this extensively in the next two chapters). Motivation encourages the student to devote more attention, time, and effort to the learning task, leading to better learning. However, this is not what is usually meant when we say that emotion modulates learning. This idea refers to the emotions students experience during an educational activity, which can either enhance or hinder their ability to learn or remember what was learned, regardless of the time or effort invested. In other words, it refers to the fact that emotions can make an experience more or less memorable.

In this regard, and to conclude this important clarification about the role of emotions in education, two possible cases must be distinguished in which they can affect the memorability of educational experiences: when they intensify the memory of what happened in class (although not necessarily what students were supposed to learn) and when they undermine the learning process itself because they divert the student's attention to irrelevant stimuli or thoughts (for example, when students cannot maintain attention on the task at hand for fear of making a mistake or looking foolish).

In this chapter, I primarily focus on outlining what we know about how emotional episodes modulate memory—how emotions influence memory consolidation. I also discuss how emotions can interfere with the encoding process of what we expect students to learn, and the chapter concludes with a brief look at emotional regulation. But before all that, it would be useful to define what emotions are.

What Are Emotions?

Emotions are automatic behavioral, physiological, and psychological responses of our body to certain external or internal stimuli that are perceived as a threat or an opportunity (Shuman & Scherer, 2015). Even though we may feel like we have control over our bodies, emotions remind us that this is not the case. Our body acts autonomously, regulating many life processes that we cannot consciously control. But it also takes control of processes we usually manage consciously when it deems it necessary, depending on how it interprets an external stimulus or an internal physiological state in relation to our well-being or survival. For example, if we want to pet our neighbor's new dog but it shows its teeth and begins to growl, our brain immediately triggers a pattern of emotional behavior: we pull our hand back, step away, and focus our attention on the dog's snout. All of this can happen even before we are aware of what we are doing. Additionally, our heart starts beating faster and our breathing accelerates, among other things.

The above example illustrates that emotions occur automatically and involuntarily, and are activated very rapidly, sometimes even before we are aware of the stimulus that triggered them. They cause physiological changes in our body and make us react impulsively in fractions of a second. But not only that; in response to stimuli that our brain interprets as a threat or an opportunity, emotions also try to take control of our consciousness to promote behaviors that lead us to flee, fight, freeze, or approach the stimulus that generated them. When they do so intensely, we say they "cloud our consciousness."

When experiencing emotions and their effects on our consciousness, we try to define and label them just as we do with everything else. The interpretation and rationalization we do of emotions when trying to explain and make sense of them is called *feelings*. This categorization is greatly influenced by the social and cultural environment, which provides us with terms and concepts to describe them. In fact, there are differences in the emotions described by different human cultures, and even within the same society, the types of emotions can change over time (Shuman & Scherer, 2015). While the physiological processes that produce emotions do not change, the way in which we interpret and conceptualize them does, which depends on language and culture.

Meanwhile, science has sought to identify and define a set of universal emotions, but scientists have not yet reached a consensus on how many there are (and they may not do so for a long time). The simplest hypothesis reduces them to four and explains all others as combinations of these: fear, anger, joy, and sadness (Jack et al., 2014). Other hypotheses mention six, adding disgust and surprise to the previous four (Ekman, 1992), or even eight, including shame and pride (Tracy & Robins, 2004). Ultimately, there is no consensus on which emotions are basic or universal, and which ones are socially constructed.

It is worth noting that, in the field of education, most psychologists use two gradational dimensions to classify emotions. On one hand, emotions are distinguished by the level of activation or arousal they produce. For example, strong emotions are high-arousal emotions.

On the other hand, emotions have a qualitative value or valence, which, to simplify, distinguishes between pleasant or positive emotions (joy, curiosity, surprise) and unpleasant or negative emotions (fear, anxiety, sadness). Different emotional experiences then fall on a continuum formed by these two dimensions (arousal and valence), as shown in Figure 1.

Now that we have a basic characterization of emotions, we should return to the topic at hand and pose the following questions: What is the relationship between emotions and learning? Is it necessary to become emotional to learn? Are there emotions that promote learning and others that hinder it? Next, I will discuss what science knows about how emotions generated during an experience influence the memory of that event.

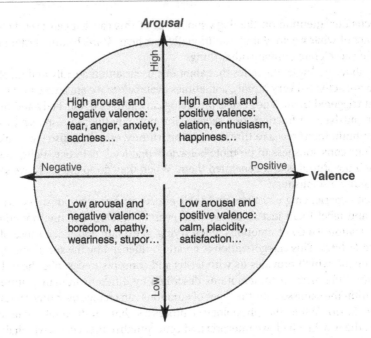

FIGURE 1 Types of emotions according to the two-dimensional gradational model composed of level of arousal and valence type.

How Does Emotion Modulate Learning and Memory?

It is obvious that experiences with a strong emotional charge (i.e., a high-arousal level) are more likely to be remembered. William James, considered the father of American psychology, wrote in 1890 that events of great emotional charge seemed to metaphorically "leave a scar upon the cerebral tissues." Several studies in cognitive psychology and neurobiology have provided ample evidence for the memory-enhancing effect of emotions. However, this claim is rather vague and open to interpretation, so let's delve a bit deeper into the details.

First, studies in which dozens of volunteers were asked to describe their clearest childhood memories (e.g., Rubin & Kozin, 1984) reveal that people mostly report moments with a high emotional charge: loss of loved ones, moments of happiness or terror, and the like. Moreover, we all agree that events that evoke strong emotions seem to hold a special and privileged place in our memory. Indeed, some researchers argue that this kind of memory, called *flashbulb* memories, must have unique encoding and consolidation mechanisms that make them especially vivid and indelible (Brown & Kulik, 1977). We all have memories of this kind, which we believe we can recall with the same clarity as on the first day.

However, are emotionally charged memories truly so special? Studying the effect of very strong emotions on memory in the laboratory is not an easy task. Suppose we told someone that they had won a million dollars only to study their reaction, and then confess that it was not true. This would not be very ethical, true, but finding someone to fund this ridiculously expensive study for the sake of ethics would not be that practical either.

The fact is that various researchers have studied the nature of flashbulb memories based on the occurrence of suddenly impactful social events. For example, Talarico and Rubin (2003) interviewed 54 students the day after the terrible events of September 11, 2001, in the United States when the terrorist organization Al Qaeda attacked the Twin Towers and the Pentagon. If you are of a certain age, you will likely remember where you were and with whom you were when you heard the news.

In their questionnaires, the researchers requested details about the circumstances in which the students experienced those events and about their confidence in their memories. They also inquired about any other emotionally significant events from that same week, usually involving parties, dates, sports events, and the like. Then the researchers contacted the volunteers again, either 1, 6, or 32 weeks later, and asked them the same questions—what they remembered from those days and how confident they were in the accuracy of their memories. The graphs in Figure 2 show the number of details provided by the volunteers that were consistent or inconsistent with their initial memory (left) and the degree to which they rated their confidence in the accuracy of those memories (right).

As observed, the accuracy of memory for the day of the terrorist attack on the Twin Towers in New York and that of the moderately emotional event gradually declined in both cases at the same rate: the number of consistent details decreased, while

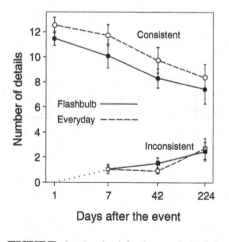 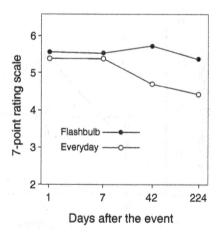

FIGURE 2 On the left, the number of details consistent and inconsistent with the initial recollection of the events, for both flashbulb memory and the memory of an emotional everyday event. On the right, the degree of confidence in the accuracy of the memories (Talarico & Rubin, 2003 / with permission of Sage Publications Ltd.).

new elements (false memories) increased. That is, forgetting influenced the two variables in the same way. However, the participants' belief in the accuracy of memory remained high for the 9/11 event and declined for everyday memories. Therefore, highly emotional events may not be more immune to forgetting than moderately emotional events, but they create an illusion of being better remembered. Studies like these have been repeated with many other events, yielding similar results (e.g., McCloskey et al., 1988).

It is evident that when an event generates emotions, it is better retained than when it does not. In a classic study (Cahill & McGaugh, 1995), two groups of students were asked to view a short slide show that told a story of a boy visiting his father in the hospital where he worked. Two different stories were created, and the narration accompanying each slide varied for the two groups. So when, in the middle of the story, very explicit and quite disturbing surgical scenes were shown, one group was told that it was a simulation with actors, and the other group was told it was a real life-or-death case. Several days later, all participants were interviewed to gather data on what they recalled from each part of the story (none of the participants knew that their memory would be tested). Figure 3 shows the number of correct details each group recalled in each of the three phases of the story, with the middle phase corresponding to the surgery episode. The group that heard the emotional story recalled many more details of the disturbing part of the story (the slight differences observed at the beginning of the story are not statistically significant).

This and many other studies have shown that emotional stimuli are remembered better than those that are emotionally neutral. But how do we know if this is due to a direct effect of emotion on memory? Researchers have argued that the cause of this phenomenon could be that the emotion elicited by the emotional stimulus causes

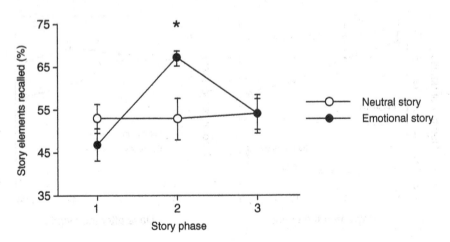

FIGURE 3 Number of details correctly remembered in each phase of the story (Cahill & McGaugh, 1995 / with permission of ELSEVIER).

us to pay a lot of attention to it, and as a result, we retain it better. This explanation is not unreasonable; several research studies have shown that in situations of high emotional impact (high arousal) caused by a specific stimulus, such as witnessing open-heart surgery or a crime, emotion triggers such an intense focus of attention that the attended object is remembered well, but memory for peripheral details is very limited. This phenomenon has important implications for the reliability of eyewitness testimonies to a crime because, while attention becomes focused on very specific details of their experience, the rest of the elements become vague in their memory. If they are pressed to explain them, their memory may reconstruct them inaccurately from other experiences and memories, a fact that has sadly led to many innocent individuals being sent to prison and even to the electric chair.

In short, the brain responds to emotionally intense stimuli by focusing its attention on them and ignoring what surrounds them. In an educational context, this might be what happens when we conduct a spectacular experiment in the laboratory and provide a good explanation of its causes. Many students only recall when that liquid exploded or changed color, but they are none the wiser as to the cause of it.

Fortunately, it seems that for emotion to promote more vivid memories, there is no need for a specific stimulus to activate an acute emotional reaction and monopolize our attention. In a series of experiments, Laney and colleagues (2003) showed that intense emotional themes were sufficient to remember an event better, not only the specific emotional stimulus but the entire event in general. For example, when a story has an emotional context, both its essence and the details of the plot are recalled much better. However, this does not answer the question of whether emotion has a direct effect on memory. Is emotion itself what makes memories more vivid, or does emotion simply make us pay more attention to them? It could also be that emotion encourages us to think more about them and retrieve them repeatedly, so we remember them better. After all, two of the cognitive processes that most enhance memory are retrieving the memory and thinking about it (with or without emotional arousal). So is the effect of emotion direct or indirect?

Well, there is evidence that points to the former. For example, Nielson and colleagues (2005) had two groups of participants learn a list of 35 words. They took an immediate recall test to see how many words they remembered, and both groups had the same average result. Next, they were asked to watch a video; one group watched a somewhat disturbing scene of oral surgery (emotional), while the other witnessed a toothbrushing scene (emotionally neutral). Thirty minutes later, participants were given an unannounced test and were asked again to write down as many words from the initial word list as they could remember. Surprisingly, this time, those who had viewed the emotionally arousing videotape remembered more words on average. The same happened when they were given the same test 24 hours later (Figure 4).

Therefore, this experiment (and many others that have replicated the same effect) demonstrates that emotions have an enhancing effect on memory that is independent of whether they encourage us to pay attention to the emotional stimulus or

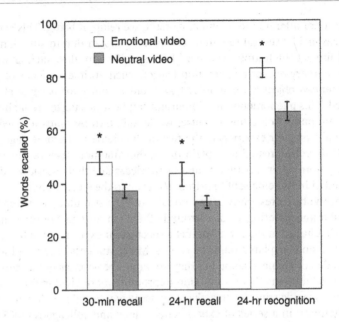

FIGURE 4 Percentage of words recalled after the preliminary test, based on whether the video viewed after the study was emotionally neutral or arousing (Nielson et al., 2005 / with permission of ELSEVIER).

think about it repeatedly. It is as if they intensify our ability to consolidate memories of anything we have encoded in memory during the emotional event, and even memories of experiences that occurred before and are in the process of consolidation (such as the word list that the participants in the previous study were asked to learn before viewing the videos). In the chapter on memory processes, I mentioned that memory consolidation is a process that continues in our brain even when we are no longer thinking about the objects that generated them (i.e., after leaving working memory).

In this regard, neuroscience has shed light on how emotion enhances memory (McGaugh, 2013; Phelps, 2006). Today, we know that in response to an emotional stimulus (that is, one relevant to our survival or goals), a region of our brain, the amygdala, is activated, and it can modulate the hippocampus—the brain region involved in explicit memory formation. The amygdala sends signals to the hippocampus that enhance its ability to encode and consolidate the experiences it is processing. Since consolidation mechanisms continue in the hippocampus minutes and even hours after the learning experience, the effects of the amygdala on the hippocampus not only affect the memory of the experiences that activated the amygdala but also memories of earlier experiences. In fact, the effect of the amygdala on the hippocampus also has some duration, so it also influences the formation of memories of experiences immediately following the emotional event.

From an evolutionary perspective, the effect of the amygdala on memory makes perfect sense. For example, when our ancestors suddenly came across a dangerous animal on the savanna, it was useful to recall not only the experience of the threat (the animal itself) but everything that preceded and followed it. Those details could be important for anticipating similar situations in the future before they happened.

In addition to influencing the memorability of episodic memories generated by the hippocampus, the amygdala also learns on its own, without our conscious awareness (Phelps, 2006). Specifically, we understand the role the amygdala plays in what is known as *fear conditioning*—the learning process by which our brain associates a stimulus with danger and assigns a fear response to it. When we encounter this stimulus again, the amygdala triggers an emotional reaction, even before we are consciously aware of having seen it. For example, if the neighbor's new dog bites us, the amygdala will remember it and elicit a fear or stress response when we see the dog next time. This capacity of the amygdala to learn is independent of the hippocampus, and, therefore, it is a part of implicit (unconscious) memory. So if a person's brain were to sustain hippocampus damage but retained an intact amygdala, they could still associate stimuli with fear and respond to them, but the person would have no conscious recollection of why they feel fear toward a stimulus they have no conscious memory of ever encountering before. Without the hippocampus, we would feel fear of the dog that bit us, even though we would not consciously remember ever having seen it.

But the hippocampus also operates independently of the amygdala. In fact, most of what gets stored in our memory does not come from emotionally arousing situations that trigger the amygdala (thankfully). A stimulus need not be emotional for the hippocampus to turn it into a memory; it continuously stores information about everything we do (otherwise, how would we remember what we did today?). To make these memories last, we only need to think about them and, in doing so, connect them with our prior knowledge. Patients who have suffered severe damage to the amygdala but have an intact hippocampus can generate memories just like a healthy person, but they do not experience memory enhancement when exposed to emotional stimuli (Cahill et al., 1995).

In short, while it is true that emotions can enhance our ability to remember the experiences we live through, they are not indispensable to do so. On the other hand, most of the research studies today on how emotion makes experiences more memorable are almost exclusively limited to cases of "strong" emotions (with a high level of arousal) that significantly activate the amygdala. These emotions are caused by intense personal experiences or induced in the laboratory using disturbing images. It would be unethical to use these types of emotions in the classroom to enhance learning. In fact, as we will see later, strong emotions often hinder the kind of learning we aim for in school.

However, in recent years, evidence has accumulated regarding the positive effect that moderately intense emotional states can have on learning—specifically, those related to emotions like surprise and curiosity, among others. I will now discuss this further.

The Effect of Surprise and Curiosity on Memory

Several recent studies suggest that it is not necessary to evoke strong emotions in students to enhance their memory of what they do in class; even mild emotions can have an impact.

Thus, we have evidence of the enhancing effect of learning through surprises that can occur in an educational context. Importantly, this does not necessarily involve shocking or startling experiences; simply deviating from the routine can produce the desired effect, and the impact of these emotions goes beyond just remembering the surprising event—it extends to remembering what students perceive before and after the surprising event.

For example, Ballarini and colleagues (2013) studied this effect in 1,676 primary school students divided into two groups. In one experiment, they read a story to the students to assess how many details the students would recall 24 hours later. While one group experienced no changes in their routine on the day of the story, the other encountered unexpected situations one hour before or after the story reading, such as a change of classroom or a lesson taught by a new teacher. The next day, the second group recalled up to 40% more details from the story than the first group. These findings have been replicated in similar tests with students of various ages, including university students, consistently showing that when unexpected elements are introduced, days later students not only remember that surprise but also recall other details of what happened during the lesson better than when it occurs in routine contexts. Specifically, these experiments revealed that everything occurring from an hour before to an hour after the novel event is remembered more vividly (Ballarini et al., 2013; Nielson & Arentsen, 2012).

On the other hand, research in recent years has also shown that emotional states associated with curiosity increase people's ability to recall what they perceive in that state. For example, Gruber and colleagues (2014) presented participants with a set of trivia questions and asked them to rate their level of curiosity about knowing the answer before revealing it. After a series of questions and answers, a surprise test was conducted to record which answers participants remembered. For questions that generated greater curiosity, participants recalled an average of 70.6%, while they only recalled 54.1% of those that did not pique their curiosity as much.

Naturally, this result might not be a direct consequence of curiosity but rather related to participants' prior knowledge. Often, we are more curious about topics we already have some knowledge of because they interest us more. The more prior knowledge we have about something, the easier it is to learn about related things. As you may recall, learning occurs by making connections between prior knowledge and new information. Hence, the more knowledge we have about something, the more connections we can make with any new data or ideas related to it, resulting in stronger and more easily retrievable memories.

To rule out this explanation, however, the researchers in the previous study also showed participants pictures of faces while they awaited the answers to the trivia questions. At the end of the procedure, participants were also assessed for their memory of those faces. Participants were better able to recall the faces they saw during states of high curiosity, as if curiosity indeed enhanced their ability to retain stimuli presented at that moment. The results showed that this effect was small but statistically significant, providing some evidence of the influence curiosity can have on memory.

Emotions for Learning

With all of this in mind, we could conclude that teachers should try to make their classes exciting to promote more lasting learning. After all, emotions enhance memory, right? Paradoxically, though, the fact that strong emotions intensify our memories does not necessarily mean that students learn more during an emotionally charged classroom activity.

To understand this paradox, it is essential to note that what we commonly refer to as memory—technically known as explicit memory—can be divided into episodic memory and semantic memory (Tulving, 2002).

As explained in the chapter on memory components, episodic (or autobiographical) memory records the events of our daily life—information associated with our experiences, whether routine details of daily life or more significant, isolated experiences. On the other hand, semantic memory stores our knowledge.

While both types of memory are closely related, ample evidence suggests that they differ functionally. One key difference between them is that episodic memory always includes contextual references, meaning that memories are always linked to details about the circumstances in which they were acquired—such as the place and time they happened and the emotions we experienced when they were formed. In contrast, the information stored in semantic memory usually lacks contextual references (such as when, where, or how we learned it). We may know what an elephant is but may not necessarily remember when or where we learned it.

In other words, episodic memory is closely tied to a specific context—the experience that generated it—while semantic memory is more "abstract" and detached from that reference. Actually, much of the information in semantic memory is in the form of meanings, which are constructed gradually from multiple experiences. Ideas and concepts are part of semantic memory.

For this and other reasons, the memory-enhancing effect of intense emotional states primarily influences our episodic memories and does not have as much impact on semantic memory—the type of memory we ultimately want to strengthen in the classroom. Therefore, when students engage in an emotionally charged activity in class, the next day they mainly remember what happened during the lesson but often recall very little of what they were supposed to learn.

Moreover, often, what triggers the emotion is not exactly the learning object but some peripheral aspect of the activity, which becomes the focus of the student's attention at the expense of the lesson's goals. In other words, emotions in the classroom, especially if they are intense, often cause extraneous cognitive load that makes it difficult for students to focus on the learning goals.

While the strengthening of episodic memory triggered by intense emotions can eventually aid in recalling specific learning goals, its effect often hinders the reflective activities necessary for conceptual and procedural learning, which aim for transfer (Vogel & Schwabe, 2016).

But this does not mean that emotions do not play a crucial role in learning. As we will see shortly, students experience emotions in the classroom continually, whether we intend for it to happen or not—the social interactions in class and the challenges presented by learning activities inevitably evoke them. These are indeed the emotions that have the most impact on learning and to which we should pay real attention. These emotions may alter a student's performance at a given moment but also determine their motivation to learn. I will now discuss the former and dedicate the next two chapters to motivation.

Emotions and Performance

The challenges a student faces in the classroom, along with the numerous interactions with the teacher and peers, continually shape their emotional state. The resulting emotions will influence their learning and performance. Positive emotions are evidently more beneficial in terms of motivation. However, when it comes to student performance in classroom tasks, all emotions, whether positive or negative, can have either favorable or detrimental effects. The crucial factor influencing the impact on student performance is the level of physiological and psychological activation they induce, known as their *arousal* level.

Earlier in this chapter, we discussed strong emotions and moderately intense emotions and their relationship with learning. The level of activation or arousal resulting from an emotional response—and consequently the degree to which it affects our cognitive functions and behavior—is an essential variable when discussing the effects of emotions in an educational context. This is because, depending on the level of activation, the effectiveness of a classroom learning task will be either enhanced or weakened. Even so-called negative emotions, such as anxiety, fear, or stress arising when facing a challenge, can be beneficial for learning as long as they remain at moderate levels of arousal for short periods. Let me insist again: moderate intensity and short duration are key.

The intensity of emotions and their effects on our cognitive functions varies, ranging from overactivation, as seen with intense emotions or states of alertness, to underactivation, as observed in states of relaxation or drowsiness. In either case, our ability to perform conscious tasks requiring attention, reflection, or reasoning (such as learning) is compromised. But when activation falls in an intermediate range, we are in an optimal state for performing such tasks.

In the case of stress or anxiety, this phenomenon has been a topic of research in psychology since the early 20th century. In 1908, Yerkes and Dodson formulated a law that describes the relationship between the level of stress experienced and the effectiveness in performing a task that demands cognitive resources. According to them, this relationship can be expressed using a bell-shaped curve, as shown in Figure 5.

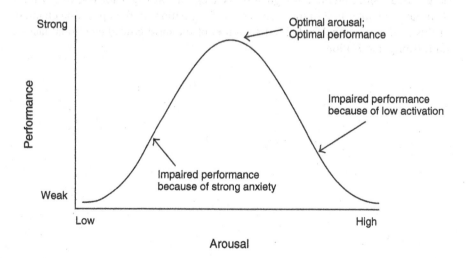

FIGURE 5   Yerkes-Dodson Law for cognitively demanding tasks.

In short, performance is optimal when levels of arousal are moderate. If arousal is too high or too low, it will adversely impact the outcome of the task.

This principle can be extended, with nuances, to any type of emotion that can arise in the context of an educational activity. Thus, positive emotions are not solely beneficial for learning; they can also be disruptive to learning if the level of arousal is too high. Just imagine a student in a state of extreme excitement when you are trying to teach them how to solve a problem that requires concentration.

Strong emotions, in general, are not usually conducive to learning or performance in the school setting. Whether positive or negative, they hinder reasoning and overwhelm working memory. Sometimes, strong emotions arise in the classroom due to a testing situation, a public presentation, a group project, or simply a wrong answer to a question posed by the teacher. Other times, students come to class in intense emotional states resulting from personal life situations. In either case, emotions divert students' attention and fill their working memory with superfluous thoughts about the learning task, negatively affecting their performance (and, of course, their well-being). Neuroscience has a good understanding of how the activation of the amygdala affects the functioning of working memory (Arnsten, 2009).

Furthermore, it is crucial to consider that the level of arousal triggered by a stimulus is not the same for every student. For example, one student may experience high levels of stress during an exam, while another may not be as affected. Similarly, the valence of emotions that students associate with stimuli also varies, so one student may feel joy when studying mathematics, while another may experience anxiety.

Therefore, it should not come as a surprise that the ability to manage emotions correlates positively with academic performance (Mega et al., 2014; Graziano et al., 2007). It is also a fact that emotional education interventions aimed at improving students' ability to identify, understand, express, and regulate their emotions properly can have positive effects on their academic performance (Jamieson et al., 2010). Since emotional regulation is a significant factor for learning, I have dedicated a chapter to it in the section on self-regulation. In the upcoming chapters of this section, nonetheless, I discuss another of the most crucial emotional factors for learning: motivation.

Motivation

An Overlooked Factor

The renowned pedagogue, psychologist, and philosopher John Dewey wrote in the early 20th century, "In one sense there is no such thing as compulsory education. We can have compulsory physical attendance at school; but education comes only through willing attention to and participation in school activities" (Dewey, 1913). Indeed, motivation has always been a key factor in promoting our students' learning, and yet, for decades, formal education did not give it much consideration, especially in the middle and higher stages of education. As we will see later, paying attention to this emotional component of the learning process—and embracing it as a fundamental part of the teacher's task—can be a small educational revolution in itself.

Science also ignored the role of motivation in the learning process for a long time, focusing on studying almost exclusively cognitive processes (Schunk et al., 2013). Consequently, for much of the 20th century, the field of educational research was primarily concerned with identifying what makes us *learn*—which actions and circumstances are most effective in generating and consolidating learning. It became clear later that it was also necessary to find out what makes us *want to learn* and, thus, what motivates us to take the actions that allow us to learn. Taking this variable into account, science has been able to describe the processes of classroom learning more precisely and validly in real-world situations (Pintrich, 2003a). In other words, the educational phenomenon cannot be understood without considering the role of motivation.

Early scientific research on human motivation provided theories based on internal impulses that drive us to satisfy biological needs, balance situations of mental or physical discomfort that cause distress, or simply seek pleasure and avoid pain (Weiner, 1990). Although these theories, primarily constructed from research with laboratory animals, may be useful for explaining the motivation that drives us to seek food when we are hungry or go to the bathroom when we feel the urge to do so, they soon proved to be inadequate to understand much of human behavior, especially to explain what motivates students to learn in the school context. In response, cognitive theories of motivation began to gain momentum during the last quarter of the 20th century. Unlike their predecessors, these theories posit that the motivation to learn depends on the conscious decisions the student makes based on how they interpret the information they receive. That is, motivation is an emotional response mediated by cognitive factors. Today, cognitive theories dominate the field of educational research on motivation; a wealth of evidence has been accumulated from a number of studies conducted in actual classrooms, rather than with laboratory animals (Schunk et al., 2013). Therefore, the focus of this chapter is to describe the main ideas that emerge from cognitive theories of motivation in the school context.

What Is Motivation?

Motivation is an emotional state that drives us to initiate and sustain a specific behavior with a particular goal. It is a predisposition toward action in a specific direction. There is no motivation without goals, because it always has a purpose: we are motivated to achieve or do something specific. In the context at hand, motivation acts in relation to learning goals or academic objectives. In short, when students are motivated to learn something, they make a greater effort to achieve it. It is important to note that motivation alone does not make learning more memorable, but it enhances it because it encourages the student to put in more effort, time, and attention to the learning object.

Cognitive theories of motivation assume that humans, to a greater or lesser extent, have a natural drive to learn. The question is, to learn what? What determines what we want to learn? What makes us persevere in a subject or lose interest in it? The object of study in this research trend is not the origin of the impulse we call "motivation" but the factors that determine its direction and persistence. In essence, what we want to know is how and why students are motivated to learn certain things or in certain contexts and what makes them persevere or eventually give up. This knowledge can help us try to improve students' motivation for school activities.

Therefore, it is important to appreciate that motivation is not an end in itself but a means to an end. Increasing students' motivation should not be considered the goal of a methodological change or a school project reform; motivation should be conceived as a (very powerful) means to achieve learning goals. As discussed later in this chapter, it is very positive for a teacher or a school to decide to make changes to improve their students' motivation. Still, it should not be forgotten that the purpose of these changes is not just to have more motivated students but students who are more motivated to *learn what we propose*. After all, we can motivate students in many ways, but not all of them will lead them to focus their attention and effort on the learning object. What we want is for them to be motivated to engage cognitively in activities that lead to deep and meaningful learning.

Goals

Motivation is always focused on specific goals or objectives. That said, it is worth noting that the objectives teachers may have for their students do not always coincide with the goals students may have for themselves. This happens, for example, when our interest is focused on students truly learning the subject matter we teach, but they are only thinking about grades. Therefore, we can distinguish two types of goals or objectives that our students may pursue (Dweck, 1986; Dweck & Leggett, 1988). On one hand, there are *learning goals* pursued by students who are genuinely interested in learning—that is, in mastering the subject matter or acquiring new skills. On the other hand, there are *performance goals*, which direct the student's behavior toward overcoming the academic challenges they face, driven by the desire to demonstrate their worth or protect their reputation and image in front of others. These are the goals of students who prioritize grades above all else.

These performance goals can further be classified into two types (Elliot, 1999): *performance goals with an approach component*, typical of students who try to always get the best grades and stay at the top of the class, and *performance goals with an avoidance component*, characteristic of students who prefer to do only what is necessary and simply hope not to perform too poorly and not to end up at the bottom of the class.

Of course, in compulsory education, we also have students who, unfortunately, do not pursue any of these goals because they do not value either grades or what they can learn in school (which, as discussed later, depends on their beliefs about learning).

Research involving students of all ages has shown that the type of goals they pursue has consequences for their behavior and, therefore, their academic results. As expected, students with performance goals with an avoidance component usually coincide with those who get the lowest grades (obviously, excluding those who have no academic goals at all). However, evidence indicates that students who get the best grades are not those who pursue learning goals, as we might wish, but those who pursue performance goals with an approach component (Wolters, 2004).

How is it possible that students with learning goals—those genuinely interested in learning—do not outperform students with performance goals academically?

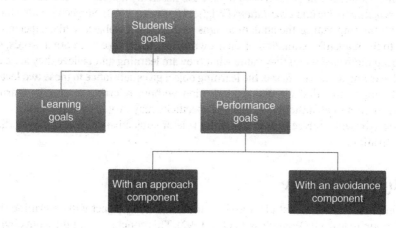

FIGURE 1   Types of goals.

Quite simply, because assessment tests that determine grades often do not differentiate between deep and lasting learning—with understanding and transferable to new situations—and shallow, short-term learning (Wolters, 2004). Most of the time, it is possible to get good grades through study strategies that prioritize memorization with very little understanding, leading to short-term learning. In other words, students can achieve academic success without truly learning (or, strictly speaking, learning to pass a test and then forgetting). Studies show that when learning is assessed through tests that emphasize understanding of the subject matter and its transferability, students with learning goals outperform students with performance goals, and their learning is also more lasting. Furthermore, these students are more engaged in activities, use active strategies that lead to deeper and more transferable learning, seek more learning opportunities (inside and outside of school), are more open to facing new academic challenges—especially when they are optional—and, ultimately, continuously seek opportunities to learn (Harackiewicz et al., 2002; Barron & Harackiewicz, 2001). These features are not correlated with performance-oriented goals in any of their two variants.

It is important to note that competence goals and performance goals are not mutually exclusive; students can have both, only in different proportions that vary depending on the subject. The fact is that learning goals and performance goals with an approach component are desirable because they have complementary positive effects. Avoidance goals, on the other hand, do not seem to lead to any positive results (Pintrich, 2003b).

In short, evidence indicates that the type of goals students adopt can influence their motivation. But, as is discussed next, the nature of the learning object itself will be even more critical for motivation.

Factors Determining Motivation

According to cognitive theories of motivation, there are two main factors that determine whether a student will be motivated to take the necessary actions to achieve a learning goal: *subjective value* and *expectations* (Wigfield & Eccles, 2000). Subjective value has to do with the importance the student assigns to the learning object, while expectations refer to the student's estimation of their own ability to achieve it. In other words, students are motivated when they value what they are learning and believe they are capable of learning it. As we can see, the learning object gives substance to these two factors, which emphasizes that discussing motivation without referring to specific learning goals is nonsensical (although the level of specificity may vary in each situation).

Next, we will analyze the fundamental role of subjective value and expectations in motivation.

Subjective Value

The importance that the student assigns to the learning object will determine their motivation to learn it (Wigfield & Eccles, 1992). This conclusion might seem obvious at first glance, but if we delve deeper into it, we can better appreciate its nuances and implications for learning and academic outcomes.

First, there are various reasons why a student may assign value to a learning goal. Educational psychology distinguishes up to three (Figure 2). On one hand, *intrinsic value* refers to the situation in which the student has a genuine interest in what they are about to learn per se. For example, many children are fascinated by dinosaurs and would spend hours learning about them. When students are motivated solely by the desire to learn about something that interests them, they are driven by what is called *intrinsic motivation*.

Traditionally, teachers have considered this type of motivation as something dependent on each student's individual interests and therefore beyond their control. If the topic of the class does not pique the interest of all students, teachers resign themselves and assume that the duty to learn it takes precedence over whether the students find it interesting or not. However, interest does not depend solely on the preferences of each individual; it can be modulated and promoted contextually (Hidi & Harackiewicz, 2000). Thus, a distinction is made between *individual interest*—what the student inherently possesses because of their nature and beliefs—and *situational interest*—what we, as teachers, can promote based on how we structure and develop learning activities. There are various specific strategies that we can use to generate situational interest effectively, but we will address them a bit later (hopefully, I motivated you to learn about them, if you were not interested in them already).

Another reason that can make the student assign value to the learning object is its utility. Thus, *extrinsic* or *instrumental value* does not directly result from the satisfaction of learning about something but from the desirable consequences that learning it may entail (or from the undesirable consequences of not doing so). For example, a student may be motivated to learn English because they want to communicate with their online chat friends; they may be motivated to participate in an optional activity because they want to please their teacher, or they may be motivated to get good grades because they feel it is their duty, which will bring personal recognition or allow them to aspire to specific higher-level studies. As you may have noticed, extrinsic value is related to performance goals, while intrinsic value is associated with learning goals.

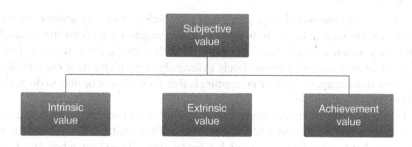

FIGURE 2   Types of subjective value in relation to learning goals.

Although extrinsic value may be seen as less desirable than intrinsic value, it actually plays a very important role in complementing or replacing the latter when it is lacking. In fact, extrinsic value is often the only possible value while the student discovers what they are learning. There is nothing wrong with a student initially approaching a subject or topic driven solely by extrinsic motives because that can give them the opportunity to discover and develop a personal interest as they learn (Hidi & Renninger, 2006).

It is important to keep in mind that extrinsic value is not only associated with seeking rewards (e.g., good grades, prizes, praise) or avoiding punishments. It also includes more "noble" goals, such as those related to the utility or the social or environmental impact of what is learned. In other words, when a school task (for example, a project) not only pursues academic learning goals but also serves social objectives or has an impact on the wider educational community or beyond (the neighborhood, the town, the country, etc.), the student's motivation dramatically increases. Therefore, when designing activities that transcend the classroom and even the school, we are relying on the extrinsic value provided by these complementary goals. We also make use of extrinsic motivation when we show the utility of what is being learned by connecting it to aspects of the students' lives.

Finally, educational psychologists also distinguish *achievement value*—the value we assign to learning something based on the perceived difficulty it entails. Thus, we assign more value to learning something that seems difficult than something that seems easy because we assign greater merit to it. Therefore, learning something that is seen as ridiculously simple is not motivating.

Nonetheless, we also do not feel motivated when the learning object is extremely complex. In reality, no matter how interesting or important something may seem to us (that is, no matter how much subjective value we assign to it), if we perceive it as too difficult, we may end up abandoning it. Subjective value is related to the choices we make when starting to learn something and contributes to our persistence in learning it, but the expectations we develop about whether we will be able to learn it have a greater impact on our persistence. Now let's explore the other determining factor of motivation: expectations.

Expectations

People are only motivated to pursue goals they believe they can achieve with the effort they are willing to put in to achieve them (which results from the subjective value they assign to those goals) (Wigfield & Eccles, 2000). Thus, when a student faces a learning task, they immediately make judgments about their own ability to complete it successfully. If their perception is that they will not be able to do it, their motivation will plummet.

This is because we do not like to fail—or rather, we do not like to experience the negative emotions that come with failure. On the other hand, we take pleasure in the emotions that success brings (Carver & Scheier, 1990). Therefore, when faced with a challenge, we immediately assess the likelihood of one outcome or the other, and if failure weighs more heavily than success, we tend to avoid the task. If the task is inevitable, as it often is in school, we do not invest the effort it requires because failure is only understood if a genuine attempt has been made. If there is no real effort made, it is not seen as a failure.

Researchers distinguish between two types of expectations. On one hand, *efficacy expectations* (Bandura, 1997), which are the judgments students make about their ability to achieve learning goals. On the other, *outcome expectations* (Carver & Scheier, 2001) are the beliefs students have that a specific set of actions—for example, a new learning strategy taught to them or a work plan proposed to them—will help them achieve learning goals. Of course, if their efficacy expectations are non-existent, they will not have any outcome expectations either: for them, there is no method that leads to success. This situation is known as *learned helplessness* (Maier & Seligman, 1976). But if efficacy expectations are merely low, we can work on the students' outcome expectations; for example, making them trust a new work strategy to achieve success, which can, in turn, improve their efficacy expectations if they achieve some success through it.

The concept of efficacy expectations is linked to the term *self-efficacy*, a psychological construct of great interest for educational research as it is widely correlated with learning and academic success. In this context, student self-efficacy—not to be confused with self-esteem—is the measure of how capable the student sees themselves of reaching a learning goal (Bandura, 1997). It is specific to each domain or learning object (just like subjective value), meaning that the student can have a different level of self-efficacy for each subject or each learning task. Moreover, self-efficacy is limited to making rational judgments about the ability to learn specific things. In contrast, self-esteem is the general and emotional perception of one's worth or value, determining how satisfied the students are with themselves and accept themselves as they believe they are. A person believing they will never be able to learn how to dance does not necessarily have low self-esteem.

Another very important difference between self-efficacy and self-esteem is that the former has a stronger correlation with academic results. But not only that—unlike self-esteem, self-efficacy has a direct effect on learning and academic results. In other words, changing students' self-efficacy regarding a subject or learning goal leads to improvements in their learning and grades. This is not the case with self-esteem since, as noted earlier, correlation does not always imply causation. For example, a study by Schunk and Hanson (1985) analyzed what happened when a group of elementary students with learning difficulties in mathematics underwent an intervention to improve their sense of self-efficacy in this subject. First, the students were split randomly into three groups, and all of them completed an initial test where they had to solve 25 subtractions with numbers with three digits or more. Then two of the groups received an intervention to increase their self-efficacy and were subsequently taught strategies to solve the type of operations in the test they had taken. The third group received the same math instruction but did not have an

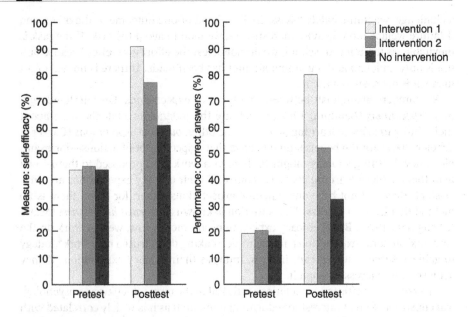

FIGURE 3   Self-efficacy measures and results in a mathematics test for three groups of students before and after a lesson that included an intervention to increase their self-efficacy (Adapted from Schunk & Hanson, 1985).

intervention to increase their self-efficacy. Finally, all groups completed a final test, again with 25 subtractions to solve. The results are shown in Figure 3.

As can be seen, interventions in students' self-efficacy (two different interventions were used) made a significant difference in the final tests. These results have been replicated in numerous studies with different content areas (Schunk, 1989), all suggesting that the judgments students make about their own ability to learn impact their learning. The reasons for this effect are quite logical: if a student believes they cannot learn something, they will self-limit—they will not invest the time, effort, or concentration required for learning tasks, and therefore they will end up confirming their initial assumption. This phenomenon is known as a *self-fulfilling prophecy* (Merton, 1948).

Motivation and Academic Performance

What do studies tell us about the correlation between value, expectations, and students' academic performance? As expected, research shows a correlation between the subjective value that students assign to each subject and their grades in those subjects. In a review of 121 studies conducted in 18 different countries, where students' interest in subjects was measured and compared with their academic grades, a moderate but consistent correlation was found (Schiefele et al., 1992). However, this correlation does not tell us whether students' preferences for certain subjects explain their results or if, conversely, the fact that they get good results is the cause of their preferences. Nor does it inform us if there is a third variable that causes this correlation, such as the student's initial ability in each subject. Nevertheless, many studies confirm that subjective value contributes to driving students to engage in and sustain behaviors that lead to good academic results.

As for expectations, as noted earlier, self-efficacy correlates highly with academic performance. This correlation is known to be causal: if we increase students' sense of self-efficacy for a subject, their academic performance in that subject will improve. This causality, however, is bidirectional: self-efficacy is in a reciprocal relationship with success. Thus, having higher self-efficacy leads the student to put in more effort, persevere, and become more involved in the learning task, resulting in better outcomes. In turn, positive results contribute to increasing or sustaining their sense of self-efficacy at high levels (Pintrich 2003a; Valentine et al., 2004). For the same reason, when the student perceives progress in the learning process, their motivation is reinforced, encouraging them to continue.

In conclusion, motivation and academic performance maintain a relation of mutual reciprocity: motivation affects learning and performance, and, in turn, what the student learns and achieves affects their motivation. Moreover, this reciprocal causality is not equivalent; self-efficacy is important for achieving success, but success is even more critical for sustaining high self-efficacy (Muijs & Reynolds, 2017).

How Can Students' Motivation Be Increased?

From what has been discussed so far, it is evident that the way to promote students' motivation for the learning goals we desire for them is to intervene in their subjective value and expectations associated with these goals. Next, we will explore some evidence-based methods that contribute to this.

Promoting Subjective Value

As I noted earlier, it is possible not only to modulate subjective value at an extrinsic level (by attributing utility to the learning object) but also at an intrinsic level (by making the learning object inherently more interesting). This involves acting on *situational interest*, which arises when we design, present, or develop learning activities in a way that makes them more appealing.

In this regard, the first trap we must avoid is to confuse *interesting* with *fun*. Of course, there is nothing wrong with learning activities being fun, but what really matters is that they are interesting. Back in the early 20th century, John Dewey cautioned against seeing interest as an embellishment added to a task that would otherwise be dull (Dewey, 1913). At this point, though, I would like to clarify what I have said about there being nothing wrong with activities being fun. In fact, there can be a downside.

First, when the fun aspect of a task is not directly related to what is being learned, the student may lose focus on what they should really be thinking about. You may recall from the chapters on cognitive processes of memory that it is important for the student to think about what they are learning and not about trivial matters. So "fun" should not come from elements unrelated to what is being learned but from the learning object itself. In this sense, many studies have shown that including eye-catching or fun details in the learning task that are superfluous to the genuine learning goal is counterproductive (Wade, 1992). These details interfere and compete advantageously with what should be the student's focus of attention, disrupting their ability to learn what we want them to learn. (Note that this is related to Cognitive Load Theory, specifically extraneous cognitive load.) Moreover, attention-diverting details also cause students to activate prior knowledge schemas that are not relevant and make them associate what they learn with ideas that will later be irrelevant for retrieving what they have learned.

Second, it does not make sense to present fun as an alternative to effort. What we want is for the student to enjoy the learning process, even to enjoy the effort it requires, not to avoid it. In the chapters on memory, I also discussed the importance of expending effort and overcoming challenges to optimize learning. The brain learns more when the learner puts forth the effort. Thus, we should not try to avoid the effort but rather ensure that students are motivated to expend it. In fact, the satisfaction associated with learning occurs especially when they succeed in learning, not necessarily while they are trying to achieve it.

Finally, we must not forget that the difference between *interesting* and *fun* draws the fine line between a moderately intense emotion (interest) and a highly intense one (fun). As was noted in the previous chapter on emotions, it is advisable to keep emotional states at moderate levels of arousal to optimize learning.

The actions that have been shown to better promote contextual interest are:

- *Facilitating understanding of what is being learned*

  When students understand what they are learning, their interest in what they have learned increases substantially. In fact, when we understand what we learn (just as when we solve a problem), the brain activates reward systems associated with feelings of pleasure and motivation. By appreciating that we are progressing in the learning process, those small achievements that occur when we connect the dots or clearly grasp new ideas reinforce our motivation to continue. Therefore, properly sequencing learning goals and adjusting task difficulty not only has positive consequences for the effectiveness of our memory, as discussed in earlier chapters, but also indirectly affects our motivation. Cognition and motivation are interconnected.

- *Using examples or contexts related to students' interests*

  Interest in a subject can be increased by embedding it in situations or examples that are intriguing to students—for example, when we compare poetic duels of improvisation between troubadours centuries ago with today's freestyle rap battles. This should not be confused with giving it a sense of utility, which would act on the extrinsic value of the learning object, but rather on making it more interesting in and of itself by connecting it with topics of interest.

- *Demonstrating passion for what is being taught*

Situational interest can also be promoted emotionally. Our social brain has a weakness for learning through the imitation of models and is particularly sensitive to the emotional component in the behavior of our peers. It is only when the teacher openly shows enthusiasm or passion for what they teach—through gestures, expressions, intonation, and words—that emotion spreads and generates curiosity in the students. This is a psychological effect that makes sense from an evolutionary perspective; if something can interest a member of our species so much, perhaps that something is genuinely important and we should find out why.

The other way to act on the subjective value of the learning object is by giving it extrinsic value. For example:

- *Explicitly stating the importance of what is to be learned*

It is not always easy to explain the utility of learning goals. (Utility is understood here as anything that fulfills a personal, intellectual, emotional, or social goal.) But although there are many times when we could do it, we choose not to. In the previous section, we talked about expressing this utility indirectly, such as when we show our passion for what we teach. However, what I mean here is to express it explicitly, like when a student asks, "What's the use of this?" Expressing the importance or utility of what is being learned contributes to increasing its extrinsic value.

- *Connecting what is being learned with contexts or examples that reflect its utility*

In addition to explicitly emphasizing the importance or utility of what is being learned, we can reinforce its extrinsic value in class by using contexts or examples where the learning object comes into play, demonstrating its utility. Of course, this includes strategies like problem-based learning, provided that these problems occur in meaningful contexts. Through this method, students understand that what they are learning is to solve a problematic situation or a need in a plausible scenario. If this problem or need aligns with their interests, even better.

- *Engaging in activities that go beyond the classroom*

As I mentioned earlier, combining academic goals with other types of goals can increase the value of learning and, hence, motivation. For example, proposing a project whose result is not only assessed by the teacher but is also presented or has an impact beyond the classroom significantly multiplies the value that students assign to it. This is the case for activities that involve the educational community, individuals or entities outside the school, students from other schools, or which end up taking part in local, national, or international projection contests.

Improving Expectations

As we have already seen, enhancing students' expectations of successfully completing learning tasks can increase their motivation and promote behaviors leading to engagement in school activities and study. The student's estimation of their ability to overcome a learning challenge can be modulated in two ways: we can adjust the task's difficulty or the student's perception of that difficulty, or we can directly intervene in the student's perception of their ability to succeed in the task. That is, we can act on the task's difficulty or on the student's self-efficacy—their confidence in their ability to accomplish it. For the first case, some strategies would be the following:

- *Adjusting the level of difficulty*

   By properly adjusting the level of activities, we not only facilitate comprehension—and, therefore, interest—but also promote positive learning expectations. It involves finding that sweet spot where the task is neither too easy nor too difficult, as tasks that are too easy bore us, while tasks that are too difficult overwhelm us. To adjust the level of difficulty, diagnostic activities are useful, allowing us to assess students' prior knowledge or their initial skill level. However, any teacher is right to point out that determining the appropriate level is not easy in a class with two or three dozen different students, so we must settle for an approximation to the average.

- *Providing early success opportunities*

   When the student is aware that they are making progress in the learning process, their expectations for completing it successfully are reinforced. Therefore, it is beneficial to break down the task into partial milestones and give the student opportunities to experience success by demonstrating mastery of these components. Partial and low-risk assessment tests not only serve to use retrieval practice and promote more solid learning (for more, see the chapter on memory processes) but also to improve success expectations and promote motivation. This strategy is particularly important in subjects or topics perceived as particularly difficult and potentially anxiety-inducing.

- *Providing clues on how to tackle the task*

   Many times, rather than decreasing the level of difficulty of a learning goal, it may be more appropriate to help students overcome it. One way to do this is by breaking down the learning object and allowing students to work on its components and gradually integrate them. We can also teach them specific strategies to tackle the learning task with greater chances of success. Indeed, each learning object may have its peculiarities, but there are also general learning strategies that can make students' efforts more effective. I discussed these in the chapters on cognitive processes of learning.

- *Specifying learning goals and providing rubrics*

   Clearly stating the learning goals usually contributes to improving student expectations because it allows them to understand what is expected of them and where to focus their efforts. Conversely, when students do not understand what is expected of them, they cannot even develop expectations of success, leading to insecurity and anxiety. In the case of highly complex tasks, it is very useful to use rubrics that guide the student on what we will evaluate in their work and where they should focus their attention and energy.

- *Aligning learning activities with assessment*

  When students perceive that assessment tests in a subject are not connected to what they are learning in class, their expectations of success are reduced. As is discussed later in the chapter on assessment, it is important for there to be good alignment between learning tasks and assessment activities.

The Foundations of Values and Expectations

Although we can adjust the difficulty of tasks, it would be foolish to fall into the trap of systematically lowering the standards of learning goals. It is best to maintain goals at the desirable level and help students feel they can overcome the difficulty through specific strategies (with our support) or directly act on their sense of self-efficacy—their confidence in their ability to achieve it. This issue is addressed in the next chapter.

Therefore, before concluding, it is important to note that this chapter on motivation is incomplete without the next one. Values and expectations are profoundly influenced by students' prior knowledge, specifically by the type of knowledge known as *beliefs*. That is, students' beliefs about the phenomena of learning form the basis of their expectations and values. Therefore, beliefs are of utmost importance in understanding motivation and, incidentally, a very relevant factor on which we can intervene to modulate motivation. For this reason, I dedicate a whole chapter to them to complete this discussion.

Beliefs

3.3

Subjective Knowledge

Just because a student believes that a subject is not important for their future does not mean that is true; likewise, the belief that they will never get good grades in mathematics does not mean it is a foregone conclusion. The values students assign to learning goals and their expectations of achieving them are subjective. Students' values and expectations are based on beliefs.

In educational psychology, beliefs specifically refer to the ideas students have developed intuitively about the nature of knowledge and learning (Schommer-Aikins, 2002). This includes how they believe learning occurs best, how they see themselves as students compared to others, and what their perceptions are about the value or complexity of learning objects and academic goals. These are called *beliefs* because they are subjective estimations about reality, but in practice they are nothing more than a form of knowledge. Knowledge that modulates students' behavior in relation to learning tasks.

As we will see in this chapter, students' prior knowledge comes back into play as a decisive factor that conditions the learning processes. This time, though, it is not because of the role it plays in the cognitive mechanisms that make acquiring new knowledge possible—due to how memory works, which relies on prior knowledge—but because of its influence on motivation. Therefore, it is worth emphasizing once again: prior knowledge is one of the most significant differences among students.

We saw in the previous chapter that motivation ultimately depends on the value students assign to learning goals and their expectations of achieving them. Values and expectations, in turn, are built on the foundation of their beliefs (see Figure 1). Therefore, this chapter will focus on how students' beliefs influence their motivation. Specifically, we will look at how their beliefs affect their expectations, as this is the aspect that has received the most attention from educational research.

FIGURE 1   Relationship between beliefs, values, expectations, and motivation.

Beliefs and Expectations

When a student faces a learning challenge, such as starting a new school year or diving into a new topic in class, they instinctively assess their ability to overcome it (Weiner, 1986). The estimation is specific to each goal and is primarily based on what they know about it. What they know comes from their previous experiences with that learning object, whether they are direct experiences—if they have already studied that subject or topic in previous courses—or indirect experiences—those derived from what other people, including the teacher, say about that subject. Thus, if the student previously succeeded with that subject or topic, their expectations are likely to be positive—their sense of self-efficacy will be high for that task. Conversely, if past experiences resulted in failure or if they consistently hear that the subject is very difficult, their expectations tend to be pessimistic. As explained in the previous chapter, students are more motivated if they believe they can achieve the learning goals set for them. After all, why invest effort if there is no hope of succeeding?

In short, a student's self-efficacy beliefs are shaped by their past experiences. But this is only half of the story. For better or worse, it is not that simple. What truly influences students' expectations is not their past experiences themselves, but how they interpret them, specifically the causes they attribute to them (Weiner, 1986; Pintrich, 2003b).

Attributions

Throughout their school journey, children develop a self-image as learners, shaped by their experiences and environment. This is what we call *self-concept* (Bong & Skaalvik, 2003). For example, some children consider themselves good students, while others think the opposite. As we will see in the chapter on feedback, school grades play a pivotal role in the development of self-concept (Butler, 1987).

Self-concept is closely related to the sense of self-efficacy because it encompasses the set of self-efficacy values that a student holds for different subjects or tasks. In other words, self-concept usually includes ideas of competence for some tasks and incompetence for others; we believe we are good at some things and not so good at others. In essence, self-concept is a type of self-labeling.

When a student with a specific self-concept receives a grade, they immediately interpret it through the lens of that self-concept. If the grade matches their self-concept, they attribute it to the same reasons that underpin their self-concept—for example, their ability or their dedication: "I got this grade because I'm smart" or "I got this grade because I study a lot." However, if the new grade does not align with their self-concept, they experience cognitive dissonance. Therefore, they immediately seek an explanation that justifies it without compromising their previous beliefs. If it is a bright student who received a low grade, they will likely assign their failure to a specific lack of effort, the unusual difficulty of the test, or some external factor that hindered their performance, such as noisy neighbors disrupting their study session. If it is a less diligent student who got a good result, they might attribute it to luck or an exceptionally easy test.

The type of causes that students attribute to their successes or failures in a task or subject has an impact on the development of their sense of self-efficacy for that task or subject (Weiner, 1986). In other words, whether students feel capable or incapable of learning something depends on the causes they attribute to their previous successes or failures with that learning object. Numerous studies have conducted surveys to identify the most common causes, and these causes, almost always consistent, can be classified into a few main categories: those related to ability, those linked to effort, and those associated with external factors, including the relationship with the teacher. Nonetheless, the most important aspect among them all is the student's perception of whether these causes are stable or, conversely, modifiable, and if they are modifiable, whether it is within their control to change them.

To be more precise, Weiner[1] (1986) identified three dimensions that describe the possible causes that students attribute to their successes or failures, and whose value has consequences for self-efficacy:

- **Locus** refers to whether the cause is viewed as external to the individual (luck, task difficulty, evaluator subjectivity, environmental contingencies, etc.) or whether it is viewed as internal (ability or effort, primarily).

- **Stability** refers to how unchanging or fluctuating this cause is over time. For example, ability is usually viewed as a fixed cause, while effort is viewed as variable depending on each situation.

- **Controllability** relates to whether the cause is within the student's control or, conversely, beyond their control. For example, luck or task difficulty are considered uncontrollable causes because the student cannot do anything to change them, while effort or study strategies are considered controllable causes.

When a student attributes their failures to fixed and uncontrollable causes, their sense of self-efficacy is seriously compromised (Schunk, 1991). This happens when students attribute their failure to innate abilities, such as saying "I'm not good at math" or "I'm not good at languages," or to any other factor beyond their control, like claiming "The teacher doesn't like me" or "The tests are too difficult." The extreme manifestation of this phenomenon is *learned helplessness*, where the student believes there is nothing that they can do to achieve a learning goal (Maier & Seligman, 1976). In all these instances, it is highly likely that the student will persevere less when faced with a learning challenge they previously failed.

Attributing failures to fixed and uncontrollable causes is also detrimental for a student who usually succeeds (and has a high self-concept). If they attribute success to such a cause, like ability, and not to effort or study strategies, they may struggle to identify the real problem when they fail. Initially, they will assign it to uncontrollable external factors that allow them to maintain their belief in their ability—for example, blaming the teacher or the difficulty of the tests—and will not seek a solution. If these

---

[1] Weiner's work was based on the attribution theory of psychologist Fritz Heider (1958).

failures persist, the student may eventually give in, lowering their perception of their own ability and, consequently, their self-efficacy. They may think, for example, that they were not as good as they thought. This can happen in cases where students did not need to invest much effort in the early years of school but begin to face challenges in higher grades, where effort and proper learning strategies become more necessary.

Conversely, when students believe that their successes or failures depend on controllable and flexible variables such as effort, dedication, or learning strategies, their self-efficacy is more robust, and in case of failure, it is less compromised (Schunk, 1991). As we will see later, perhaps this relationship is mediated by the success experiences that effort and good learning strategies usually bring. In other words, effort and effective strategies increase successful experiences, and success, in turn, boosts the sense of self-efficacy.

Attributional Training

As you may recall, not only do we know that self-efficacy beliefs influence motivation, but we also have evidence indicating a direct relationship with learning and academic outcomes. In other words, if we can change a student's sense of self-efficacy regarding a task, they are more likely to succeed in learning it. Therefore, if the causes that students attribute to their successes and failures play such a key role in their self-efficacy, several questions arise: Is it possible to change attributional beliefs? If we can change them, will students' self-efficacy, motivation, and learning outcomes also change? This is precisely what Weiner and other psychologists have extensively investigated, starting from the so-called *attributional training hypothesis*.

In summary, studies in this area reveal that educating students about success and failure, with the aim of encouraging them not to attribute these outcomes to stable and uncontrollable causes but rather to factors within their control—such as effort and study strategies—can have positive consequences on their self-efficacy and learning outcomes (Robertson, 2000; Haynes et al., 2009).

For example, in a study by Borkowski and colleagues (1988), a group of 75 upper elementary students with reading difficulties were asked to take two tests (the pretest). In one, they had to read a text and summarize it, while in the other, they had to answer comprehension questions after reading another text. Then the students were split into two groups. The first group received lessons on reading comprehension strategies and summarization. The second group also received these lessons but underwent "attributional training." Essentially, the teacher delivering the lessons included multiple explicit messages highlighting the importance of not attributing errors to fixed and uncontrollable causes, such as ability or task difficulty, and encouraged attributing success to effort and the use of appropriate strategies. After the class sessions, the students took two tests similar to the initial ones (the posttest). The results of each group are shown in Figure 2.

As can be seen, students who received attributional training improved more significantly than those who did not. Although other studies show that attributional training alone leads to improvements, the greatest gains are observed when it is combined with the teaching study strategies or problem-solving strategies, such as those

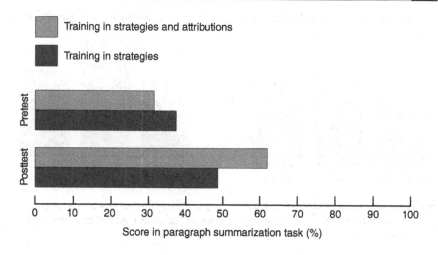

FIGURE 2   Results in reading comprehension tests before and after receiving an intervention on reading strategies that included or did not include attributional training (Adapted from Borkowski et al., 1988).

included in the previous study (Van Overwalle & De Metsenaere, 1990; Curtis, 1992). Moreover, the same studies indicate that teaching strategies without motivational training has a much smaller impact.

In conclusion, strategies are of little use if students do not believe they will make any difference and, as a result, do not even put them into practice. Let's say that the positive impact occurs when students are motivated to expend effort because they believe in the strategies they have learned to turn that effort into success. Remember that *outcome expectancy* is defined as the student's confidence in a specific procedure to achieve learning goals. If indeed, the learning strategies used are effective and lead to success, the student's sense of self-efficacy will increase. It is essential to keep in mind that motivation is important for achieving success, but success is perhaps even more important for sustaining motivation.

Feedback and Attributions

As we will discuss later in the chapter on feedback, an important way to help develop a culture that attributes success to effort and not to ability is precisely to focus feedback on the work done and never on the student's qualities. There is substantial evidence of how the praise students often receive in the educational (or family) context emphasizes ability and thus prompts them to attribute the causes of their successes or failures to their ability.

For example, in an experiment conducted by Mueller and Dweck (1998), two types of praise were used to provide feedback to a group of students about a series of tasks they had successfully completed. These activities were adjusted in difficulty so that everyone could solve them correctly. On one hand, praise was directed at their intellectual ability, such as "You must be smart at these problems," and on the other,

Student enjoyment in a highly difficult task

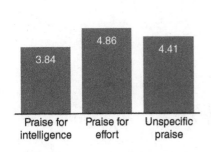

Student performance in a highly difficult task

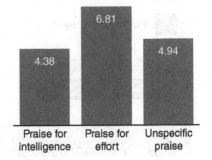

FIGURE 3 Student enjoyment and performance in a highly difficult task after receiving praise for either their intelligence or their effort, or unspecific praise (Adapted from Mueller & Dweck, 1998).

praise was directed to their effort, such as "You must have worked hard at these problems." Next, the study analyzed the effect of each type of praise on their motivation to face a new task that was much more difficult than the previous ones.

Figure 3 shows that students who received praise that appealed to their intelligence achieved lower performance in the final task and enjoyed it less. These students were mainly concerned about losing their status as "smart students" if they did not solve the new task, so they showed more anxiety, persevered less in the face of difficulty, and enjoyed the task less. In contrast, students who were praised for their effort were more engaged, persisted longer, and felt more satisfied, probably because they held the belief that effort is key to their performance.

Beliefs About Ability

As can be seen, the attributions students make about their successes or failures are part of their beliefs. For example, considering a fixed factor like ability more critical for academic success than a variable factor like effort is a belief, not necessarily a reality. In fact, believing that abilities are fixed and uncontrollable (innate) is also a belief.

Most of us know that skills improve with practice and training, but for some reason—probably cultural—we assume that this is not the case with some of them. For example, most of us believe that intelligence or academic skills in general are innate and fixed. Moreover, we cannot help but believe that there are certain skills we will not be able to perfect no matter how much we practice, unlike other people ("I'll never learn how to dance"). In these cases, we adopt a *fixed mindset* about these skills. However, as noted earlier in the chapter on deep learning, this perception is nothing more than a belief, as there is substantial evidence to the contrary: all of us (except for people with severe disorders) can develop expertise in any discipline with the right training. We can even improve our intelligence, creativity, and memory.

In this sense, psychologist Carol Dweck (2000) argues that when students maintain a *fixed mindset* regarding the skills that come into play in school, especially intelligence, their motivation and learning are compromised. On the other hand, students with a *growth mindset* believe that their ability is changeable and are more motivated to learn and improve it. In short, in Dweck's view, thinking that intellectual ability is fixed and uncontrollable is a self-limiting belief.

Carol Dweck's theory of the two types of mindsets has been well received by the educational community in recent years, so I will elaborate on it a bit more. However, it is worth noting that the evidence we currently have regarding this theory is mixed, showing both promising results and difficulties in replication and generalization (I discuss this at the end of the chapter).

Mindsets

In Dweck's theory, people can adopt a growth mindset or a fixed mindset regarding each type of skill, depending on whether they believe they can improve them with practice or assume they cannot change them (i.e., they consider them innate and stable). In the school context, these two mindsets are established with respect to academic skills, which are related to intelligence. Thus, there are students who believe that their performance in school is entirely conditioned by innate intellectual ability, while there are others who believe that this ability can improve with effort. This is the difference between a student who says, "I'm not good at math," and another who says, "I'm not good at math yet."

The development of these mindsets has consequences for how students interpret their successes and failures and the type of goals they pursue. Thus, students with a fixed mindset do not handle mistakes and failures well. For them, mistakes are a sign of inability, and since they believe that intelligence is fixed, the meaning they attribute to making a mistake is devastating—it defines them for life. Therefore, these students usually do not pursue learning goals but focus on performance goals, as they want to protect their self-concept and the image they project to others.

In the previous chapter, we addressed two types of performance goals: approach and avoidance. Students with a fixed mindset who have consistently received good grades from a young age prioritize goals with an approach component. Even though these students usually put in the effort to achieve these grades, they believe that their success is truly due to their ability and that it defines them. Therefore, they prefer to lie about the time they spend studying—when asked, they say they study very little—and typically do not seek help if they encounter difficulties. Children with a fixed mindset believe that effort is a sign of low ability and that if one needs to make a lot of effort or ask for help, it is precisely because they are not intelligent.

As for students with a fixed mindset and low grades, their performance goals usually have an avoidance component. They may not even pursue any school goals at all. In general, they shy away from challenges and avoid learning tasks for fear of making a mistake and revealing supposed innate incompetence. Moreover, they often self-limit, explicitly reducing their effort or sabotaging their own opportunities to study so they can attribute their failure to external causes rather than a lack of ability. These students avoid participating in class, adopt behaviors justifying not knowing how to answer a question by claiming they do not want to or are not interested, and, ultimately, focus on avoiding looking foolish.

On the other hand, students with a growth mindset accept error as a natural part of the learning process. This does not mean that mistakes and failures do not bother them; these bother them just like they bother anyone else, but their mindset allows them to overcome frustration and eventually interpret mistakes as an opportunity to improve. This leads them to persevere in adversity, where a student with a fixed mindset would likely give up. Therefore, the growth mindset is mainly associated with learning goals, although it can also be typical of students with performance goals with an approach component.

It is important to note that, according to Dweck, these two mindsets do not exist exclusively as two extremes separating one group of students from another. All students have both in varying proportions, and these proportions vary depending on the skill in question. For example, some students may tend to have a fixed mindset for mathematics but lean toward a growth mindset for English.

Table 1 Characteristics of students with a fixed mindset or a growth mindset regarding academic skills (Adapted from Dweck, 2008).

Fixed Mindset	Growth Mindset
They believe that ability is fixed.	They believe that ability is malleable.
They perceive mistakes as a stigma.	They see mistakes as something logical and necessary in the learning process.
They focus on protecting their own image.	They focus on learning.
They don't take risks; they don't put themselves to the test.	They take risks; they try; they put themselves to the test.
Challenges or criticism make them defensive.	Challenges or criticism motivate them.
They are not open to accepting mistakes and learning from them.	They are open to accepting mistakes and learning from them.
When they don't do something well, they quit.	When they don't do something well, they persist.
They believe that those who need to expend effort are not skilled.	They believe that to be good at something you must work hard even if you have talent.
They feel threatened by those who stand out.	They are inspired by people who stand out.
They believe that seeking help shows weakness.	They seek help to learn more and better.

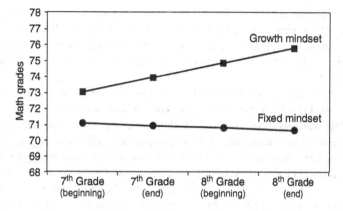

FIGURE 4 Mathematics grades of 373 high school students distributed according to their mindset (fixed or growth) with respect to this subject (Blackwell et al., 2007).

Mindsets and Academic Results

Several studies have gathered evidence of a positive correlation between the growth mindset and academic results (Stipek & Gralinski, 1996; Blackwell et al., 2007; Romero et al., 2014). For example, Blackwell and colleagues (2007) explored the association of the two mindsets with the mathematics achievement of a group of 373 high school students over two years. Participants who believed that intelligence is malleable (growth mindset) showed an upward trajectory in their grades throughout the study, while those who believed that intelligence is fixed (fixed mindset) showed a flat trajectory (Figure 4).

On the other hand, Romero and colleagues (2014) assessed the type of mindset that 115 high school students fit into and compared it with their grades and the elective subjects they took. They found that students with a growth mindset regarding intelligence got better average grades and were more likely to enroll in advanced mathematics courses.

In summary, this evidence shows a certain correlation between the type of mindset students hold and their academic results. However, these studies do not tell us if this relationship is causal. To determine that, it is necessary to conduct experiments in which we can change students' mindsets and see if this affects their results. But is this possible?

Can We Promote a Growth Mindset?

A general finding across several studies is that it is possible to shift students' beliefs toward a growth mindset. Not only that, but some research shows that by doing so, positive changes may occur in their learning outcomes. This is crucial because one might think that the growth mindset is the consequence of results, not the other way around. In this sense, it is likely that a growth mindset influences the student's self-efficacy (their expectations of success) and that this leads them to make more effort and persevere. Similarly, we now know that successes contribute to reinforcing their beliefs, so the relationship between a growth mindset and success could be a two-way street.

In the same study by Blackwell and colleagues mentioned earlier, an experiment is also described in which these hypotheses were tested with 91 first-year high school students. The students were randomly divided into two groups, and their math grades were analyzed on two occasions. In both groups, the grades were slightly lower the second time. Next, both groups received instruction in the physiology of the brain and study skills. The experimental group also received an intervention to promote a growth mindset (specifically, sessions discussing the malleable nature of intelligence), while students in the control group had a lesson on memory. A few weeks later, data on their math grades were collected, and it was observed that the students in the experimental group had reversed the downward trend, unlike the students in the control group. The results are shown in Figure 5.

Paunesku and colleagues (2015) reported a study along the same lines but on a larger scale, analyzing the effect of an intervention on 519 students at risk of dropping out of high school from 13 diverse Chicago high schools. In this case, the intervention was straightforward and administered online. Students in the treatment group read an article describing the brain's ability to grow and reorganize as a result of effort and the use of effective strategies in solving challenging tasks. The article highlighted the major findings of neuroscience about students' potential to become more competent through study and practice. It also emphasized that effort and mistakes in school are not indicators of limited potential but rather opportunities for learning. After reading the article, these students engaged in two activities to reflect on what they had read. On the other hand, students in the control group completed a

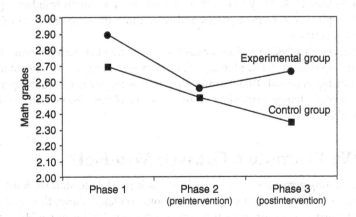

FIGURE 5   Results of an intervention to promote a growth mindset on math grades of two similar groups of high school students (Blackwell et al., 2007).

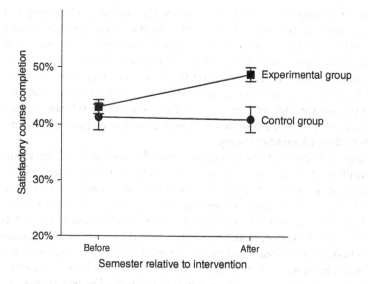

FIGURE 6   Percentage of courses completed satisfactorily before and after an intervention to promote a growth mindset (Adapted from Paunesku et al., 2015).

similar activity about the brain but did not discuss its potential for learning. For both groups, grades in all subjects were analyzed before and after the intervention, and the number of satisfactory grades (passing or higher) they obtained was analyzed. The results are shown in Figure 6.

As can be seen, the students who received the intervention improved their academic achievement, increasing the percentage of satisfactory grades by up to six percentage points. These are promising results, especially considering that the intervention was limited to two 45-minute sessions and was administered online.

Even more astonishing is the study conducted by Paunesku (2013) in collaboration with Khan Academy, an open educational platform that provides videos and activities for self-directed math learning. With a sample, if we can call it that, of 265,082 students, Paunesku found that including short messages of encouragement in the activities that conveyed a growth mindset influenced students' persistence in solving them correctly. For example, students who were randomly exposed to messages such as "When you learn a new kind of math problem, you grow your math brain!" showed a slight increase in the number of problems solved compared to those who were not exposed to such messages.

How to Promote a Growth Mindset

The studies mentioned earlier provide evidence of the possibility of promoting a growth mindset in students and the impact it can have on their outcomes. Although the description I provided of these studies already offers some clues, you may be wondering how to achieve this.

In brief, fostering a growth mindset is much like attributional training; it involves educating about the meaning of error and promoting a culture that recognizes the value of effort over innate talent (Dweck, 2008). According to the cited studies, this can be done through explicit interventions that inform students about what science has discovered regarding how the brain learns and changes with experience, and, ultimately, what we now know about learning and skill development: practice is more important than talent. (These ideas are extensively developed in the chapter on deep learning.) From a certain age, it may also be useful to explicitly introduce students to Dweck's mindset theory.

However, beliefs are not easily changed by merely providing an explanation; we saw how difficult it is to modify students' preconceived ideas about how the world works in the chapter on conceptual change ("Reorganization of Memory"). The messages that students receive must be reiterated, diverse, and consistent. As noted earlier, focusing feedback on effort is critical. (We will delve further into this in the chapter on feedback.)

Moreover, for this conceptual change about the nature of abilities—including intelligence—to occur, new ideas need to prove fruitful. In other words, students need to see that effort is related to success. Beliefs about learning can be important for achieving success, but success is even more critical in shaping these beliefs (Pajares, 1997). Therefore, as we discussed in the previous chapter, it is essential to sequence learning activities properly and provide short-term opportunities for success. This does not mean lowering the standards but structuring learning goals progressively, with various opportunities for the student to see progress. This educational practice is often called *cognitive and motivational scaffolding* (Lajoie, 2005). As suggested in the chapters on cognitive processes of learning and instruction, it is essential to use effective teaching methods if these opportunities are to lead to actual success.

Finally, it is also critical to help students develop effective learning strategies (see the chapter on metacognition). That is, it is not only a matter of expending effort. Effort alone is often not enough, and yet, exerting a lot of effort and failing is very frustrating. Therefore, it is important for students to understand that effort needs to be channeled through effective strategies that increase their chances of success. If we insist on effort but do not provide ways to make the work effective, we may achieve the opposite of what we intend. So, when a student fails despite putting in effort, we should avoid giving feedback such as "Well, at least you tried." This may lead the student to believe that the cause of their failure is a lack of innate ability, and that without ability, there is no success. Instead, in such situations, we should focus our feedback on strategies, such as "Maybe we should try a different approach, don't you think?" There is no doubt that the way we provide feedback contributes to the type of mindset students develop (more on this in the chapter on feedback).

Labels

In essence, Dweck's theory of mindsets informs us about the disadvantages of students assigning themselves unchangeable labels that define their ability to learn—whether positive or negative—and highlights the benefits of not believing in such labels; that is, considering their current ability as provisional and not predictive of how far they can take it. But it is very hard to ignore labels when they have become a staple in our culture and even an object of reverence. Despite the evidence showing that practice and effort are more important than innate talent in mastering any skill, our society still believes the opposite (Dweck, 2008).

At the beginning of this chapter, we discussed the importance of promoting, for motivation and learning, the idea that students should place greater value on effort (and the way they exert effort) than on ability when explaining their successes or failures. With the theory of mindsets, the importance of understanding that, in fact, effort has a direct impact on ability is also added to the equation—we can be born with more or less ability, but practice makes us better. Yet the world around our students insists on telling them otherwise. For example, celebrities who excel in their skills (athletes, artists, scientists, etc.) are often defined as special or talented individuals ("Serena Williams is a genius!"), with little or no mention of the countless hours and sacrifices they have made and continue to make to achieve their successes. We only see them outperform their peers and quickly attribute it to talent, unaware of the difficult road they have had to travel to get there. The picture below illustrates this idea—a picture is worth a thousand words.

The fascination with talented individuals is inherent to our culture. Take, for example, the fictional heroes that pervade our students' popular culture. Most of them owe their extraordinary qualities to their birth (Superman, Wonder Woman, Thor, Harry Potter, etc.) or to some fortuitous circumstance (Spiderman, Hulk, Flash, etc.), but almost never to their effort. And even those who strive to improve their skills—interestingly, often Japanese heroes—eventually stand out over others because they have "something special" (Son Goku, Naruto, etc.). Every time I explain this in a talk, Iron Man or Batman are mentioned as counterexamples, but apart from being a few rare exceptions, these two fictional characters owe their power to being born into a wealthy family and to an ability we consider innate: intelligence. In the comic book story about Batman's origin, only one panel refers to his training; one page in and he has already become the justice-seeking bat. We cannot deny that the concept of the "chosen hero," one who harbors a hidden innate power inside, seduces us (Gasca & Gubern, 2001).

Mindsets and Stereotypes

Cognitive theories of motivation caution against the dangers of labeling. In this regard, it is worth noting that labels attributed to us, whether by others or ourselves, often result not from our individual behavior but from social stereotypes. These stereotypes comprise a set of features that society irrationally attributes to a specific group of people simply because they share a trait, such as gender or nationality. For example, a common stereotype is that Japanese people are hardworking.

Stereotypes are beliefs ingrained in our social and cultural imagination, supported by cognitive biases that lead us to make fallacies of inappropriate generalization. Specifically, these fallacies occur when we associate two completely unrelated personal features simply because some individuals share them. Unfortunately, these are not just anecdotal phenomena but have relevant psychological consequences (Steele, 1997; Taylor & Walton, 2011). In education, gender stereotypes are particularly concerning (mostly detrimental to girls), as are ethnic stereotypes (primarily affecting children who are not of Caucasian or Asian ethnicity) and socioeconomic stereotypes (which undermine children from deprived families).

In all these cases, stereotypes suggest that there are demographic groups whose ability to excel academically is lower than others due to innate factors, rather than environmental ones. It goes without saying that all scientific evidence points to this not being true, but social stereotypes persist in this belief and contribute to making it a reality. For example, several research studies show that girls' abilities in mathematics and scientific–technological subjects are equal to or even surpass those of boys (Halpern et al., 2007). However, as they reach a certain age, despite maintaining the same level of grades as boys, their self-efficacy for these disciplines gradually diminishes, along with their interest in them. Tellingly, some studies show that girls begin to adopt gender-related intellectual ability stereotypes from as early as the age of six (Bian et al., 2017). Specifically, from that age, girls are less likely than boys to believe that members of their gender can be "very smart." Also, at six years old, girls start to avoid activities that are said to be for "very smart students." These findings suggest that notions about the presumed intellectual ability of each gender are acquired early and have an immediate impact on young children's interests.

In this situation, most experts agree that gender stereotypes, which affect both boys and girls from all areas of their social environment, are responsible for instilling certain ideas in them that influence their self-concept and, consequently, their values and expectations (Steele, 1997; Dweck 2000). In the case of girls, who often find themselves continually exposed to explicit and subliminal messages about their presumed inferiority in certain disciplines, the effects on their motivation lead them to put in less effort and pursue other goals, ultimately resulting in poorer long-term results and steering clear of scientific and technological careers (Leslie et al., 2015). It is a clear case of a self-fulfilling prophecy.

As for stereotypes related to socioeconomic status, these beliefs are as cruel as they are unfortunate, attributing the academic failure of children from disadvantaged families to innate causes rather than their actual reasons, such as the limited educational opportunities these young people usually have from a very early age, among other factors (Hart & Risley, 1995; Willingham, 2012). These stereotypes, therefore, do nothing but contribute to their failure unjustly, undermining their motivation—as if they did not have enough disadvantages already.

There is no doubt that schools work to develop values and attitudes that distance children from stereotyped thinking. Of course, many families also make efforts to instill these values, but the social environment in which children are immersed is persistent, uncontrollable, and inevitable. Therefore, it will always be worthwhile to intensify efforts in schools to combat stereotypes continuously and explicitly, through concrete actions based on a shared culture that pays special attention to these aspects. In any case, it is a matter of everyone doing their part. Let's not forget that, over the course of a year, children spend only about 25% of their time in school (excluding sleep hours).

The good news is that when we take steps to lower our students' stereotypical beliefs—just as when we address any belief that affects their self-efficacy—there is a positive impact on their academic outcomes (Good et al., 2003; Aronson et al., 2002). After all, stereotypes are societal beliefs that label us and, therefore, affect motivation.

There Are No Positive Labels in School

If I were to summarize this chapter in one sentence, I would say that to promote motivation and learning in all school areas, it is crucial to do everything possible to help students develop a label-free culture that places effort in the foreground and has (innate) talent in the background. We saw how not even positive labels are beneficial; when a student self-labels as a "good student," their goals can be set to maintain that reputation, potentially diverting them from behaviors that promote learning. Choosing to motivate a student by praising their presumed talent ("Don't worry, maybe math isn't your strong suit, but you have a talent for music") does more harm than good; the student may cling to that label and see no reason to put in effort in other areas. It is important to bear in mind that we are always talking about the school context, where we aim for them to acquire basic knowledge and skills for life, as well as values and attitudes that open up new opportunities. A child who believes they cannot learn math from school, for example, is a child who may cause that belief to become true for not having tried or persevered (Bloom, 1985).

When we use positive labels, we clearly do so with the best of intentions—to boost the student's self-esteem. But, as discussed earlier, self-esteem and self-efficacy are different things. Considering everything discussed in this chapter and the preceding one, we can conclude that, when it comes to achieving school goals, one the best ways to motivate students is to help them believe in the value of effort over talent (which, of course, does not mean that talent does not play a role).

Criticisms of the Impact of Beliefs on Learning

Carol Dweck's insights into the growth mindset have received a great deal of attention—perhaps a bit prematurely if we are to be scientifically strict—from the educational community. Many schools, especially in the United States and the United Kingdom, have adopted her premises as part of their school culture to motivate their students to learn. However, just as with any other new proposal entering education, caution is warranted, even with some evidence in its favor.

While the previously mentioned studies are quite promising, it is fair to note that some researchers have pointed out various irregularities in the experimental design or statistical analysis of some of them (Yeager, 2018). Furthermore, attempts to replicate their results and predictions have been unsuccessful in several studies (Li & Bates, 2019; Bahník & Vranka, 2017; Rienzo et al., 2015). For example, Glerum and colleagues (2019) replicated Mueller and Dweck's experiment that assessed the effect of praise directed toward effort or intelligence, and they observed no differences among students based on the type of praise they received.

Even more relevant is the study by Foliano and her colleagues (2019), who investigated the impact of a project implemented by the University of Portsmouth in the United Kingdom to promote a growth mindset among students in Year 6. Funded by the Education Endowment Foundation, the project involved 5,018 students and was implemented through training courses for their teachers and the provision of materials designed to work explicitly on the growth mindset in their classes, for approximately two hours a week over eight weeks. Additionally, teachers were encouraged to integrate recommendations on how to promote a growth mindset into their daily routines. At the end of the course, grades on standardized language and math tests were analyzed, and the results did not show significant differences between the students who participated in the project and those who did not. This study also examined the impact of the project on self-regulation and three socioemotional variables (intrinsic value, self-efficacy, and test anxiety). Again, no differences were observed following the intervention.

To sum up, replicability issues raise doubts about the potential of interventions aimed at promoting a growth mindset. These criticisms certainly do not completely negate the evidence in favor, but they do remind us of the need for caution and a critical mindset. It may be that there is indeed a positive effect on learning and academic performance when developing a growth mindset for such goals, but it could also be very small or only noticeable in certain students. Some recent high-quality studies have revealed that interventions aimed at promoting a growth mindset may have modest effects on the academic outcomes of students at risk of school failure. These effects are diluted when considering all students (Sisk et al., 2018; Yeager et al., 2019).

On the other hand, promoting a growth mindset in students within the school context may be much more challenging and complex than it seems. In fact, Carol Dweck acknowledges the difficulty of transferring these ideas to the classroom in a scalable way and laments how they have often been misinterpreted and incorporated into educational practice as mere proposals to promote self-esteem (Dweck, 2015). In this sense, it is crucial not to be driven by naïve interpretations and assertions such as "where there's a will, there's a way," or "anything is possible if you believe in it." First, remember that Dweck's theory of mindsets is limited to the capacity to learn and develop abilities (including intelligence). Second, as noted in the chapter on deep learning, effort is essential for learning and achieving academic goals, but it is not always sufficient, so we cannot expect effort alone to save the day. In reality, nothing said so far implies that everyone can achieve any learning goal with effort (rather, that without effort, no goal is achievable) but that if we give up effort because we do not expect to succeed, we will simply fall into a self-fulfilling prophecy. In any case, the most important thing will be to instill in students the *sine qua non* value of effort and, above all, promote their ability to take their skills beyond where they currently are.

To conclude, it is important to be cautious about assuring that merely changing the students' beliefs about learning will bring about change in their behavior. We humans are, if anything, inconsistent. Knowing that something is good for us—even when we are convinced of it—does not necessarily mean that we will act accordingly. How many things do we do every day, knowing they are not good for our health? Ultimately, it is important to put into perspective the power that a change in our ideas can have on our habits.

The Social Dimension of Learning

3.4

Made to Learn from Each Other

If one thing has contributed to the development of human civilization and the rise of *Homo sapiens* as the dominant species on Earth, it is undoubtedly our ability to learn from each other. This means that we have excelled as a species due not only to an exceptional ability to learn but also due to an extraordinary capacity to teach.

Learning and teaching are ingrained in our nature. While learning may occur without the need for social interaction, teaching by definition is a social act. It is therefore reasonable to claim that learning through social interaction is inherent to our species. Moreover, we may even have an evolutionary predisposition to do so and to be particularly effective at learning in this way.

Of course, social learning does not only occur through a voluntary act of teaching. Our brain continually learns from our experiences and, by extension, from all the interactions we have with the people around us. In the classroom, our students learn not only by interacting with us—their teachers—but also from interactions with their peers.

The learning that arises from these social interactions almost always has both a cognitive and an emotional aspect. It is especially important to keep this second aspect in mind. As we will see in this chapter, the way students perceive their relationships with their teachers, their peers, and, in general, the social environment around them has a decisive influence on their emotional state and, especially, their motivation. As for the cognitive aspect, in this chapter we will also explore how social interactions can promote meaningful learning in a unique way.

Emotions in Social Learning

Teachers have a major influence on students' motivation and performance through their educational practices, the feedback they provide (including grades), and all the other interactions they have with their students on a daily basis (Stipek, 1996). The way we manage all these interactions and, especially, the extent to which we offer support to our students, not only in terms of teaching but also emotionally, is crucial for their learning and development. Thus, teachers who build a positive emotional climate and express enthusiasm for their work provide an environment in which students are more motivated to learn and more inclined to cooperate and participate in classes (Hattie, 2009; Patrick et al., 2012).

What we communicate verbally and convey with our tone of voice, gestures, and attitude is interpreted by students based on their values and expectations, which ultimately affects their motivation. In the previous chapters, I discussed how students' subjective value of the learning task and their expectations for completing it successfully (i.e., self-efficacy) drive their motivation to engage in it, and I presented some strategies we can use to influence these key motivational factors. But the truth is that we continually exert this influence in each and every one of our interactions with our students—whether we want to or not, and whether we are aware of it or not.

In this regard, some researchers have suggested a third variable that, in combination with the student's subjective value and self-efficacy, determines their motivation for a task in class or a subject in general: the extent to which they perceive their environment as supportive (Ford, 1992). The environment in this case refers to the role that teachers—and other adults of reference for the student—play in it. If the student perceives that the teacher supports them in their learning process—regardless of how demanding the teacher is—they will be more motivated. Otherwise, their motivation may be compromised, even if their subjective value for the subject is high and their expectations of success are promising.

When we combine this variable with the subjective value and expectations, or self-efficacy, we can construct a theoretical three-dimensional model that describes the possible behaviors that students tend to adopt based on their individual cases for each of these factors. Drawing on the work of Hansen (1989) and Ford (1992), Ambrose and colleagues illustrate this model with the diagram in Table 1.

Therefore, there are two combinations for value and self-efficacy in this model in which the environment barely changes the situation, and two others in which the environment can make a difference. Thus, in both a supportive and an unsupportive environment, students who attribute no value to the learning goal and find it easy to achieve it will tend to behave evasively. They will find it difficult to pay attention and may get distracted thinking about other things or doing other tasks, such as doodling in their notebooks. To avoid this affecting their reputation, they may choose to do the bare minimum to get the grades they think are expected of them. As for those students who not only care little about the learning goals but also have no expectations of success, their perception of support from the environment will not be decisive

Table 1 Behaviors that students tend to adopt based on subjective value, expectations of efficacy, and their perception of the support they receive from their environment (Adapted from Ambrose et al., 2010).

| | The Student DOES NOT Perceive a Supportive Environment | | The Student Perceives a Supportive Environment | |
	Low value	High value	Low value	High value
Low self-efficacy	APATHETIC	FRUSTRATED	APATHETIC	FRAGILE
High self-efficacy	EVADING	DEFIANT	EVADING	MOTIVATED

either. In either case, their behavior will tend to be apathetic—they may disengage from learning tasks due to a complete lack of motivation. It may even happen that, in a supportive environment, the student takes it the wrong way and interprets the support as coercive.

On the other hand, in cases where the student attributes value to the learning goals, the model shows differences in their behavior depending on whether they perceive support or not. Thus, when the student is eager to learn but has low self-efficacy and does not perceive support from the environment, they tend to feel frustrated and helpless, and consequently, demotivated. In contrast, if they perceive support from their environment, they may feel vulnerable: since they are interested in achieving the goals and feel supported but lack confidence in their abilities, they will be inclined to worry about not disappointing those who support them and, therefore, feign understanding, avoid situations that might expose them, and make excuses in case of failure.

In this model, the two most desirable situations for a student are those that combine a high interest in achieving learning goals and a high sense of self-efficacy. However, in this scenario, the student does not respond in the same way whether they perceive a supportive environment or not. Motivation will be at its highest when the student senses an encouraging environment. However, their response can become challenging if the environment sends messages that contradict their values or expectations. For example, a well-intentioned teacher may start the course by warning about the number of students who usually do not pass their subject. This teacher likely believes that such a provocation will motivate students to work hard to avoid failure—it may have motivated them when they were a student. But this type of "incentive," at best, may cause students to become defiant. And this is in the *best* case. Just imagine the effect it can have on those who do not appreciate the value of the subject, and especially those who have doubts about their self-efficacy.

It is worth clarifying here that the above model explains how a student's perception of the environment affects their motivation and how this effect depends on the values and expectations they hold in a given situation. But the environment can also directly intervene to change the student's values and expectations. This aspect was discussed in the chapters on motivation and beliefs: the way the environment modulates values and expectations is slow and progressive, feeding on multiple interactions. In contrast, the above model tells us what happens when a student with a set of values and expectations for a given situation assesses the support they will receive from their teacher or those they believe can help them achieve their goals. In any case, this model once again emphasizes what we already highlighted in the previous chapters—that the best way to influence students' motivation is to focus on the value they place on the learning task and work on their sense of self-efficacy (their expectations of success).

The Pygmalion Effect

The influence of our treatment of students on their motivation is inevitable and occurs even without us realizing it. In fact, evidence suggests that the expectations we unconsciously place on our students shape our behavior toward them, contributing to the fulfillment of those expectations. This phenomenon is known in educational psychology as the *Pygmalion effect* (Rosenthal & Jacobson, 1968). You may recall the concept of a self-fulfilling prophecy, a situation in which a student who does not believe in their ability to learn something ends up not putting in the effort to achieve it, causing that belief to come true. The Pygmalion effect is a type of self-fulfilling prophecy that occurs interpersonally—one person's expectations (the teacher) about another person's ability (the student) influence their motivation and, consequently, their performance.

In a famous study, Rosenthal and Jacobson (1968) administered an intelligence test to elementary school students in California. Teachers were informed that the test measured the children's intellectual potential and could detect those who would flourish in the coming months (if two reputable researchers from Harvard told me that, I would probably choose to believe it). They then randomly selected 20% of the students and told the teachers that these boys and girls would intellectually excel that year. After a few months, the researchers returned to the school and administered the same test, a regular intelligence test. Surprisingly, the students labeled as promising showed a significantly greater increase in the average scores of the second test than their peers. Rosenthal used this evidence to suggest the existence of the Pygmalion effect in the classroom, highlighting that teachers can unconsciously behave in a way that facilitates and stimulates their students' academic performance.

In the natural classroom setting, without researchers trying to convince us of the potential of certain randomly selected students, teachers also form expectations about our students based on what we can observe and how we interpret it in relation to our beliefs. In fact, studies comparing teachers' expectations of their students and the academic performance they achieve in their subject show strong correlations. This situation is quite different from Rosenthal and Jacobson's study. In fact, a wealth of evidence indicates that the correlation between teachers' expectations and students' performance is largely due to the fact that teachers are very often correct in their assessment of how well their students will do in their subject (note that we are always talking about performance in their own classes). Although the Pygmalion effect is accepted by the scientific community, its impact is considered very small (Jussim, 1989; Babad, 1993; Jussim & Harber, 2005). In fact, Rosenthal and Jacobson's original experiment has faced criticism for methodological issues, the possibility of explaining their results through mere statistical artifacts, and the serious difficulties encountered when trying to replicate it (Thorndike, 1968; Brophy & Good, 1974; Raudenbush, 1984).

While it is true that the Pygmalion effect is typically small, it may still be relevant for students from social groups affected by stereotypes (Jussim & Harber, 2005). These effects, it turns out, can be either positive or negative. Therefore, when teachers' beliefs are influenced by stereotyped ideas about these students' ability, the teacher's behavior can negatively influence them, even when acting with the best of intentions to favor the group they consider disadvantaged. This can happen when a differential behavior by the teacher toward these students is detected and interpreted by them as a sign of less confidence in their ability—even the most innocent comment can trigger the activation of the stereotype and affect students' sense of self-efficacy.

We should keep in mind that when students assess their expectations of success in relation to a learning goal, the activation of the stereotype can work against them. For example, a well-known study found evidence of how activating racial stereotypes before taking an exam affected the performance of African American students (Steele & Aronson, 1995). In the study, some of the students were told that the exam would measure their intellectual ability—likely activating the stereotype—while others were informed it was a simple problem-solving test. Students in the first group achieved significantly lower results, possibly due to anxiety resulting from the focus on the stereotype. Although one might be tempted to think that the difference could simply be due to the tension generated by what the students believed was being assessed in each test, the experiment was conducted simultaneously with Caucasian students, and they achieved the same average results in both tests (equivalent to the results by the second group of African American students). Of course, we could argue that African American students regulate their emotions worse (which would be discussing a stereotype). The fact is, though, that similar results have also been obtained with other social groups affected by stereotypes, such as women (Inzlicht & Ben-Zeev, 2000), students from underprivileged families (Croizet & Claire, 1998), or older people (Levy, 1996).

The negative effect that the activation of stereotypes can have on students' performance is known as *stereotype threat*. Research findings suggest that its impact is because alluding to the stereotype generates emotions of anxiety or anger that can disrupt cognitive processes, such as filling working memory with irrelevant thoughts that do not allow students to focus or reason clearly (Steele & Aronson, 1995). It is worth noting, however, that the *stereotype threat* hypothesis continues to be an intensely debated and researched topic in educational and social psychology (Spencer et al., 2016).

Learning Through Social Interaction

So far we have addressed the emotional consequences, especially those linked to motivation, that arise from social interactions in teaching and learning processes. But what about the cognitive aspects? Earlier in the chapter, I mentioned the social nature of human learning and how evolution has likely shaped us to learn cooperatively. In this sense, research on the relationship between learning and social interactions (both teacher–student and student–student) has drawn mainly on two theories whose origins can be traced back to the insights of Piaget and Vygotsky, respectively.

On one hand, Piaget (1959) posited that learning in social interactions occurs when the exchange of ideas leads to cognitive conflict in the child—that is, a discrepancy between their knowledge and that of their interlocutor. Through dialogue and discussion, the child gradually advances to a higher level of understanding, leading to conceptual change and restoring cognitive equilibrium (recall everything related to conceptual change discussed in the chapter on the reorganization of memory).

This process is viewed as a phenomenon of internal and individual construction that occurs in the child's mind as they try to fit new ideas into their cognitive schemata, which will subsequently manifest in their behavior (Garton, 2004).

On the other hand, researchers from the Vygotskian tradition argue that learning is inherently social. In social interactions, meaningful learning occurs more effectively when two people, who differ in their initial level of competence, work cooperatively on a task to achieve shared understanding (Garton, 1992; Johnson & Johnson, 1994). In Piaget's theory, the learning mechanism is based on conflict, while in Vygotsky's theory, cooperation is key. Unlike Piaget's view, learning through social interaction as suggested by Vygotsky is a process of external co-construction that arises from sharing knowledge to achieve a common goal, which will later be internalized by each individual (Garton, 2004).

Vygotsky's theory incorporates a key concept that you may find familiar: the so-called *Zone of Proximal Development* (ZPD) (Vygotsky, 1978). This concept is defined in relation to a student's ability to solve problems. Essentially, ZPD is the gap between what the student can do independently and what they can achieve with the guidance of an adult or in collaboration with more competent peers. Learning occurs when the individual bridges this gap through cooperation. As Vygotsky writes, "What the child can do with assistance today, she will be able to do by herself tomorrow."

To achieve this, the "expert" individual must assess the preexisting skills and instructional needs of their less experienced partner and break down the task or problem into manageable components. In other words, the more capable individual takes on the responsibility of providing cognitive scaffolding to facilitate their partner's transition through the Zone of Proximal Development (Lajoie, 2005).

Both studies, whether based on Piaget's theoretical framework or grounded in Vygotsky's ideas, confirm that social interactions typically provide greater benefits for meaningful learning than when students learn alone (De Lisi & Golbeck, 1999; Garton, 1992). Perhaps the most notable conclusion from research in either paradigm is that communication between individuals through dialogue or discussion is key to explaining the advantage of learning through social interaction. For example, a study by Kruger (1992) showed that children who engaged more in a discussion obtained greater cognitive benefits than those who remained passive listeners. In another study by Barbieri and Light (1992), student pairs who explicitly discussed and verbalized their planning during the development of a task typically performed better on an individual test later. In similar fashion, Forman and McPhail (1993) observed that students generally showed greater learning when they listened to their peers' explanations and reflected aloud on their accuracy and logical consistency.

Therefore, for social interaction-based learning to be effective, the individual must actively participate, assess explanations, explore and clarify inconsistencies, and express their ideas in light of their peers. From a cognitive perspective, these findings align with what we know about how the brain learns: dialogue compels us to evoke our ideas, compare them, and connect them with new ideas. It also compels us to reflect on them, structure them, and make sense of them. In essence, dialogue is a cost-effective and efficient way to perform the actions that allow us to learn the most (Teasley, 1995).

Cooperative Learning

Cooperative learning is an educational methodology rooted in Vygotskian principles that is widely used in schools, although not all group activities can be considered as such. From the various definitions provided by educational literature regarding cooperative learning methods, personally, I would adopt two. One definition, proposed by Johnson & Johnson (1999), describes methods in which a group of students, generally small, work together to achieve common goals or complete a task. The other, proposed by Slavin (2018), describes a method in which students work in small groups to help each other learn. The second definition emphasizes one of the most important keys for cooperative learning methods: collaboration among group members to ensure each and every individual achieves the learning goals. This feature distinguishes true cooperative work from situations where students are assigned a group task, often resulting in one or a few students doing all the work while others remain disengaged or sidelined. In cooperative work activities, the goal is for all students in a group to learn, and the only way to achieve this is by helping each other. Cooperative learning methods may or may not involve the creation of a product by students; it is included only if this creative activity helps students achieve the desired learning.

There are indeed multiple strategies within cooperative learning. Some are suitable for activities with very specific goals that last only one class session, while others are suitable for much more complex activities that extend over time. A popular strategy that is widely used in schools is Project-Based Learning (PBL). In this case, students are tasked with creating a product that contributes to the group's overall learning. The specific way projects or other types of cooperative learning activities unfold is so diverse I could devote an entire book solely to that topic. Nonetheless, it is worth noting that due to the wide diversity of existing approaches, some of these methods are more effective than others.

Cooperative learning is likely one of the most studied topics in educational research (Johnson & Johnson, 2009). Most studies comparing cooperative learning methods with more traditional methods, where students work individually or even compete, show the advantage of the former in promoting learning and achieving academic goals—so much so that research on this matter has shifted from comparing its effectiveness against other methods to trying to understand what factors make it more effective (Cohen, 1994). Depending on the circumstances and the way it is applied, the effectiveness of cooperative learning can vary and even diminish. In fact, a large number of studies have not found evidence of its advantage over traditional methods and have even provided evidence to the contrary in certain cases. These studies have taught us that, for cooperative learning to be more effective than traditional methods, a series of requirements must be met (Slavin, 2013). The three most important ones are as follows:

- First, student groups must be heterogeneous in terms of their ability and initial knowledge, so it is important for the teacher to put them together.

- Second, the summative assessment or recognition of learning resulting from the task must be done at the group level, meaning all group members should know they will get the same grade.

- Third, the assessment mentioned above must be based on the individual performance of each group member—the group's success should be assessed in terms of the learning achieved by each member separately, not in relation to a common product.

The last point is perhaps the key factor that distinguishes a group task that does not end up in cooperation from one that does. In this sense, one of the most common mistakes when proposing group activities that aim to be cooperative is confusing the task to be performed with the learning goals—the means to achieve learning (the task) becomes mixed up with the presumed learning acquired. Consequently, the assessment focuses on the developed product and not on the learning achieved by each student. If we assess the product, students understand that to get a good grade, they must deliver a good product (and for this, it is not necessary for everyone to participate).

On the other hand, since our ultimate goal is for the creation of the product to serve as a means for students to acquire knowledge or skills, the evaluation should focus on those learning goals. Evaluation should not be limited to assessing the task's end product; rather, it should include an assessment activity to check what each team member has learned individually. To promote this learning, there is no better approach than establishing that the grade all members receive depends on each student's individual performance in the assessment test (such as averaging the grade). The key aspect is for group members to be aware of the importance of each member mastering the learning goals of the activity. Only then will all group members channel their energies into learning and supporting each other in the learning process, reducing the likelihood of some slacking off and others taking on all the work (Slavin, 2013).

When cooperative learning methods are timely selected, aligned with the learning object, and applied while meeting the requirements mentioned earlier, they become a powerful tool to enhance both learning and academic outcomes. However, it is important to bear in mind that the findings from educational research always refer to the group of students as a whole and not necessarily to each individual student. In this case, it is particularly important to bear this in mind because the potential of cooperative methods is best understood in relation to their impact on the class as a whole—that is, cooperative learning contributes particularly to improving the overall performance of the class, implying greater equity. While some studies suggest that, overall, its effects are greater in less advanced students (Slavin, 1995), multiple studies show that students who usually get good grades with traditional methods not only maintain or improve them (Slavin, 1991) but also improve the consolidation of their learning, making it more meaningful and transferable. This is likely because teaching their peers contributes to this process (Webb, 1992; Teasley, 1995).

Learning to Cooperate

Organizing students into groups and assigning them a common task or goal does not necessarily mean they know how to cooperate effectively and get the maximum educational benefit from it. Often it is stated that cooperative learning activities teach students a life skill as important as cooperation. However, this is not necessarily the case; what cooperative activities really provide is an opportunity to practice cooperation. If students are not guided on how to do it and are expected to learn it spontaneously, the opportunity to practice cooperation loses much of its potential, both to help them develop this skill and to promote learning through it. On the other hand, if we provide students with basic guidelines for communicating, organizing teamwork, and resolving conflicts, then cooperative learning becomes much more effective. For example, several studies show that if students are taught communication skills (Senn & Marzano, 2015) or specific teamwork strategies (Saleh et al., 2007), their learning improves more than those engaged in cooperative work without these guidelines.

Moreover, teaching metacognitive methods (as will be discussed in the chapter on metacognition) also seems to enhance the effectiveness of cooperative work in improving learning (Friend, 2001). In this regard, it is essential to highlight the role of the teacher as a guide, especially promoting and modeling behaviors that enhance cooperative learning. For example, it is not common for students to engage in reflecting on the information they manipulate, ask questions that provoke reflection, and spontaneously resort to their prior knowledge unless there is some external guidance promoting them to do so (King, 2002). Nor do they usually involve themselves in high-level discourse or provide arguments for their conclusions unless explicitly taught to do so (Chinn et al., 2000). When the teacher teaches students to converse and reason together and apply those skills in their interactions, this benefits both their ability for group problem-solving and their learning (Webb, 2009).

Diverse Classrooms?

To conclude this chapter, I would like to emphasize an interesting aspect of cooperative learning. When one realizes that, cognitively, prior knowledge is key to learning, there may be a temptation to think that students should be grouped according to their initial performance to give better opportunities to each. However, research supports quite the opposite. Diversity in the classroom can benefit the learning of all students if properly utilized—for example, through cooperative learning. Moreover, evidence indicates that separating students by ability only benefits the more advanced ones, to the detriment of others, while well-managed mixed groups contribute to the improvement of all students (Oakes, 2005). This is a good example of how, when making methodological decisions, we must consider not only cognitive aspects but also socioemotional ones.

SELF-REGULATION OF LEARNING

In the previous chapters, we delved into the processes of learning, examining the cognitive processes at play and how emotions modulate them. In this regard, successful students are often those who deliberately engage in actions aligned with the way the brain learns (even if they do so unknowingly), regulate their emotions, and fuel their motivation to optimize performance and stay on task until they reach their goals. The successful student self-regulates on two levels: cognitive and emotional.

In this section of the book, I explore the importance of self-regulation in learning. First, I dedicate a chapter to aspects related to cognitive self-regulation, or metacognition, linked to the competence of "learning to learn." Next, I address the significance of self-control and emotional self-regulation as skills that complement the self-regulated learner. The last chapter of this section focuses on resilience in the academic context, a capability that emerges from success in cognitive and emotional self-regulation.

These concepts may seem unfamiliar to many educators. However, their relevance to learning and academic performance is enormous, to the extent that the ability for self-regulated learning could be a predictor of academic success even greater than intelligence (Gomes et al., 2014). Hence, an introduction to this concept is essential in a book like the one you have in your hands. Let's begin by exploring the processes of self-regulated learning from a cognitive perspective—the processes related to learning how to learn.

Metacognition

Learning to Learn

Among the eight basic competencies defined by the European Union as priority objectives in education, perhaps the most crucial is the competence of learning to learn. Initially, this concept may seem peculiar. Learning to learn? First, if we need to learn how to learn, how do we learn in the first place? Second, it is obvious that all humans learn naturally. So what is the point of learning something we already do spontaneously?

At this point in the book, you may have already formed an idea (if you didn't already have one) of what "learning to learn" means. Indeed, learning is a natural and automatic process carried out by our brains. Just as we cannot prevent our brains from "seeing things" when we open our eyes (assuming there is light), we also cannot prevent our brains from learning from our experiences. We are constantly learning. But as we saw in earlier chapters, there are ways to approach knowledge that boost our ability to learn, help us retain what we have learned for longer, or determine what we can do with what we have learned. Thus, understanding learning strategies based on how memory works is an example of learning that can make us better learners; learning these strategies is a way of learning to learn.

However, there is more to it than that; learning to learn involves becoming aware of one's own learning process, monitoring its progress, and being capable of taking actions to deliberately improve it. It is, therefore, a metacognitive skill—it requires the individual to think and reflect on their own cognitive processes.

The term *metacognition* refers to the act of "thinking about one's own thinking." It occurs, for example, when we reflect on how we have gone about solving a problem or have managed to learn something. Therefore, it includes processes such as task planning, monitoring progress, and assessing the results. It also involves modifying the chosen strategy—if necessary—to improve the outcome or optimize the effectiveness of the procedure used. Furthermore, reflecting on our beliefs about learning or our self-efficacy could also be thought of as a metacognitive skill. Ultimately, metacognition occurs when we reflect on our ideas, mental processes, and cognitive performance and consciously intervene in any of these aspects.

Therefore, self-regulated learning includes all those metacognitive skills specifically involved in managing one's own learning. These skills, like all skills, can be learned and developed. Research provides a wealth of evidence that acquiring these skills may significantly improve students' academic outcomes (McClelland & Cameron, 2011). After all, one of the most important factors distinguishing successful students from those lagging behind is the ability to regulate their learning autonomously (Zimmerman & Martinez-Pons, 1986).

Metacognitive Skills for Self-Regulated Learning

There are multiple metacognitive processes that help regulate our learning. Any learning task can be broken down into several stages based on the metacognitive processes involved. These processes include:

1. Assessing understanding of learning goals

2. Assessing personal strengths and weaknesses regarding the learning goals

3. Planning the learning task

4. Selecting strategies to achieve learning goals

5. Implementing the plan and monitoring its progress and outcomes

6. Reflecting on the suitability of the chosen plan and making adjustments

These six types of metacognitive processes characterize the development, from start to finish, of a self-regulated learning task. Let's discuss them in more detail.

1. Assessing Understanding of Learning Goals

Often when students respond to questions in a way that lacks coherence or submit work that does not align with the requested criteria, we attribute it to them "not reading the instructions" or "not paying attention." While these may be the causes in some instances, at other times the problem is that they do not understand what is asked of them. This lack of understanding may stem from an interpretation biased by the student's preconceptions; it is important to bear in mind that even the way we remember something can differ from our initial interpretation, as memory processes modify what is learned based on our prior knowledge. That is, students often reinterpret tasks based on their past experiences, either ignoring or forgetting the instructions given. For example, a study with university students revealed that half of them completely disregarded the professor's instructions on the type of writing they should produce, opting for the same writing structure they were accustomed to from high school (Carey et al., 1989).

The same happens when we inform students that they will have an exam assessing their understanding, and they can refer to the textbook or their notes during the test, but they ignore this fact and prepare in the same way they would for a more traditional exam. Therefore, it is important for students to learn to pause and evaluate their understanding of the given task; they need to integrate this habit as the first step before starting to solve it. To do this, they can begin by asking themselves if they understand what they should do and assess if they have overlooked any important details.

As teachers, we can help our students in this aspect in several ways. First, we can try to be more explicit than may seem initially necessary when describing the objectives of a task. As mentioned above, students may interpret instructions differently based on their prior assumptions. In this sense, providing rubrics that highlight the aspects we will value when assessing the task will help them better understand what is expected of their work. For example, if the task involves preparing a presentation on a topic, we can emphasize the importance of their ability to synthesize ideas over other evaluation criteria, such as the graphic design of the slides.

Moreover, drawing from our previous experiences, we can underline what we do *not* want them to do—especially if it is not the first time we assign a specific task, as we likely have insights into potential challenges. Therefore, it is worth sharing these insights with students to reduce the likelihood of them recurring. For example, regarding the slideshow presentation mentioned earlier, we can ask them not to clutter the slides with too many words and animated effects, or to avoid reciting the same text projected on the screen (considering the extraneous cognitive load that imposes on the audience).

Finally, particularly when students encounter new tasks, we can help them assess their understanding by asking them what they think they need to do to complete them or how they plan to solve them. It may also be helpful to ask them to explain the task objectives in their own words and, at the same time, teach them to pose these questions to themselves before starting any task. If their responses to these questions are not on the right track, we can always provide feedback to help them refine their understanding of the task objectives.

2. Assessing Personal Strengths and Weaknesses Regarding the Learning Goal

Once the student has understood the objectives of the learning task, they must assess their ability to achieve them. In this sense, it is common for students to overestimate their knowledge or skills (Dunning, 2004). In fact, the less mastery they have of the learning object, the more inaccurate their estimates become (Hacker et al., 2000). The tendency to overestimate their ability is fueled by the illusions of knowledge resulting from familiarity with the task—remember that familiarity gives us a false sense of knowing something, but it does not guarantee that we can retrieve it when necessary. Thus, when students study by rereading notes or the coursebook, or when they check the procedure to solve a problem without trying to solve it themselves, they likely form a mistaken idea about their ability. They believe they can provide an answer or solve a similar problem when, at best, they are only capable of recognizing the answer if given to them. To help them avoid such inaccurate assessments, we can recommend using the retrieval technique—instead of rereading notes or reviewing solutions to class problems, they test themselves as if taking an exam.

On the other hand, when students overrate their ability for a task, they may underestimate the time or effort required to complete it or ignore the need for support or resources to undertake it. This can lead them to procrastinate until the last moment, leaving them with insufficient time to finish the task or seek the necessary help. In these cases, when the task is to be done outside the classroom (such as homework or exam preparation), the student may experience anxiety. This anxiety might be transferred to their parents when asking for help they no longer have time to seek at school. Therefore, it is worth advising students to address tasks as soon as they are assigned, regardless of the deadline (even if they may not be inclined to follow the advice, it is still worth suggesting).

Finally, it is important to appreciate that the metacognitive capability to estimate one's own ability is closely related to the student's beliefs about their self-efficacy. Remember that these beliefs influence the student's expectations regarding the outcome of their effort and, therefore, can determine their motivation. Modulating one's motivation regarding a task can indeed be considered a metacognitive skill, as we will see in the chapter on resilience. In this sense, working on students' beliefs about their self-efficacy to promote a growth mindset can help them improve their motivation to apply their learning strategies.

3. Planning the Learning Task

Studies show that students, unlike experts, hardly spend time planning the tasks they must perform. For example, Chi and her team (1989) examined how various physics experts (graduates and professors) solved problems in this discipline compared to the methods used by first-year students. While experts spent a significant amount of time planning their approach, students barely hesitated to apply formulas and check results. Nevertheless, the experts solved problems correctly much faster, whereas students often needed multiple attempts to find the correct solution. Similar observations have been replicated in other fields, such as mathematics (Schoenfeld, 1987), or writing (Carey et al., 1989).

To instill the habit of planning in students, the first step is to make explicit how we, as experts, do it. Thus, we can start by giving concrete examples of how we would plan the resolution of the type of task assigned, along with guidelines for them to apply. While this might not directly help them practice planning, it fosters awareness of the need to perform this step in approaching any task and helps them understand the logic behind planning. Subsequently, we can have them practice their own planning skills in solving new tasks by asking them to make their planning explicit. In fact, proposing activities where planning is the final goal or part of what will be assessed can be effective. This can be reflected in a rubric if deemed appropriate.

Assisting students in planning their tasks can be done at various levels, from solving simple activities to developing large projects and, of course, in preparing for assessment tests.

4. Selecting Strategies to Achieve Learning Goals

How many times have we heard students complain about not understanding why an exam or another task went poorly despite having "tried so hard"? As I will discuss in the chapter on resilience, sometimes putting in effort is not enough if the effort is not directed in the right way—if the strategies used are not suitable or the most effective. However, students spontaneously develop strategies to tackle school tasks, and not always in the most effective way. Some persist with these strategies despite their lack of success, attributing their poor performance to other factors, from what they believe is an innate inability (e.g., "This is not my thing") to the presumably malevolent actions of their teachers (e.g., "He's biased against me!"). Others may choose to stop trying as a self-protective reaction, so they can always claim they "don't want to put in the effort" to justify their poor performance, instead of having to come to terms with a presumed innate and fixed inability.

On the other hand, students who do get good results with the strategies they have developed spontaneously may run into serious problems when the type of tasks requested changes, especially when their strategies have proven useful for a long time. For example, when exams shift focus from factual knowledge to assessing understanding and transferability, these students often struggle to get the same results they were used to. You surely recall the first time you had to take an exam where you could consult the book and notes. In our educational system, these exams are often feared and seen as "very difficult." But the truth is, they are not—they are simply different. The study strategies needed to succeed are different from those for traditional exams. But to change them, one must first realize and accept this fact. Precisely when students who have always got good results using certain study strategies face tests that ask for different methods, their self-regulation ability is laid bare. Some of these students will reveal their metacognitive weaknesses by blaming the exam (or the teacher who set it) without ever considering that the problem might lie in their learning strategy. Others, however, will understand the need to adjust their strategies to overcome these academic challenges.

In summary, many students are unaware that their academic performance may depend not only on their effort but also on the type of actions they take to learn. Therefore, when students use inappropriate strategies, whether these were effective in the past or never were, it is advisable to explicitly discuss these strategies with them. Educating in this area can significantly benefit students (McClelland & Cameron, 2011).

To help students improve these metacognitive skills, we can provide recommendations on which strategies to use when tackling tasks or studying. In this book, we have already discussed the effectiveness of retrieval practice—trying to remember what was learned instead of rereading it. This practice takes various forms, such as self-assessment with questions or problems to answer without checking the solution in the book or notes until having made an effort to solve them first; writing summaries of what was learned; creating concept maps without looking at notes or the book; or explaining to someone (real or imaginary) what was learned as if they were the teacher, among similar techniques.

If the goal is to improve understanding, retrieval practice should not involve rote reciting what was read but rather trying to explain it in different words, with new examples, comparing it with other similar ideas, or arguing its plausibility, among other options. In other words, it involves using elaboration and self-explanation, practices that were also discussed in the section on cognitive processes of learning. There is compelling evidence that the most successful students spontaneously resort to elaboration and self-explanation very frequently (Chi et al., 1989).

Also, you may recall the importance of spaced practice—not leaving everything for the day before the exam but working on it a bit every so often—and even interleaved practice—focusing attention on a topic for a short period of time and combine it with the study of other topics or the practice of other skills, especially when they are similar.

On the other hand, there are learning techniques specific to each discipline or even tailored to a particular learning object. To teach them, it is useful to have a deep knowledge not only of the learning object but also of the process that the student usually follows to achieve it.

However, it is true that making students aware of various learning strategies is often not enough (Blackwell et al., 2007). Many times, they believe they do not need them, do not appreciate their value, or simply are not motivated to put them into practice due to their self-efficacy beliefs or outcome expectancies. Moreover, as noted in the chapter on memory processes, many of these techniques require more cognitive effort and make us feel that we are progressing more slowly in the learning process, while less effective techniques are easier and produce illusions of knowing.

5. Implementing the Plan and Monitoring Its Progress and Outcomes

When students finally proceed to put their work plan into action, they should get used to continuously checking whether it aligns with the initial plan and how effective it is in achieving the set goals. Thus they need to compare the task's progress with the defined plan and make adjustments as unexpected events arise or if it becomes evident that they have misjudged some variable. Therefore, students should develop the habit of constantly asking themselves questions such as "Am I achieving the plan's milestones within the expected time?" "Is the strategy I'm following effective?" or "What am I learning?" In other words, the ability to self-assess one's own learning is a crucial metacognitive skill.

For tasks aimed at consolidating knowledge, students must learn to assess the level of learning they have achieved. As mentioned earlier, this is usually not easy for them; they tend to overestimate their mastery of a skill or knowledge. This may be due to the use of study strategies that create illusions of knowing, or because many students—especially younger ones—do not take into account or do not know how to measure the effects of forgetting (Schoenfeld, 1987). We also noted that one of the best ways to strengthen memory and, at the same time, assess one's own learning as realistically as possible is to use retrieval practice. This practice involves self-assessment that allows the learner to identify their real weaknesses and have the opportunity to address them. In contrast, less demanding practices such as rereading what is presumably learned are deceptive and do not provide a good understanding of the level of learning achieved.

6. Reflecting on the Suitability of the Chosen Plan and Making Adjustments

After assessing their own performance, the self-regulated student must make decisions about what to do next based on the results. However, as mentioned earlier, students may resist questioning their strategies, even when they fail. The cognitive dissonance caused by unexpected failure leads them initially to point to other factors, such as task difficulty. Research shows that students most adept at problem-solving are those who change their strategies based on results, while less effective students resist changing their methods, often because they simply do not know others (Bransford et al., 2000). But even when students overcome their cognitive biases and acknowledge that other strategies may be better, they may resist adopting them if the perceived cost seems too high and they do not see clear benefits that outweigh the additional effort (Fu & Gray, 2004). We should keep in mind that, in the end, we are talking about changing habits, which is not trivial. Usually, the most effective strategies require more effort and, while learning them, more time. They are also more frustrating for students because they do not produce illusions of knowing but reveal the (often stark) reality that there are things they have not learned well. As noted earlier, knowing better strategies than the ones they use does not guarantee that students will adopt them. Motivation will be key for them to do so.

Autonomous Learners

The skill of learning how to learn, or the ability to self-regulate one's own learning through metacognitive strategies, aims to turn students into effective and, above all, autonomous learners. After all, as they grow older, the time they spend learning will be much greater outside the classroom, without a teacher guiding them at every step.

Therefore, the support we provide them to develop these learning skills must be significant at the beginning and then gradually decrease, just like in learning any other skill. The teacher should start by helping the student become aware of meta-cognition processes and use them appropriately. This involves making them explicit, promoting and guiding their practice, and providing ample feedback at each step. Gradually, the teacher will withdraw, giving learners increased control over their own learning. This scaffolding process is similar to what we can use in teaching any skill.

The educational impact of students developing their metacognitive skills for self-regulated learning is very relevant, given the evidence provided by research. Studies show that students who have developed these skills, either with help or spontaneously, achieve better academic results (McClelland & Cameron, 2011; Zimmerman, 2001). Moreover, studies on how we achieve expertise provide convincing evidence that one of the features that differentiate experts from beginners is the superior metacognitive skills that the former have developed (Bransford et al., 2000).

Of course, we cannot ignore the numerous factors determining our students' ability to develop their metacognitive skills.

First, self-regulation depends on higher cognitive functions (executive functions) supported by neural circuits that take a long time to mature, and they do so at very different rates depending on the individual. Consequently, we must assume that metacognitive skills must mature progressively throughout schooling, and some students will find it easier to develop them earlier than others.

Second, motivation plays a crucial role in the development and implementation of metacognitive skills. After all, there is a significant positive correlation between the ability to self-regulate and the sense of self-efficacy (Schunk, 1989). In other words, students with higher metacognitive skills for regulated learning usually have greater confidence in themselves to achieve learning goals and, therefore, they have higher motivation to learn.

It is likely that motivation and metacognition mutually reinforce each other. The motivation to achieve learning goals is key to implementing metacognitive strategies that can increase the effectiveness of the learning task—no matter how much we teach metacognitive strategies to a student, they need to be motivated to use them in the first place. On the other hand, metacognition can influence motivation by helping the student reflect on and manage their own self-efficacy and outcome expectancies. Moreover, since applying metacognitive strategies usually contributes to better results, this also positively influences the student's self-efficacy level and, therefore, their motivation. Finally, metacognitive strategies help explicitly outline a work plan and clear milestones to gradually achieve, which improves the student's outcome expectancies.

In the next chapter, I will discuss a cognitive skill that has important implications for the development of self-regulated learning: self-control.

Self-Control

Self-Control for Learning

Consider the following situations:

1. Pablo is in his junior year of high school (11th grade) and has to submit an essay to his philosophy teacher on Monday morning. For different reasons, he could not work on it during the week as planned, so he will have to tackle it over the weekend. However, there are sunny days ahead, and his friends have sent him a message inviting him to go to the beach. After weighing his options, Pablo politely declines the invitation and stays at home to work on his essay.

2. Elaine and Natalie are in class working on a challenging math problem. Natalie has solved it and is now explaining it to Elaine. Despite the noise in the class and the glass walls through which primary school children pass by, Elaine is not put off by these distractions. She remains fully focused on her friend's explanation of the math problem.

3. Claire is sitting an official exam to get her certificate in advanced German. While it is natural to be nervous before the exam, she manages to stay relatively calm and focuses on completing the test.

These three cases, though distinct, share a commonality: the individuals involved must contend with the emotional or cognitive impulses generated by their situations. To overcome these impulses, they need to redirect their behavior toward actions that will benefit their learning and academic outcomes. Despite the differences in these situations, studies indicate that individuals who can act in this way in any of the described cases are also likely to do so in the other two, or at least have a higher probability of doing so. In other words, there is a significant correlation in these behaviors (Duckworth & Kern, 2011; Carlson & Wang, 2007), suggesting that they depend on the same set of skills that allow regulating behavior to free it from automatic impulses. Neuroimaging studies reveal that the same brain region—the prefrontal cortex—is involved in all these situations, further suggesting their interconnectedness (Cohen & Lieberman, 2010). Therefore, despite differences in each case, we can use the concept of *self-control* to encompass them all.

In essence, self-control is the cognitive function that allows us to inhibit the automatic responses of our body in certain situations, especially emotional responses, but also learned and automated responses (such as looking left or right before crossing the street) or genetically programmed responses (such directing attention to the place where we heard a noise). When managing the intensity and type of emotions we experience—such as in the third situation described, where a student remains calm during an important exam—we specifically refer to emotional self-regulation. As this is a feature of self-control of particular interest to both the scientific and educational communities, I will dedicate the next chapter to delve deeper into it.

However, the capacity for self-control refers to the ability not only to regulate the experience and expression of emotions but also to overcome motivational impulses or automatic behaviors. This enables individuals to assess the situation and provide a reasoned response that yields greater benefits (Baumeister et al., 2007). For example, in the second situation where a student tries to concentrate on her friend's explanation despite all the distractions around her, cognitive self-control is at play: the student manages to focus her attention where she wants, not toward other competing stimuli. This is not easy, considering that our attentional system is designed to automatically shift our attention to any outstanding sensory stimulus.

In the first situation, where a young man decides to stay home to finish his philosophy essay instead of going to the beach, we see an example of what is known as *delayed gratification*—the ability to resist taking an immediate reward to receive a greater reward at a later time (Mischel et al., 1989). In other words, it is the ability to resist the temptation of an immediate reward to obtain a greater benefit in the future. Undoubtedly, this capability is closely related to motivation—it involves a struggle between two mutually exclusive goals, between which the individual must choose based on their values, that is, what motivates them more. But for this choice to be fair, the person must inhibit the motivational impulse that favors the immediate goal and rationally assess the two goals in light of their priorities. This is the type of self-control needed to follow a diet, quit smoking, or, in this case, give up short-term wants or pleasures to achieve medium or long-term academic goals.

In summary, self-control is a multifaceted skill studied from various, often unrelated scientific perspectives (Hofmann et al., 2012). Only recently have the various approaches to studying this psychological construct begun to converge, pointing to the existence of an underlying skill involved in any situation that requires the suppression of impulsive and automatic responses. Along with working memory and cognitive flexibility, this capability is another of the so-called higher *cognitive functions* or *executive functions* that characterize, by their degree, the human species: inhibitory control (Diamond, 2013), the higher cognitive function underlying the ability for self-control in all its facets.

Self-Control and Academic Achievement

Scientific studies suggest that the capacity for self-control is positively correlated with lifelong academic attainment. In fact, some studies find that self-control in preschool children predicts their performance in mathematics and reading in childhood even better than intelligence does (Blair & Razza, 2007). In adolescents, self-control can outdo IQ in predicting academic achievement (Duckworth & Seligman, 2005). A high level of self-control is associated with multiple personal benefits beyond the school context, such as enhanced social skills and better health (Tangney et al., 2004).

While there are thousands of studies linking self-control to various desirable features, perhaps some of the most famous are Walter Mischel's studies on delayed gratification using the "marshmallow test" (Mischel et al., 1988). Between the 1960s and 1970s, Mischel conducted a series of experiments where children around the ages of four and five years old were placed in a room with only a chair and a table. On the table, the researcher left a treat (for example, a marshmallow) and told the child to wait there for 15 minutes while he went out to do some things. If the child wished, they could eat the sweet, but if they waited, the researcher would give them another upon returning, and they could then eat both. The rewards did not necessarily have to be marshmallows, but the idea was always the same: the child had to choose between an immediate reward or a greater but delayed reward. Most importantly, while waiting, the child had to overcome the temptation of the immediate reward, which was constantly within reach.

Nearly a hundred children participated in Mischel's original experiments. Some managed to resist the temptation using various strategies, such as looking away from the marshmallow and reminding themselves why they should endure, while others ate it as soon as they were left alone in the room. The researcher did not end his experiment there; he followed these children for years—a longitudinal study—and found that the group of children who had shown greater inhibitory capacity in the marshmallow test statistically coincided with those achieving better academic results in adolescence. That is, the capacity for self-control was a predictor of academic success. High levels of self-control identified in the test were also associated with enhanced social skills, a better ability to manage stress and cope with frustration, and a greater ability to pursue goals in adolescence (Mischel et al., 1989).

Numerous subsequent studies replicating Mischel's work have produced comparable results. It seems logical that self-control should provide benefits for behavior directed toward long-term goals and contribute to success in interpersonal relationships. However, as always, it is better to be cautious and not assume that self-control alone explains the personal and academic benefits observed in the aforementioned studies. Self-control is indeed correlated with many other variables also associated with these outcomes, from intelligence to the type of family environment. Therefore, the maxim that correlation does not imply causation should be kept in mind, so we cannot rule out that part of the relationship observed between capacity for self-control and success in various areas of life may be mediated by other factors that are the cause of both. Moreover, tests like the marshmallow test are not perfect: there are many reasons unrelated to self-control why a child might prefer to eat the treat right away—namely, a bird in the hand is worth two in the bush. In any case, a takeaway from this is that studies suggest self-control is part of a set of interconnected skills that play a relevant role in students' academic performance, as well as in other aspects of their personal and professional lives.

Finally, the works of Mischel and other researchers not only suggest that the capacity for self-control is essential for success in life but also that this ability develops early, starting from early childhood (Mischel et al., 1989). As expected, inhibitory control has a hereditary genetic component, but its development also depends significantly on the environment (Beaver et al., 2009; Goldsmith et al., 1997). That is, inhibitory control is shaped by experience and can be improved through learning at any age (Meichenbaum & Goodman, 1971; Strayhorn, 2002). Of course, the earlier it is learned, the better, but it is never too late to nurture it. The environmental factors contributing to children developing their capacity for self-control are explored in turn.

Factors Modulating Self-Control Capacity

As mentioned earlier, although inhibitory control—which underlies self-control—has a hereditary component that we cannot overlook, researchers agree that the child's environment and experiences play a remarkable role in the development of this cognitive ability. Since inhibitory control begins to take shape in early childhood, the child's family environment likely plays a relevant role in its stimulation (Bernier et al., 2010). In this sense, despite the recent and diverse research on this matter showing small to moderate-sized effects (Karreman et al., 2006), psychologists generally agree that a key factor in self-control development is the degree to which a child's family environment provides emotional and cognitive support (Schroeder & Kelley, 2010; Grolnick & Farkas, 2002).

First, emotional support refers to displays of affection, trust, and backing that the child receives from caregivers, as well as the sensitivity these caregivers have toward the child's physical and psychological needs and how they regulate the child's behavior. Indeed, studies show that children growing up in warm and nurturing family environments often develop better self-control skills than those in cold and indifferent environments or those subjected to physical or verbal control (Calkins et al., 1998).

Research examining this relationship is conducted through direct observation of interactions between parents and children, either in their own homes or in the laboratory, where they may be asked to perform a task together, such as assembling a puzzle or a card castle. Researchers use rubrics to categorize observed parent-child interactions in various scenarios, thus establishing behavior patterns. They then assess children's self-control through tests or interviews and compare the results of both studies. Through this approach and after assessing various research studies, psychologists conclude that there is a correlation between warm, supportive parenting and capacity for self-control (Evans & Rosenbaum, 2008; Eisenberg, 2005). Furthermore, these studies are complemented by others providing evidence of the positive impact of such relationships on children: they improve their ability to identify and interpret their emotions and those of others and learn to behave sensitively and appropriately on each occasion, based on the models provided by adults (Howes et al., 1994).

In addition to emotional support, the development of the capacity for self-control seems to also depend on the cognitive support provided by the child's environment (Evans & Rosenbaum, 2008). This translates into, among other things, the intellectual stimulation the child receives from their family—for example, when parents frequently engage in conversations with the child, encourage them to express themselves, expose them to a rich vocabulary and complex linguistic structures, or provide opportunities for them to explore and experiment with their surroundings. This is also related to access to intellectually stimulating resources such as books, games, puzzles, and the like. However, two specific features of the family environment stand out as particularly influential in the development of self-control: the child's level of autonomy (Bernier et al., 2010) and the presence of well-structured and consistent rules at home (Steinberg et al., 1989).

Regarding the first aspect, children whose parents are high in autonomy granting tend to develop better self-control. Obviously, this does not mean leaving the child to their own devices and expecting them to figure everything out on their own without help. Rather, it involves promoting their autonomy by placing them in situations that encourage them to deal with the challenges of everyday life, with the guidance and support of adults, for example, through appropriate feedback. It is also crucial that the child exercises this autonomy responsibly (Lamborn et al., 1991). In short, the child should have multiple opportunities to solve problems, make decisions, take responsibility for their actions, and not expect everything to be done or resolved for them.

As for the second aspect, studies suggest that households with well-established and consistent rules of coexistence contribute more significantly to the development of children's self-control. It could be hypothesized that the existence of these behavioral norms provides an opportunity to exercise the ability to inhibit impulses to adjust behavior to social norms. Indeed, numerous studies show that self-control is reinforced through its practice with activities that involve the restraint of impulses to follow rules that lead to specific goals (Diamond & Lee, 2011). In this sense, games provide interesting opportunities to practice self-control.

Situations forcing children to practice self-control may result in improvements of this capacity because they encourage them to seek strategies that help them achieve it. For example, some of the children who participated in the marshmallow test employed strategies such as looking away from the treat, singing, repeatedly reminding themselves of their goal, and sitting on their hands, among others. These strategies can develop spontaneously or through imitation of models provided by adults and, of course, can be taught explicitly. In either case, learning them probably requires opportunities to put them into practice.

In conclusion, within the family context, parental practices that contribute the most to the development of children's self-control skills could be summarized as what some researchers define as a "demanding yet supportive" environment. This environment promotes autonomy within a framework of consistent behavioral rules and provides emotional and cognitive support to exercise it (Grolnick & Ryan, 1989). But what about the school environment? Children come to school with a capacity for self-control built on their genetic heritage and shaped based on their family environment. With this in mind, can teachers contribute to improving students' self-control skills? Let's explore this further.

Promoting Self-Control in School

When reviewing the scientific literature on the effect that teachers can have on their students' self-control skills, at first glance, the impact—if any—appears to be very small (e.g., Skibbe et al., 2011). Upon closer examination, however, the effect is actually relevant for the children who need it the most—those who come to school with underdeveloped self-control skills because their homes have not provided the best opportunities to promote them (Rimm-Kaufman et al., 2002). The impact on the overall group of students, of course, is generally small; children who already possess these skills do not experience any significant improvement in school, which lowers the average and the corresponding effect size in the group of all students.

In any case, the important aspect is that evidence suggests that teachers can precisely help those children who have the greatest room for improvement, namely those who have not developed their self-control potential in the family environment. Research also indicates that the same ideas valid for self-control development in the family context are applicable in the school setting. When teachers provide a well-organized, demanding yet supportive, affectionate and comforting learning environment that promotes autonomy through consistent rules, students develop better self-regulation skills, especially those with fewer competencies in this area (Connor et al., 2010).

For example, a study by Connor and colleagues (2010) examined the impact of providing training to first-grade teachers regarding class planning and organization, classroom management, and activities promoting student autonomy, both when working individually and in small groups. The results revealed that only those students with greater self-regulation deficits benefited from the classroom environment created by their teachers through the new organizational and methodological skills they had acquired. Although the overall group's effect may be irrelevant, the impact on the most disadvantaged students contributes to improving equal opportunities, which is no doubt one of the most fundamental goals of school.

In addition to creating a comforting and well-organized atmosphere, certain types of activities can also contribute to the development of inhibitory control in younger students. While activities promoting student autonomy have been mentioned, it is also worth noting activities that challenge children to practice self-control, putting them in situations where they must inhibit their impulses to adjust their behavior to interaction rules with their peers.

In this regard, it is appropriate to mention educational programs such as *Tools of the Mind*, a preschool program offering activities designed to develop higher cognitive functions, including inhibitory control. Some of these activities involve learning to collaborate in a task by taking turns while a peer intervenes or following a set of increasingly complex instructions. The implementation of this program in preschool over periods of one to two years has provided evidence of its positive impact on improving children's self-control skills (Diamond et al., 2007).

Of course, it is also possible to help students improve their self-control skills by learning strategies to regulate their emotions (see next chapter). To conclude this chapter, I will discuss the importance of not unnecessarily forcing students' inhibitory control capacity and provide some final comments on the neurobiological foundations underlying its development throughout life.

The Limits of Inhibitory Control

One interesting feature of inhibitory control is that it behaves as if it were a limited resource that depletes over time. In this sense, numerous studies have shown that the capacity for inhibitory control works in a manner analogous to a muscle, meaning it fatigues after intense exercise (Hagger et al., 2010; Muraven 2012). Indeed, tasks involving the intervention of inhibitory control require effort, and like all activities that demand effort, they cannot be sustained indefinitely without taking a break. Moreover, research suggests that the depletion of a higher cognitive function, such as inhibitory control, also depletes other higher cognitive functions involved in planning, decision-making, and problem-solving (Hofmann et al., 2012).

Furthermore, inhibitory control also fatigues when overly demanded. For example, as seen in one of the situations at the beginning of the chapter, inhibitory control allows us to ignore distractors in the environment to focus our attention on stimuli relevant to our goals. In a way, inhibitory control helps us voluntarily determine what will enter our working memory, excluding irrelevant stimuli. However, doing so requires a considerable number of cognitive resources (Baumeister, 2002). Therefore, when students are in an environment full of prominent stimuli, whether noise or visual distractions (such as people passing by windows), they need to employ a greater capacity for inhibitory control to maintain attention on the task. Excessive decoration on classroom walls, for instance, can act as negative interference during learning tasks. In fact, several studies indicate that students pay more attention to class activities when the walls are less decorated (Fisher et al., 2014). Additionally, similar effects have been observed concerning noise in the classroom (Klatte et al., 2013).

Therefore, cognitively speaking, it is not advisable to have students in environments rich in stimuli that force their inhibitory control (and working memory) while they perform learning tasks, as this negatively impacts their performance. It is crucial to avoid confusing the inhibitory control training mentioned earlier—done through explicitly targeted activities—with the presumed training that would occur if students were constantly in a distracting environment. There is no need to train inhibitory control in this manner, and the detrimental effects it has on learning strongly discourage it.

Development of Inhibitory Control

Finally, it is worth noting that, much like working memory, inhibitory control gradually improves with age. This should not come as a surprise; adults clearly differ from children in their ability to behave according to established social norms—hence the existence of children-free restaurants. Jokes aside, the reason for this phenomenon has a neurological basis. The explanation is the same as I provided in the case of working memory; after all, it is another higher cognitive function closely related to inhibitory control.

Higher cognitive functions, or executive functions, are supported by the prefrontal cortex—one of the last brain regions to mature during neurodevelopment. This region continues maturing until well into the 20s, sometimes even beyond (Sowell et al., 2003). Therefore, it is not uncommon for this ability to spontaneously develop throughout the academic life of our students, much like their working memory. However, a significant difference from working memory is that inhibitory control can apparently be improved overall through practice, whereas there is no compelling evidence regarding the capacity of working memory.

You will likely recall this limitation of working memory. And surely, you will also remember that, despite this limitation, it can be optimized through acquiring meaningful knowledge and task automation. Inhibitory control, on the other hand, can also be enhanced through learning, specifically through the acquisition of strategies for emotional management. I will explore this in the following chapter.

Emotional Self-Regulation

4.3

Untimely Emotions

In our daily lives, we constantly encounter situations that automatically trigger emotional responses of varying intensities. These response patterns are adaptive; they evolved throughout the course of human evolution as they contributed to the survival of our ancestors in their environment. While emotions continue to be crucial for our preservation today, the social and cultural context differs significantly from that of our ancestors. Consequently, certain emotions can sometimes hinder rather than advantage us. Indeed, emotions impact fundamental cognitive processes, such as attention and working memory, and can even "take control" of our behavior, making tasks more challenging than they would be without them (Gross, 2002). For example, both anger and fear can influence our ability to make sound decisions, hindering efforts to solve problems that require intellect. Needless to say, untimely emotions can impede learning and performance in an academic setting. Too much anxiety, for example, can block us during an exam or a public presentation—a topic I discussed in the chapter on the role of emotions in learning.

Fortunately, as explored in the preceding chapter, humans have also developed the capacity for self-control, undoubtedly another evolutionary milestone of our brain. This ability enables us to inhibit or redirect various automatic responses our brain generates to specific stimuli, including emotional responses. In scientific terms, when self-control refers to the management of one's emotions, the term commonly used is *emotional self-regulation* (Tice & Bratslavsky, 2000). Emotional self-regulation involves the ability to control one's emotional responses, either by regulating the physical and psychological experiences they generate or by suppressing or modifying their external expression (Gross & Thompson, 2007). While this ability, like others, has a genetic hereditary basis, it is also influenced by the environment. Therefore, it is possible to learn to regulate emotions through specific strategies. In fact, we all employ regulation strategies spontaneously, such as looking away from something that disgusts us, writing to express our feelings, or taking deep breaths to calm ourselves (Koole, 2009).

In this sense, scientific research has found that developing emotional self-regulation skills has significant consequences for both academic and social success (Graziano et al., 2007; Gross & John, 2003). To be fair, this is one of those conclusions that seems evident without the need for scientific evidence. Just think how much easier many tasks would be if we could control fear or anxiety, and how many decisions would be less ill-advised if not driven by, say, anger or pride. However, it would not be the first time that something seemingly logical lacks support from evidence, so it is better to rely on scientific findings.

Research on emotional regulation is one of the most productive areas of the psychology of emotion. Among its key findings related to the educational context are that children can learn to self-regulate and teachers can help them improve this skill—especially those who need it most—thereby contributing to making them better students (and happier individuals, if you will).

In this chapter, I will first discuss how students developing emotional self-regulation skills contributes to their learning in the school context. Then I will present some of the strategies they can learn that have yielded the most promising results when analyzed through the lens of the scientific method.

Self-Regulating Emotions for Learning (and Performance)

There are several reasons why being able to regulate one's emotions is beneficial for becoming a good student. In the previous chapter, we stressed the importance of inhibiting immediate impulses to decide between two or more mutually exclusive options that differ in value and immediacy—delayed gratification, as exemplified by the marshmallow test. To choose the option that is not immediate and less likely to happen, it is necessary to overcome emotions that push students to automatically opt for the benefit already within their reach. Only in this way do they have the chance to weigh the pros and cons of each option. The student who could forgo immediate pleasure—going to the beach with friends—in favor of working on a philosophy essay that, in the student's eyes, would bring a greater reward in the long run, provides a good example of what this type of regulation can mean for learning in the academic context (Duckworth & Seligman, 2005).

However, another important scenario where emotional regulation plays a fundamental role in the school context is in situations where the student's emotional state or reaction can affect their performance during a task or their motivation to tackle it (Kim & Pekrun, 2014). As discussed in the chapter on the role of emotions in learning, when emotions induce too high a level of arousal, the cognitive processes necessary for intellectual tasks are significantly disrupted (Arnsten, 2009). Similarly, when learning tasks are associated with negative emotions, students' motivation to engage in them is seriously compromised (Kim & Pekrun, 2014).

Emotions in the school context can occur for various reasons and can be classified into two main types: those arising from social interactions both inside and outside the classroom, and those occurring when the student interprets that a learning challenge may have positive or negative effects on their academic or personal goals depending on the outcome (Pekrun et al., 2007). This is the case with emotions that arise during exams and grades. These emotions are known as *performance-related emotions*, and they will receive much of our attention in this chapter precisely because they are an inevitable consequence of the act of learning and have been extensively studied. In fact, for decades, they were virtually the only emotional phenomenon studied in the educational context (Pekrun & Linnenbrink-Garcia, 2014). Of course, in some cases, social emotions overlap with performance-related emotions, such as when exam results are made public or when a teacher provides feedback on a student's response to the entire class. Not surprisingly, regulation strategies, which we will discuss later, are useful for all of them.

Performance-Related Emotions

Performance-related emotions are inherent to learning (Pekrun et al., 2007). When we undertake a learning task, especially when we attach high value to it, we desire to perform well. In other words, we detest failure, especially if we have put in effort. Unlike success, failure brings unpleasant emotions. Emotions tend to guide us toward actions that help us avoid the unpleasant and pursue the pleasant. In general, we tend to avoid situations where we anticipate failure and lean toward those we believe will lead to success. Therefore, performance-related emotions are key to motivation in the school context.

Indeed, performance-related emotions are nothing less than the driving force behind motivation that arises from assessing the value of the learning object and expectations of success. When I mentioned in the motivation chapter that a student with low expectations (low self-efficacy) would likely choose not to expend effort or would give up, I did not explicitly refer to the possible cause—our tendency to try to avoid the unpleasant emotions associated with failure.

Remember that when a student is faced with a challenge, the first thing they do—automatically and unconsciously—is assess both the value of successfully overcoming it and the negative impact failure would have. Above all, they assess their expectations of overcoming it. Depending on their estimation, the emotions they predict they will experience will lead them to act in one direction or another.

Obviously, if the student assigns no value to the challenge, their emotions will remain at low levels. But if the challenge is relevant to the student—whether for academic reasons or for the integrity of their reputation or self-concept—then their expectations will determine their behavior. If expectations are very low, they might choose to give up; by not trying, failure can be explained without resorting to more "painful" causes, such as a lack of ability, for example. Alternatively, they might choose to "self-sabotage," making up excuses that explain why they could not perform better. On the other hand, if their expectations are ambiguous, then their emotions will also be very present during the challenge, hindering their concentration on the task and thus affecting their performance. Finally, if their expectations are high, the student may be able to keep emotions in check—although this is not always the case—before and during the test. In either case, emotions will resurface upon receiving feedback on the task results.

Performance-related emotions, therefore, arise when the student anticipates a challenge in the future (e.g., an exam), when facing it (while doing the exam) and when confronted with its outcome (when receiving grades or other types of feedback). When these emotions arise prospectively, they condition the student's motivation to expend effort and prepare for the challenge. During the challenge, they affect performance because they alter cognitive processes. Upon receiving feedback on the challenge, they influence the motivation the student will have to face future challenges related to it (e.g., other challenges in the same academic subject). Therefore, the ability to regulate these emotions is crucial for students' learning and performance.

Promoting Emotional Regulation

Students experiencing high levels of anxiety or stress regarding school tasks, especially exams, are at a clear disadvantage compared to those who can regulate these emotions and keep them at more beneficial levels. The results they obtain in such tests attest to this (Chapell et al., 2005). While it is true that the capacity for self-regulation has a genetic component and is nurtured by experiences provided by the student's family environment from early childhood (Morris et al., 2007), studies show that it is possible to help students struggling to regulate these emotions.

The assistance can be provided by teaching the student to regulate their own emotions, that is, helping them develop their self-regulation capacity through specific strategies, or by implementing measures that provide a learning environment that reduces undesirable emotional responses. In many cases, both types of actions will be complementary. I will now discuss self-regulation strategies and later address what can be done regarding the learning environment.

Strategies for Emotional Self-Regulation

The capacity for emotional self-regulation relies on two other emotional competencies: the ability to identify, assess, and correctly understand one's own and others' emotional expressions and internal emotional states, and the ability to communicate emotions to other people through verbal and nonverbal means (Gross & Thompson, 2007). To promote emotional self-regulation, it may therefore make sense to start by working on these aspects. In fact, numerous studies reflect that, in general, adolescents have difficulty identifying their emotions and those of others, and often are unaware of the emotional regulation strategies they spontaneously use (Fried, 2010). However, they also show that these skills can improve relatively easily with the right guidance (Zins et al., 2007).

Initially, students differ in the self-regulation strategies they have spontaneously developed. While the same strategies may have different effects on each individual, there is consensus on the types of strategies that are generally more effective. Students with greater difficulties in self-regulating their emotions can benefit from learning these strategies.

Emotional self-regulation strategies can be classified according to different criteria. Thus, I will address the aspects that are most relevant in the educational context to distinguish them. On one hand, regulation strategies can differ based on when they are applied: before the intensely emotional episode is anticipated (such as an exam) or during the episode itself—that is, before they occur or once they have already occurred. Research suggests that, as a rule, anticipatory strategies are more effective than strategies that attempt to control the emotional reaction after the episode has already occurred (Gross & John, 2003). On the other hand, strategies can be classified according to the component of the emotional process they target, whether attention, bodily expressions, or cognitive appraisal of the situation (Koole, 2009). Let's explore them now.

Strategies Aimed at Modulating Attention

Among the strategies that act on attention are those that involve avoiding thinking about the object that triggers emotions. A better way to achieve this is by redirecting attention to other things (Wegner, 1994). It is indeed almost impossible to decide not to think about something (for example, try not to think about a polar bear), so we must instead focus on thinking about other things (and yet, there's the polar bear again). In any case, to apply this strategy, it is not necessary for the things we think about to trigger positive emotions; it suffices if they keep the student's working memory busy and hinder the entry of thoughts that provoke negative emotions (Van Dillen & Koole, 2007). However, it is obvious that for the context at hand, these techniques are rather ineffective—controlling attentional processes is challenging.

Other strategies that act on attention involve doing the opposite of what was previously stated: instead of diverting attention from the emotional stimulus—that is, instead of trying to suppress it—they involve deliberately focusing attention on it to express the emotions it has generated. This occurs when we write about our feelings or share them with a friend. Nonetheless, their regulatory effect may be more related to cognitive reappraisal, which involves reconstructing the emotional episode, rather than simply focusing attention on it. I will discuss cognitive reappraisal strategies after briefly commenting on strategies that act on bodily responses.

Strategies Aimed at Modulating Bodily Expressions

It is evident that different emotions provoke specific patterns of bodily and physiological reactions, including facial expressions, changes in respiratory rate, and the like. Interestingly, deliberately activating these reactions can trigger the emotions usually associated with them. Moreover, by controlling and modifying bodily reactions during an emotional episode, we can reduce the intensity of the emotion that caused them. For example, one of the most effective emotional self-regulation strategies in this category is the practice of controlled breathing.

There is ample evidence that the voluntary modulation of specific breathing patterns can selectively activate specific emotional states (Philippot et al., 2002). More importantly, it can contribute to reducing the intensity of acute emotional episodes (Varvogli & Darviri, 2011). Furthermore, focusing attention on one's own breathing to try to regulate it serves at the same time as an attention modulation strategy.

Other strategies for bodily control include the suppression of emotional expressions (Gross, 1998) or releasing and channeling them into other behaviors (Schmeichel et al., 2006; Bushman et al., 2001). However, these types of strategies have various disadvantages for overall emotional well-being or may simply be inappropriate in the classroom context, making them less advisable (Gross & John, 2003; Bushman, 2002).

Strategies Aimed at Modulating the Cognitive Appraisal of the Situation

All in all, studies on emotional self-regulation suggest that the most effective strategies are those directed at modifying the student's cognitive appraisal of the challenge they are faced with. What does this mean? Remember that emotions associated with performance arise when the student perceives that a situation they are facing may have consequences for their academic or personal goals, which will be either beneficial or detrimental depending on the outcome. In such a situation, the student makes a cognitive appraisal, unconsciously and automatically, in which they estimate the importance of the task (subjective value) and the chances they have of overcoming it (expectations). The result of this evaluation will trigger emotions of a particular kind and of a greater or lesser intensity. For example, a student who values mathematics highly but believes they are incapable of passing an exam in this subject will likely experience negative emotions. It is crucial to recognize here that what triggers emotions is not the situation itself but the interpretation the student makes of the situation. Therefore, cognitive reappraisal techniques aim to modify this interpretation.

As you may have noticed, the cognitive appraisal that a student makes when faced with a learning challenge is the same as that proposed by cognitive theories of motivation to explain when a student will be motivated or not to pursue goals—that is, it is based on the same principles: subjective value and expectations (self-efficacy). Therefore, self-regulating emotions through cognitive reappraisal means acting on the value and expectations one holds regarding a task. For example, when a student tells themselves that the result of a test is not important enough to get so nervous about it or when they encourage themselves by repeating that they can handle it, they are attempting cognitive reappraisal. In these examples, the first case seeks to reconsider the subjective value of the task, and the second, the expectations of overcoming it.

You will likely recall that the subjective value and expectations of a student regarding a learning goal are based on their beliefs—their ideas about how learning works and how they see themselves as students. Therefore, cognitive reappraisal strategies can be directed at modifying these beliefs. The student's environment plays a very relevant role in this aspect, so I will address that in the next chapter section.

Note: Confirmation Bias as an Automatic Emotional Regulation System

In the first chapter of this book, which deals with educational research, I discussed cognitive biases, particularly confirmation bias. When new information contradicts our ideas—especially when these ideas are well established and form part of our identity—we experience cognitive dissonance (Festinger, 1957). This phenomenon is usually accompanied by negative emotions because deep down we feel threatened—after all, our ideas or knowledge have been questioned. However, immediately, our confirmation bias comes to the rescue—the tendency to reinterpret the received information to fit our schemas or to directly ignore and forget it. Confirmation bias prompts us to find an explanation for why the new information must be incorrect. Moreover, it leads us to seek sources that support our position (and our position only) to dismiss the information that caused the dissonance. In this sense, confirmation bias, which is based on cognitive appraisal, may be interpreted as an automatic emotional regulation system triggered to reduce the negative emotions that arise from cognitive dissonance.

However, I would like to point out that, of the three types of emotional self-regulation strategies I mentioned based on their target (attention, bodily expressions, and cognitive reappraisal), the first two are usually employed when the emotion has already been triggered and its impact needs to be reduced. Meanwhile, the third operates especially preventively, reducing the likelihood of an emotional peak when the challenge arises in the future (although it can also be used to mitigate an emotional episode). As I mentioned earlier, in general, preventive strategies usually yield better results than those used once the emotional reaction has occurred.

Learning Environments That Support Emotional Regulation

In the classroom, teachers are not psychologists (nor do we have to be), but we may nonetheless contribute to providing learning environments that facilitate the emotional regulation of our students when they face school tasks and academic challenges. This, in turn, will help them become better students.

If the emotions associated with performance arise from the cognitive appraisal that students make about the importance of doing tasks well and their expectations of succeeding, then a good way to help them keep their emotions in check may be by intervening in their beliefs, which form the basis of subjective value and self-efficacy

(Romero et al., 2014). We discussed this in the chapter dedicated to beliefs, but it is worth revisiting some cases here in the context of emotional regulation.

First, we can promote cognitive reappraisal of the causes students attribute to their successes and failures. Some researchers contend that what really matters about the estimation that a student makes when faced with a challenge is the degree of control they perceive it provides (Pekrun et al., 2007). That is, whether they believe success depends on themselves or on variables they cannot control. For example, a student who believes their ability in a subject is deficient and unchangeable will have a very low sense of control; they will interpret that achieving learning goals will not be in their hands but probably in the hands of "lady luck." In such a case, we are reminded of the concept of attributional training, which we discussed in the chapter on beliefs (Weiner, 1986). In short, it involves educating individuals about success and failure, aiming for students not to attribute them to fixed and uncontrollable causes but to factors within their control, such as effort and study strategies.

Second, another crucial target for cognitive reappraisal is the meaning students attribute to errors. This involves promoting ideas consistent with a growth mindset, where the error is not interpreted as a stigma defining a supposed incapacity but as a natural part of the learning process. This way, we can contribute to reducing or redirecting the negative emotions resulting from difficulties that may arise in a learning activity. Of course, I would like to note here that for cases of students with severe anxiety and stress regarding school tasks, it is always best to seek the help of a specialist who works with them, providing appropriate emotional scaffolding.

Nevertheless, the key to the contribution that we as teachers can make to the emotional regulation of our students is to offer support throughout the learning process, while remaining demanding and consistent within a well-established framework of rules. As noted in the previous chapter on self-control, a demanding yet supportive atmosphere can be the best recipe for developing self-control. Remember that emotional self-regulation may be thought of as a type of self-control and, as such, depends on the executive function of inhibitory control (Joormann & Gotlib, 2010). As we will see next, the correlation also extends to other executive functions.

Executive Functions and Emotional Regulation

Emotional regulation processes, aside from automated ones, are deliberate and cognitively demanding. Given that they involve overcoming spontaneous emotional responses generated by our organism, it is evident that they require the capacity for inhibitory control. Moreover, the capability for cognitive reappraisal—the most effective emotional regulation strategy—is not only correlated with inhibitory control but also with other executive functions, namely working memory and cognitive flexibility (Schmeichel & Tang, 2014; McRae et al., 2012b).

In this regard, studies utilizing functional magnetic resonance imaging have revealed that during cognitive reappraisal, regions of the prefrontal cortex associated with executive functions are activated, while the activity of the amygdala and other areas related to emotional processing of stimuli decreases (Ochsner et al., 2002). This relationship explains why the capability for emotional self-regulation, like other types of self-control, increases with age (McRae et al., 2012a). As you may recall, the brain circuits related to executive functions are among the last to mature during neurodevelopment. Nevertheless, it appears that age alone may not fully predict self-regulation capacity; the opportunities the child has had to learn effective self-regulation strategies may also be crucial (Morris et al., 2007). Of course, the types of environments and experiences we discussed in the previous chapter, promoting inhibitory control ability in children, may simultaneously contribute to improving their ability for emotional self-regulation (Bernier et al., 2010).

Resilience and Grit

The Ability to Persevere

The term *resilience* is used in diverse fields such as psychology, ecology, and materials engineering. In all these contexts, it refers to the capacity to bounce back or recover after a disturbance. Resilience, therefore, is the property exhibited by a material when, after being subjected to a force that deforms it, it spontaneously springs back into shape. In ecology, it defines the tendency of an ecosystem to recover after being altered by natural or anthropogenic causes. In psychology, it refers to a person's ability to overcome adversity. This latter meaning is what we will explore in this chapter.

But what does resilience have to do with learning to warrant its inclusion in this book? While you may already have an idea, we will seek the answer in the work of psychologist Angela Duckworth, a researcher in the field of what is known as the *psychology of success*. To be more accurate, nonetheless, this chapter will mainly focus on a presumed quality closely related to resilience, which Duckworth and her colleagues termed *grit*—a blend of perseverance and passion for achieving long-term goals. Over the years, Duckworth's team has thoroughly studied this construct as a personality trait, observing that individuals with a high level of grit can maintain their determination and motivation over extended periods despite facing failure and adversity (Duckworth et al., 2007). Grit, in a sense, can be seen as resilience directed toward the attainment of long-term goals. Its relevance to learning is evident as it speaks to the ability to sustain motivation despite difficulties for extended periods, aiming to achieve long-term goals, such as those required for academic success.

The identification and study of grit arose from Duckworth's interest in finding a personality-related variable that could explain the likelihood of achieving personal goals (Duckworth, 2016). Until then, one of the best predictors of future achievements was intelligence (and still is), measured by intelligence quotient (IQ) tests (Gottfredson, 1997). Although the relationship between intelligence and success has been evident in both academic performance and job performance (Neisser et al., 1996), Duckworth's team has provided ample evidence suggesting that grit might be a better predictor of success than intelligence (Duckworth et al., 2007). Furthermore, they argue that these two qualities are not correlated—grit, unlike many other traditional performance measures, is independent of intelligence. In their view, this helps explain why some highly intelligent individuals do not perform well when goals are not achievable in the short term but require sustained effort and dedication over extended periods.

Before going any further, it is important to note that we will discuss grit as a quality involved in the achievement of academic goals—or any other goals—always in a comparative framework with other personal qualities. It is clear that external factors, such as the socioeconomic variables in the student's environment, factors related to the learning environment, or simply chance, play a crucial and often decisive role in the likelihood of students' academic success. However, personal factors that can contribute to the achievement of their goals—whether academic, sport-related, professional, or personal—should not be ignored. In any case, we will see that the concept of grit and its impact on academic success is not without criticism.

Successful Cases

West Point is the oldest military academy in the United States. It is located in the town that bears the same name, about 60 miles north of New York City. The admissions process is as rigorous as that of the most prestigious universities, considering grades from the last four years of high school, SAT and ACT scores (college entrance exams), and the results of a tough fitness test. Additionally, applicants need a nomination from a member of the U.S. Congress or Senate (or from the president or vice president). Out of over 14,000 applicants each year, only 1,200 secure a spot.

However, what is most surprising is that 20% of those admitted drop out before graduation, with most not even making it past the first two months—a training period known for its toughness as Beast Barracks. Although West Point has detailed information about the academic and athletic achievements of each cadet (the term for students at a military academy), none of this data has ever reliably predicted who will surpass the initial period and who will not. This intrigued Duckworth, who started her research to find a factor that could better predict the success of cadets.

Military psychologist Mike Matthews had a hypothesis about what determined success at West Point. He believed it was the attitude of "never giving up." Duckworth defined this attitude as *grit*, the perseverance to achieve personal goals, and studied how she could measure it in individuals. She developed a test that allowed her to establish a grit scale and used it with cadets newly arrived at West Point.

Two months later, at the conclusion of the demanding Beast Barracks selection period, Duckworth found that grit measures showed a strong correlation with the outcomes of early dropouts. Grit, with considerable accuracy, explained who would persist and who would not. In other words, it would not necessarily be the cadets with the best grades or those with better physical fitness—not even those with both— who would be guaranteed to make it through the selection period. Instead, it would be those who had an attitude leading them to persevere in the face of harshness, failures, and even discouragement: those with grit.

Duckworth and her team also conducted research applying their grit scale in other areas: sports, academics, arts, and business. While there were obviously particular differences in each domain, all the individuals investigated who had achieved success in these diverse fields shared a high degree of grit (see Box 1).

BOX 1 Some famous cases of grit.

MICHAEL JORDAN

Few people know that Michael Jordan, regarded by many as the greatest basketball player of all time, was cut from his high school basketball team because his skill level did not match that of his teammates. Driven by determination, Jordan spent that year training daily on his own and managed to be readmitted to the team. His path to stardom was not a walk in the park. Although his role in college basketball was outstanding, he entered the NBA draft as only the third overall pick. But he did not let it bother him, quite the opposite. Once he joined the national league, he struggled for six years before winning his first trophy with the Chicago Bulls. The player's mindset and determination are clearly stated in his own words: "I've missed more than 9000 shots in my career. I've lost almost 300 games. Twenty-six times, I've been trusted to take the game-winning shot and missed. I've failed over and over and over again in my life. And that is why I succeed."

JOHN IRVING

The renowned American writer John Irving, acclaimed for novels such as *The Hotel New Hampshire* and *A Widow for One Year* and the recipient of the Oscar for Best Adapted Screenplay for *The Cider House Rules*, serves as an example of how grit contributes to success. During his childhood, he struggled with his schoolwork. He found both reading and writing—essential skills for any writer—to be difficult. It was not until his younger brother was diagnosed with dyslexia that Irving realized his problem. Despite several occasions when he wanted to give up, one of his high school teachers instilled confidence in him, urging him to continue his education. In Irving's own words, he learned "to enhance his abilities by devoting twice as much attention to reading and writing." He reached a point where he saw a positive aspect in his dyslexia for his writing career, "as it taught him to approach writing slowly and to revise his work over and over for improvements."

Drawing from her research, Duckworth has posited that grit is a better predictor of success than intellectual talent (IQ) or other talents, because grit is a fundamental factor providing the resilience needed to "stay on course" in the face of challenges and adversities—that is, to keep striving toward goals despite (inevitable) failures and setbacks. In other words, Duckworth's work supports the claim that effort is more important than talent.

Grit, Motivation, and Metacognition

Grit has a significant motivational component. In Duckworth's view, grit is not just perseverance but also passion (in the sense of devotion) for achieving goals. Devotion is what fuels the ability to persevere and not give up. If the goals motivating a person necessarily involve long-term efforts to reach them, it is more likely that this person has a higher level of grit (Von Culin et al., 2014).

Grit also has a significant metacognitive component because sustaining motivation despite setbacks often requires conscious strategies that can be learned (Karimi Jozestani et al., 2016; Spellman et al., 2016). First, grit is always associated with long-term goals, so it can be strengthened by goal management strategies. Breaking down long-term goals (such as "I must pass math this semester") into smaller, more immediate, and concrete goals and identifying them as part of the journey can favor the sustainment of motivation. It is nonetheless advisable that short-term goals are described in terms of actions to be taken rather than milestones to be achieved. That is, a goal like "I must complete all the activities assigned by the teacher during the semester and not leave everything to the last minute" is a useful approach because it precisely states what the student must do. In contrast, a goal such as "I must achieve grades of at least a *B* on every exam" not only fails to provide guidance on how to achieve it but is also more likely to cause frustration if the goal is not reached.

Moreover, in situations of failure, grit benefits from the metacognitive ability to analyze errors and seek new strategies to overcome challenges. A person who simply tries again and again without analyzing what might be wrong in their endeavor is very likely not to reach their goal and eventually gives up. Often, it is not just about trying harder; rather, it involves changing how one expends effort, adapting strategies based on the results of previous attempts. Many times it's not even a matter of putting in more effort but rather expending effort differently.

Clearly, grit is related to the capacity for self-control, a topic explored in the second chapter of this section of the book. Specifically, it relates to the ability to delay rewards. It is not surprising, as we will see later, that grit tends to increase with age. The brain regions involved in self-control and planning are among the latest to mature (Sowell et al., 2003).

Grit and Beliefs

As you may have noticed, Angela Duckworth's concept of grit is closely related to Carol Dweck's theory of mindsets (Hochanadel & Finamore, 2015), extensively discussed in the chapter on beliefs. It is evident that, for a person to develop a persevering attitude in pursuing their goals, it is beneficial for them to adopt a growth mindset regarding those goals (Yeager & Dweck, 2012). If someone believes that the skills needed to achieve their goals are innate and unchangeable, they are likely to avoid putting in effort. Similarly, if they believe that their initial performance in a particular task determines whether they can learn it or not, they are likely to give up at the first setback and opt not to persevere. Undoubtedly, this fixed mindset is potentially detrimental to promoting the practice required for learning any skill, as mastery typically demands more than one attempt, and improvement requires perseverance.

As previously discussed, a growth mindset is characterized by destigmatizing error and viewing it as a necessary step in the learning process. Failure can be frustrating for a student with a growth mindset (as it is for anyone else), but after experiencing that inevitable feeling, the student reappraises failure as a circumstantial event, not as a definitive one. This attitude arises from the belief that skills are not fixed but can be enhanced with study or training. Skills do not define who we are or what we can become; instead, they indicate our current position and not the limits of our potential. The essence of grit lies in the ability to manage frustrations, and students' ideas about the meaning of failure or its causes are crucial for developing this ability. Thus, if students attribute failure to factors beyond their control, such as "I'm not cut out for this" or "The teacher doesn't like me," they are unlikely to persist in their efforts because they see no point in doing so. In contrast, if students believe that their failure can be explained—at least in part—by factors within their control ("I didn't study enough" or "I left everything to the last minute"), then the likelihood of them trying again with expectations of success is much higher (Dweck et al., 2014).

In conclusion, grit and growth mindset, which exhibit a positive correlation (Duckworth & Eskreis-Winkler, 2013), often coexist—just as a growth mindset can be shaped by the environment, grit can also be cultivated simultaneously.

Cultivating Grit

Perhaps one of the most interesting conclusions drawn from Duckworth's studies on grit is the evidence that it is not a fixed quality, and notably, it can be cultivated.

To begin with, there is evidence that grit tends to increase with age (Duckworth et al., 2007), likely for two reasons. The first is due to the cultural differences between generations regarding values. Second, the brain matures biologically during puberty, adolescence, and the early years of adulthood, alongside the development of skills related to self-control, goal management, and delayed gratification. However, the role of personal experiences of success or failure throughout life is likely much more critical in promoting grit development than these other age-related factors.

While grit, like any skill, has a genetic component, individuals vary in their predisposition to develop this attitude toward their goals. According to studies with twins, the genetic influence on the perseverance component of grit is measured at 37%, with the motivational component at 20% (Rimfeld et al., 2016). This implies that, although there is a hereditary component, grit largely depends on environmental factors—specifically, the experiences fostered by an individual's surroundings.

Indeed, personal experiences and the developmental environment play a significant role in the formation of grit. It is essential to recognize that a quality linked to self-efficacy beliefs—our beliefs about our own ability to achieve certain goals—is inevitably influenced by the successes and failures we encounter, as well as the causes we attribute to them. This is why fostering a culture of effort grounded in a growth mindset becomes instrumental in facilitating the development of grit (Yeager & Dweck, 2012).

However, it is likely that focusing only on the beliefs of our students and their ideas about failure is insufficient to cultivate grit. To illustrate, let's briefly revisit the case mentioned in the first chapter of the book regarding the correlation between self-esteem and academic results. Many interpreted this correlation as an opportunity to promote improvements in their students' academic performance by enhancing their self-esteem. Remember that despite the significant educational investments made to implement this approach, it ultimately proved unsuccessful. The consideration that the causal relationship could be reversed (i.e., that good results increase students' high self-esteem) or that both variables could be influenced by a third cause (e.g., socioeconomic factors) was not made. It was not even considered that causality could be reciprocal and, to achieve improvements, action should be taken on both. In any case, in light of preliminary studies showing that interventions on students' self-efficacy beliefs can have positive effects on their performance (Blackwell et al., 2007), we cannot ignore the need for students to experience success as a result of their effort more than once to build their grit. In other words, to cultivate grit, it would not be enough to address students' beliefs and expectations alone; it would also be necessary to help them make those beliefs a reality (Didau, 2018).

Ultimately, grit is more likely to develop when students experience success. Thus, it is crucial to address two key aspects: helping students improve their learning strategies, and appropriately assessing the difficulty of assigned tasks. Regarding the former, we already noted the relationship between grit and metacognition—grit has a metacognitive component that, as such, can be learned. Therefore, one of the ways we can help students develop grit, other than acting on their beliefs, is to teach them study techniques (retrieval practice, spaced practice, interleaved practice, etc.) and metacognitive strategies, such as those discussed in this section, to enhance their effectiveness as learners. Of course, devoting class time to activities based on the principles of how people learn will also impact their likelihood of success.

As for the difficulty of assigned tasks, this is related to one of the basic principles of motivation: we are driven by challenges we believe we can overcome, yet we dislike tasks that are either too easy or too difficult (Willingham, 2009). Thus, striking a balance where effort translates into success requires crucial adjustments to task difficulty. Certainly, this is easier said than done, especially in a class with over 30 students, each with varying skill levels. Nevertheless, it is imperative to acknowledge that fostering a resilient attitude is impossible if our students do not regularly associate effort with success or if they do not believe in the efficacy of persisting and adjusting strategies in the absence of success.

Helping students experience success does not imply shielding them from all possible failure or frustration; on the contrary, this is crucial for resilience development. Resilience emerges not only from successful experiences linking effort to success but also from encounters with failure that enable the practice of resilience skills. Overprotecting children, avoiding any hint of failure or frustration, and not allowing them to face difficulties from a young age (e.g., solving problems for them or trying to prevent them altogether) may result in future adults lacking resilience, unable to manage frustration or persist in adversity (Swanson et al., 2011). Therefore, experts recommend that educators adopt a demanding yet supportive approach—abstaining from direct intervention to prevent or solve problems but aiding students (or children) in tackling life's challenges and supporting them in overcoming obstacles (Duckworth, 2016). Fittingly, this support can draw upon all the concepts discussed in this book related to metacognition, emotional self-regulation, beliefs, and so forth.

Criticism of Grit

Duckworth's ideas about the combination of resilience and passion—grit—have gained significant popularity in recent years. That is why I thought it was appropriate to focus this chapter on resilience from the perspective of this concept. However, it is important to note that grit has faced numerous criticisms from other researchers, stemming from various pieces of evidence.

First, some researchers doubt that grit is a distinct quality from others that have already been identified and defined decades ago. Specifically, there is a very high correlation between grit and the personality trait known as *conscientiousness* (Credé et al., 2017), closely related to self-control and the ability to delay rewards. Additionally, several studies suggest that the impact of grit on academic achievement is small and is primarily due to its resilience component—the perseverance in maintaining continuous effort to achieve a goal (Rimfeld et al., 2016; Muenks et al., 2018). Finally, Muenks and colleagues (2018) postulated that, within the school context, grit does not seem to have as high a predictive ability for success as mere self-efficacy beliefs—students' beliefs about their ability to achieve their academic goals based on past experiences. Duckworth herself has acknowledged, relying on evidence from her research team, that grit is not correlated with academic outcomes (Duckworth et al., 2019). Ultimately, grit only refers to the ability to persevere in the goals we set for ourselves. What those goals are is another matter entirely.

Taking all factors into consideration, it has been pointed out that the concept of grit is unnecessary (Ericsson & Pool, 2016). If grit is the ability to persevere to achieve specific long-term goals driven by a high degree of motivation, we are essentially discussing a situation where motivation is sustained in the long term, and that this is what facilitates resilience. Consequently, from that perspective, it seems more sensible to focus on examining the numerous factors that determine a person's motivation in a given situation and their ability to maintain it in the long term despite adversities, as explored in the chapter on motivation.

Beyond discussions on technicalities that may occur in the scientific field, it is crucial to prevent discrepancies regarding the role of grit in education and other related concepts, such as growth mindsets, from becoming dogmatic in any case. While these may be factors to consider, it must be kept in mind that they are not infallible and do not provide the only answer to questions about students' success. Instead, a more useful approach is to focus on considering resilience as a desirable skill and concentrate on how we can help our students be more resilient with their studies. This involves addressing both their beliefs and metacognitive strategies, particularly in challenging situations. The reality of any educational system is that students will encounter failure to varying degrees, and in many cases, they are not prepared to handle these situations of academic failure productively.

KEY TEACHING PROCESSES

So far, this book has provided a scientific, evidence-based response to the question posed in its title: How do we learn? Or rather, how do students learn within the school or academic context? As outlined in the introduction, it is no wonder that learning depends on what the student's brain ultimately does. In this sense, teaching involves providing the experiences that the student needs to learn and motivating them to engage cognitively in those experiences. Teaching, in essence, is about helping to learn, about promoting learning. To quote Herbert A. Simon once again, "Learning results from what the learner does and thinks and only from what the learner does and thinks. The teacher can advance learning only by influencing what the student does to learn." This includes all the activities that the student engages in the classroom based on the methods employed by the teacher.

The role of the teacher as a promoter of learning is pivotal. However, not all teachers exhibit the same level of "effectiveness." Thus, for the same group of students, there are teachers whose methods and savoir-faire produce better results in their learning and academic performance than others. Experience, of course, plays a role, and a teacher's effectiveness typically improves with it. Nevertheless, experience alone does not explain all the variability, and researchers have tried to find out what makes some teachers more effective than others. Thus, it might be possible to design training programs that contribute to the professional development of teachers in a way that has a greater impact on their classes.

In this section, I will present some of the conclusions that research has reached by directly analyzing how teachers influence their students' learning and the effectiveness of their actions and teaching methods. Learning is undoubtedly enhanced when students are engaged in the actions we have discussed in the previous chapters. Therefore, we should expect that the most effective methods are grounded in these principles. Nevertheless, the section enables us to explicitly explore what teachers can do to foster meaningful learning and provides an opportunity to discuss one of the factors with the greatest impact on learning: feedback.

I have divided this section into three chapters that broadly describe the core actions constituting teaching: the process of instruction, wherein students are specifically engaged in learning; feedback, involving the provision of information about their progress and guidance on how to improve it; and assessment, encompassing the procurement of evidence to infer learning by assessing performance. These three processes are intricately intertwined, but since they are studied separately, it seemed like an effective way to organize them. We will start by exploring what research says about the various methods of instruction.

Instruction

Effective Lessons

In educational research, the term *instruction* is often used to refer to the actions that the teacher takes when guiding the development of a lesson with the aim of promoting students' learning. This no doubt constitutes the teacher's most common task during class time, involving the delivery of between 700 and 1,000 lessons over the course of a year.

When discussing lessons, we are not only referring to classes in which the teacher delivers a lecture. Lessons can take on diverse forms, ranging from the traditional lecture to sessions where students engage in various activities either individually or in groups. Indeed, all teachers are aware that the methods used in each lesson throughout the course can be quite different, and even within the same lesson, different methods may be combined. Therefore, debates about which methods are better are often quite futile because the reality is that various methods often need to be combined, depending on the learning goals and the context. As articulated in the report from the National Research Council of the U.S., *How People Learn* (Bransford et al., 2000), inquiring about the best teaching method is akin to asking about the best tool in the toolbox. The effective teacher does not come into the classroom with a single tool but with a complete toolbox, using various tools based on learning goals, context, and specific situations.

A lesson should be understood as the temporal unit in which learning opportunities are distributed in the classroom. These opportunities unfold based on the methods employed by the teacher in relation to specific learning goals. Therefore, the pivotal core of the teacher's task should ideally be delivering effective lessons to help students achieve their learning goals.

In this chapter, I will outline the actions that teachers take during a lesson that have been substantiated by scientific evidence regarding their effectiveness. But what do I mean by "effectiveness"? Research on instructional methods almost always measures effectiveness in terms of academic outcomes or performance on a knowledge test by students. So let's not lose sight of the fact that this is the space we will navigate because these are the data we have.

Rosenshine's Principles

Barak Rosenshine (1930–2017), a professor in the Department of Educational Psychology at the University of Illinois (United States), dedicated over 30 years to researching teaching processes, teacher performance, and student achievement. In 2010, he published a document for the International Academy of Education, UNESCO, summarizing the basic principles of effective instruction according to scientific evidence (Rosenshine, 2010). These principles are rooted in evidence from three research areas that, rather than contradicting each other, mutually support one another: research in cognitive psychology on how the brain acquires and manages information, research on educational practices used by teachers whose students show the greatest progress, and studies where teaching and learning strategies, designed by researchers based on the results and conclusions of their prior research, are transferred to the classroom and tested.

Now, I will present these principles, linking them with the ideas discussed in earlier chapters about how learning occurs, showing their consistency with established cognitive models. This presentation will also offer an excellent review of some of the ideas covered in this book, this time from the teacher's perspective. But before delving into Rosenshine's principles, it seems appropriate to position them within the theoretical framework known as *direct instruction*.

Direct Instruction

Direct instruction is a practice that involves the teacher explicitly presenting what they want students to learn and suggesting specific activities for them to consolidate that learning. In the case of a procedure, the teacher explains how to do it step by step and then directs the students to practice it, providing feedback when necessary (Clark et al., 2012). This approach stands in contrast to the expectation that students should figure it out on their own, a concept commonly known as *discovery learning* (Bruner, 1962).

For example, suppose that we want to learn how to use Photoshop and have never used a similar program. A direct instruction method would involve an expert teaching us how to use it, while a discovery method would entail figuring it out on our own (without looking at the instructions). Thus, it seems evident that direct instruction is more effective than discovery learning, as research has repeatedly shown (Kirschner et al., 2006; Alfieri et al., 2011), albeit with some nuances and exceptions.

First, when selecting the methods to use, we should not forget the crucial role of motivation (Kuhn, 2007). It is indeed more effective to receive an explanation on how to use Photoshop than to try to figure it out by randomly testing functionalities. However, following the expert's instructions step by step at the pace of the class might be a bit dull, especially when students can choose to explore the program on their own. Although direct methods are often cognitively more effective, they may be less motivating, potentially reducing their effectiveness. Moreover, how are we to know whether the student is interested in learning what we want them to learn? If direct methods do not take this into account, they also lose effectiveness. Therefore, we should never overlook the motivational dimension when using these methods or the social context in which they are employed (Herman & Gomez, 2009). As highlighted in the chapters on the socioemotional aspects of learning, unfortunately, motivation is not a given and cannot be demanded, especially in the school context.

Second, for direct instruction to lead to lasting learning beyond the short term, it must offer students opportunities to make sense of what they learn. Therefore, instruction should occur within their "zone of proximal development," allowing the connection of new information with the student's prior knowledge. Placing instruction too far from the student's prior knowledge will lead to memorization without understanding (Ausubel, 1962). Direct instruction should also include activities that prompt students to elaborate on what they have learned. The teacher must ensure that students think about what they learn (remember, that is the key to active learning). Thus, effective direct instruction involves a lot of interaction between the teacher and students.

Third, when promoting conceptual change, strict direct instruction may not be as effective; in practice, it would instead take the form of a "guided discovery" method. This means that the teacher must strategically sequence students' experiences and guide their reasoning to help them reach conceptual reconstruction (Duschl & Duncan, 2009). As noted in the chapter on memory reorganization, when learning requires a conceptual change, simply explaining the correct concept is not enough: the student must go through various experiences leading to the reconstruction of their mental schemas. However, these experiences are better when designed and structured by a teacher with the necessary knowledge than when the student tackles them alone (Alfieri et al., 2011). That is why this method is known as "guided discovery." Therefore, direct instruction should be broadly conceived as any method in which the teacher plays a relevant role as a designer and guide of learning experiences, not just someone who imparts knowledge to be learned (Hmelo-Silver et al., 2007).

Finally, it should be noted that direct instruction is more effective the more "novice" the student is. Indeed, when the student has a certain level of knowledge about the subject, the efficacy of direct instruction diminishes. This is known as the "expertise reversal effect," which essentially states that methods which are more effective with students who are starting to learn something lose efficiency with those students that are already knowledgeable, and may even be detrimental (Sweller et al., 2003). Therefore, as the student advances in their mastery of the subject, it is better to step aside and only intervene at the right moment. For example, when a student faces a geometry problem for the first time, it is better to explicitly explain how to solve it and show several examples before they try to do it themselves. But when the student already has significant knowledge of geometry and faces a new type of geometric problem, it may be better to let them try to solve it before explaining how to do it, if needed at all.

Note: Discovery Learning

There is a belief that the most effective learning occurs naturally through discovery, without the guidance of a teacher. It stands to reason to think this way, as there are indeed things for which we are born with the ability to learn through mere exposure, without explicit teaching. However, evolutionary psychologist David Geary (2007) suggests distinguishing between two types of knowledge and skills: those that are *biologically primary* and obtained instinctively because our brain has evolved to learn them seemingly effortlessly (for mere survival reasons), and those that are *biologically secondary* and exclusively cultural, requiring teaching for acquisition. The former includes speaking the native language, developing social skills, and solving simple everyday problems, learned seemingly effortlessly through interaction with the physical and social environment. Children learn to speak their native language without explicit teaching, and they grasp the basics of how the world around them functions through exploration. Our brain possesses functional structures that have evolved in such a way that this type of learning becomes effortless and appealing. Hence, we acquire this primary knowledge with apparent ease, and we are motivated to learn it.

In contrast, culturally oriented knowledge and skills are not learned as spontaneously; they typically require deliberate cognitive effort. This category includes mathematics, literature, science, history, or skills such as reading, writing, and learning other languages—the kind of knowledge schools have always aimed to provide. Our brain has only been grappling with this type of knowledge for a few millennia, so it has not had time to evolve specific and explicit biological structures to support it. Instead, the brain employs the resources it has to make this learning possible. Fortunately, this organ has the remarkable ability to adapt structures not originally intended for a function to fulfill that function if our behavior promotes it. However, this adaptation is not spontaneous and requires conscious effort. This is the basis of our capacity to learn.

Research leaves little doubt that strict discovery learning is much less effective than learning guided by teaching for this latter type of knowledge (Alfieri et al., 2011; Mayer, 2004). It is essential to note, nonetheless, that in learning that requires conceptual change, the discovery method can be more effective, provided it is structured and guided by the teacher—termed *guided discovery*. This fits into direct instruction due to the crucial role of the teacher in it (Hmelo-Silver et al., 2007; Furtak et al., 2012).

While you might think that direct instruction is incompatible with methods like project-based learning, this need not be the case when we recognize that direct instruction includes any method closely guided and regulated by the teacher. On one hand, the effectiveness of a project as a learning activity relies on meticulous design, a responsibility assigned to the teacher. On the other hand, a successful project requires continuous teacher monitoring and intervention to ensure it stays on the right track. Additionally, the development of the project requires students to learn things to carry it out, many of which are learning goals of the project. At that stage, direct exposure may be the most effective way for them to acquire the necessary knowledge. It is worth noting that project-based learning with novice students can be more effective when the project serves as a motivating context, providing meaning to what is to be learned because it is necessary to achieve a goal. The project itself, however, is developed once students have acquired the necessary knowledge, offering them an opportunity to apply what they have learned in a meaningful context (Rosenshine, 2010). Finally, in cooperative learning, which often accompanies project-based learning, students help each other learn, and its effectiveness relies on the fact that students who need more help have "assistant teachers"—their peers (Slavin, 2013). Given these considerations, direct instruction and project-based learning need not be in conflict unless project-based learning is interpreted in a way that deprives students of guidance on what to do or how to do it, lacking the frequent intervention of a teacher. Indeed, evidence suggests that project-based learning organized in this way is much less beneficial for academic performance than that guided by the teacher (Alfieri et al., 2011).

Ultimately, research suggests that when students are beginners in what we want them to learn, direct instruction methods—where the teacher plays a significant role—are more effective for learning than methods that relegate the teacher to a secondary role. However, this effectiveness depends on the specific practices the teacher employs, which should be tailored to the learning object and the characteristics of the students. (As noted earlier, there are many different ways to guide learning and important factors to consider such as motivation.) To clearly understand the practices that make direct instruction effective, I will proceed to outline them in more detail.

Sequencing and Dosing

I discussed the principles of sequencing and dosing in the last two chapters of the section on the cognitive processes of learning, in relation to working memory and cognitive load—recall the example I used from the movie *The Karate Kid*. These principles involve breaking down the learning process into small steps ("wax on, wax off"), allowing students to progressively learn them in a sequence coherent with comprehension building.

The body of evidence supporting these principles is the same that backs the theory of cognitive load (Sweller et al., 1998). As you may recall, working memory can be regarded as the mental space where we hold and manipulate the information we are paying attention to, whether from the external environment or our long-term memory. It is where we reason, imagine, and, ultimately, connect our prior knowledge with new information—where learning occurs. However, working memory has limited capacity, capable of handling only a certain amount of information at once. If it surpasses its capacity, it overflows, hindering learning and affecting motivation.

The amount of information working memory can handle simultaneously depends on the knowledge we have in long-term memory and how well consolidated it is. What is already well learned demands resources from working memory and becomes a support for learning the next thing (provided that it is related). But what is still new for the student generates cognitive load. That is why we cannot expect students to learn many new things at once (or something overly complex that requires combining many new ideas) because they simply cannot. It is crucial to dose and sequence learning appropriately.

This practice, known as *cognitive scaffolding*, involves always placing instruction in the student's zone of proximal development (requiring identification of their prior knowledge) to provide the necessary help at each moment while progressively developing and integrating each component of the learning goal. The scaffolding metaphor also underscores the importance of gradually reducing assistance as the student advances in knowledge (Wood et al., 1976).

As I discussed in the chapter on expertise development, a wealth of evidence supports the idea that students learn more effectively when components of the learning object are temporarily worked on separately and progressively integrated (White & Frederiksen, 1990; Salden et al., 2006; Wightman & Lintern, 1985). Even a small dose of practice in one of the components of the learning object significantly improves overall learning (Lovett, 2001).

This aspect is an essential part of teaching techniques in sports or dance disciplines. For example, in learning the high jump using the Fosbury flop, coaches do not have beginner athletes perform the jump from the outset. Instead, the technique for high jumps is broken down into four phases (approach, takeoff, flight, and landing), each trained separately with specific exercises. Next, these phases are gradually integrated to achieve the goal of clearing the bar. The effectiveness of this progressive process is evident not only in physical skills acquisition but also extends to academic disciplines (Hmelo-Silver et al., 2007).

Modeling

Modeling involves providing explicit models that students can use to guide their reasoning. These models can take various forms:

- First, models can be examples of completed tasks that meet (or do not meet) the desired requirements, such as when showing a sample text and highlighting its virtues or flaws.

- Modeling can also involve demonstrating how to perform a task, such as step-by-step solving of a mathematical exercise or creating a summary or concept map from a text.

- We also provide models when we show students how we, the experts, approach tasks in our discipline to solve them. This involves not only explaining how we solve a problem or task step by step but also externalizing the metacognitive strategies we employ while doing so.

- Similarly, we model our attitudes as learners when showing that we also make mistakes and how we manage errors, for example.

- Finally, we can provide conceptual models, such as diagrams, animations, manipulatives, or any resource that allows students to visualize and make sense of what they are learning, such as showing how an eclipse occurs with a model of the Sun-Earth-Moon system.

In any of these cases, for effective modeling, it is crucial to use multiple examples and make explicit the connection between the concrete (examples) and the abstract (the concept, the procedure, etc.).

A particular case of modeling highlighted by Rosenshine, especially for being one of the most studied, is the *worked example*. This involves explaining step by step how to perform a task or solve a type of problem, instead of leaving students to figure it out themselves. According to proponents of cognitive load theory, the worked example effect is the most well-known and thoroughly examined aspect within this framework (Sweller, 2006). This effect suggests that learning through the study of practical examples is more effective than trying to solve problems from the outset, a conclusion supported by multiple studies providing consistent evidence of this phenomenon (Clark et al., 2006).

Worked examples are beneficial for learning by reducing the cognitive load on students facing a type of task or problem for the first time, especially when they lack sufficient knowledge or experience (Paas et al., 2003). However, it is important to note that the use of worked examples to enhance learning becomes less effective as students gain experience (Kalyuga et al., 2001), in line with what was mentioned earlier regarding direct instruction, namely the expertise reversal effect. The worked example method also has limitations, such as when students focus solely on the solution rather than the procedure, or when they merely memorize algorithms (Renkl et al., 2004).

Given that worked examples are effective as a teaching method for less experienced students but lose efficacy with increased experience, a gradual transition to problem-solving based methods is necessary. To achieve this, it is effective to provide increasingly less structured partially solved examples until students can independently solve them from start to finish (Renkl et al., 2004). Furthermore, this method becomes more effective when students are asked to explain how they solved them and why they followed the steps they did (Atkinson et al., 2003).

Although learning through worked examples is common in mathematics and sciences, its use extends to various disciplines. Researchers have studied the impact of worked examples in diverse areas such as music, chess, athletics, and computer programming (Atkinson et al., 2000).

Review

You surely remember the benefits associated with retrieval practice for learning, which involves actively trying to recall what was learned. This is particularly so when the acquired information has started to fade, and even more so when repeated at spaced intervals (Roediger & Pyc, 2012). Therefore, it comes as no surprise that teachers who allocate time to review activities, where students are required to recall what they learned in previous lessons, achieve better results (Roediger et al., 2011). These activities may involve quizzes, asking them to create concept maps (without looking at notes or the book), or simply asking them to explain what they remember, among many other methods. Another option in this vein is conducting multiple low-stakes assessment tests, with minimal impact on final grades.

In some programs based on this principle, teachers were asked to spend about eight minutes each day on such activities at the beginning of each class. Moreover, on Mondays they had to spend more time on reviewing the previous week, and every fourth Monday, conduct a review of the entire month. Obviously, these multiple tests involved revisiting the same contents several times, following the principles of spaced practice. As a result, students whose teachers implemented these measures achieved better results in final exams (Good & Grouws, 1979).

This outcome is to be expected, given the robust effects of retrieval and spaced practice on learning, as previously explored in the chapter on the cognitive processes of memory.

Asking Questions

Research suggests that teachers who ask many questions during their lessons generally help their students achieve better results (Cotton, 1988). There are several reasons for this. On one hand, at the beginning of a lesson, questions can help students activate their prior knowledge related to what they will learn, promoting their learn-ing (as discussed in the chapter on memory organization). On the other hand, ques-tions during the lesson allow assessing the students' level of understanding and taking appropriate measures if necessary, such as providing feedback or revisiting explanations with new examples or alternative perspectives. Additionally, when stu-dents realize that they may be required to participate at any moment, they tend to pay more attention. Finally, questions force students to retrieve what they have learned, prompting them to structure it for explanation. This, in turn, promotes connections with their prior knowledge (Chi et al., 1994).

The effectiveness of this practice, however, relies on the type of questions used. For example, the common approach of asking, "Does anyone have any questions?" and proceeding if no one raises their hand is generally not very helpful. A more effec-tive strategy is to directly ask them what they have understood from the explanation, how they would explain it in their own words, and what examples they would pro-pose, among other approaches. In this regard, King (1994) provides some ideas for productive questions (Box 1).

BOX 1 Examples of productive questions in the classroom (Adapted from King, 1994).

What do _____ and _____ have in common? How do they differ?
What is the main idea of _____?
What are the strengths and weaknesses of _____?
How does _____ relate to _____?
What do you think causes _____?
How does _____ relate to what we have learned before?
Which is the best _____ and why?
What solution would you propose for the problem of _____?
In relation to what we have learned, do you agree or disagree with this statement: _____?

As can be seen, these questions always focus on demonstrating understanding of the learned material rather than a simple recall of facts, although including the latter is also useful (Wilen, 1991). When dealing with a procedure, it is very produc-tive to ask students to explain the steps they have followed to perform it (Fonseca & Chi, 2011). In essence, this involves encouraging *self-explanations* (Chi et al., 1989), the practice where students try to explain what they have learned in their own words, the benefits of which were discussed in the chapter on memory reorganization.

Finally, as you can probably imagine, for this practice to be useful, we need to find ways to engage all students as much as possible. For example, instead of posing the question to the entire class and waiting for (the usual) hands to be raised, a more effective approach may involve directing the question specifically to the student we consider appropriate, based on our knowledge of the class and the observed situation. Alternatively, we can use a box containing slips with the name of each student and randomly draw them (returning the names to the box after drawing). This will keep everyone on their toes "in case it's their turn." If we notice that this frustrates students eager to participate, we have other options, such as having everyone write their answer on a piece of paper and exchange it with their peers; providing multiple-choice answers on the board and using cards they lift with the chosen response; using small whiteboards where everyone writes the answer and shows it at the same time; and using two-colored cards (e.g., red and green) for them to respond if they think a statement is correct or not, and so forth. Of course, we can also use digital tools for real-time surveys.

Structuring and Guiding Practice

To conclude, evidence suggests that the most effective instructional practices include careful planning of the tasks students will perform and providing feedback while they do them.

Regarding planning, it essentially involves giving students enough time to practice through the type of activities that best contribute to achieving their learning objectives. In the section on cognitive learning processes, I outlined the difference between learning "in depth" and learning "in breadth." Depth entails mastery of the subject and transferable skills, while breadth focuses on accumulating extensive knowledge about a subject, even if it may be superficial. Given the constraint of time in the classroom, we usually find ourselves having to choose between depth or breadth. If we opt for depth (assuming such a choice is allowed, as our decision may be conditioned by curriculum or school policies, for example), it is important to plan the practice required for students to achieve a good mastery of what they have learned. The same holds true if we want students to automate a process, such as reading decoding or typing, for example. I extensively discussed this in the chapter on deep learning.

However, neither extensive and well-structured practice nor the other teaching practices discussed in this chapter fully realize their potential without one of the most important actions that teachers contribute to learning: feedback. This is a factor so relevant to learning that I have dedicated an entire chapter to it.

Feedback

5.2

A Relevant Factor with Mixed Effects

Feedback, or information provided to students about their performance and indications on how to improve it, is a fundamental—some might say, a natural—educational practice. It is one of the factors that most contribute to students achieving learning objectives (Hattie & Timperley, 2007). For this reason, it has become a subject of special attention in educational research. The evidence obtained to date confirms its relevance, but it also reflects that the type of feedback and the way it is provided can substantially vary its effectiveness. Studies even reveal that, depending on these variables, its effects can be negative (Kluger & DeNisi, 1996). Thus, feedback is a double-edged sword, and its use for the benefit of student learning depends on a thorough understanding of its details.

As teachers, we incorporate feedback into our daily routine—whether it is correcting school tasks, scoring evaluative tests, assessing project outcomes, responding to a student who just completed an activity on the board, or even adjusting our facial expressions upon hearing a student's answer in class. Therefore, understanding the variables that contribute to positive feedback effects or those that might have unfavorable consequences is of great interest to teachers. In this chapter, I will outline what research has revealed about this ubiquitous factor in our daily learning environment.

The Nature of Feedback

Feedback aims to promote actions by the learner that help bridge the gap between their current performance and the explicitly stated learning objectives (Sadler, 1989). To achieve this, feedback must address three questions: "Where am I going?" "How am I going?" and "Where to next?" (Hattie & Timperley, 2007). A fitting analogy for feedback is a GPS navigation device—it indicates the destination, informs us about our current position in relation to our destination, and also gives us directions on how to get there from our current position.

For feedback to be effective, the first requirement is that the learner is aware of their destination—they need to know and understand the learning objectives. Often, students are not very clear about the learning goals or interpret them differently from us. This situation occurs, for example, when the student, while correcting exercises in class, simply copies answers and is not aware that what we actually intend (and will ultimately assess) is for them to learn the procedure leading to those answers.

Additionally, feedback needs to inform the learner about their current level of performance, which, as we will see below, can be done in several ways. Indeed, this is the question ("How am I doing?") that we most often address through the feedback provided in school tasks.

Finally, effective feedback must provide clear and precise information on what the learner needs to do to progress from their current position to reach their objectives. In fact, this is arguably the most relevant aspect of its enhancing effect on learning (Hattie & Clarke, 2019). Returning to the GPS analogy, the directions it provides on how to reach our destination are the key to its success as a navigation tool.

The ways we address the three previous questions when providing feedback to students can vary widely, and their impact depends on the approach used. Therefore, I will now explore the types of feedback that exist and then explain how their effectiveness varies according to how we apply them, based on the evidence at our disposal.

Types of Feedback

First, feedback can be classified based on whether it is positive or negative (Freedberg et al., 2017). Positive feedback emphasizes milestones achieved and progress made. In contrast, negative feedback focuses on highlighting flaws in the learner's performance and areas for improvement. Let's say it is the difference between seeing the glass half full or half empty.

Second, in the context of school tasks, feedback can be distinguished by the aspect of the task they refer to. Up to four types of feedback can be differentiated based on four distinct aspects of the task (Hattie & Timperley, 2007):

- **Feedback on the outcome of the task (FT):**

    It refers to the assessment made of the outcome of a specific task. This type of feedback is the most common in school tasks: "This is correct," "That is wrong," "This is missing," "That is unnecessary." It offers superficial and very specific information, often provided through numerical scores, symbols indicating correct-incorrect, or rubrics. Task-level feedback basically addresses the second question ("How am I going?") and can only answer the third question ("Where to next?") by including correct answers or comments indicating improvements needed.

- **Feedback on the process undertaken to achieve the outcome (FP):**

    In this case, feedback focuses not on the specific outcome but on the process necessary to reach it. For example, it concerns the procedure followed to solve a math problem or emphasizes a spelling rule to explain why a word is misspelled. This feedback goes beyond correcting an error in a specific outcome (*"happily* is spelled with an *i*") but can be generalized to avoid new errors in analogous cases ("when a word has two consonants before -*y*, it is changed to -*i* before adding the suffix -*ly*"). Process-level feedback has enormous potential for addressing the third question ("Where to next?") and is one of the most effective types of feedback.

- **Feedback on the metacognitive processes involved in the task (FM):**

  This type of feedback goes a step further than the previous one, focusing on the metacognitive processes that can contribute to improving the learner's overall performance (recall the metacognitive processes involved in self-regulated learning discussed in the previous section). These processes are habits and strategies that allow the learner to plan, monitor, and assess their own learning. Feedback at this level, therefore, is aimed at emphasizing higher-order skills.

- **Feedback on the learner's qualities in relation to the task (FL):**

  This level of feedback is used when referring to the learner's abilities or the effort they have put in to complete a task. As we will see, this feedback is also given implicitly, even if unintentionally, based on how the student interprets the other types of feedback, especially that related to the outcome of the task (FT). For example, a student interpreting a grade on a task as a sign of their skill level or effort.

Effectiveness of Various Forms of Feedback

Unfortunately, there are no simple, universal recipes for effective feedback. The effectiveness of feedback depends on who gives it (the relationship they have with the learner and the trust they inspire), how it is given (types of feedback, social context, etc.), when it is given (timing and frequency), and also how the learner receiving it interprets it (Hattie & Clarke, 2019). To simplify, our focus here will be on the effects of the last three variables, as they have been the most extensively researched: when we give feedback, how we give it, and how students interpret it.

1. According to the Timing and Frequency of Feedback

What is preferable: for the student to receive feedback immediately after completing a task (or part of it), or for the feedback to be delayed for a certain period? The available evidence is contradictory; both situations come with their advantages and disadvantages (Erev et al., 2006). The effectiveness of immediate versus delayed feedback depends on the nature of the task and the type of feedback provided. When feedback focuses on the outcome of the task (FT), evidence shows that it is much more effective if it is immediate. For example, if a student answers a question or solves a problem, having the opportunity to know if they did it right or wrong as soon as they finish the exercise provides greater benefits than having to wait to find out (Kulik & Kulik, 1988). However, notice the nuance in the phrase "as soon as they finish the exercise." Completing the task (or considering it done) implies that the student has had the opportunity to apply self-correction methods, if known, before seeking external feedback. If the student replaces possible self-correction processes (such as using another method of solution to see if they get the same result) with immediate, easy-to-obtain feedback that carries no consequences, then its effect will not be as positive (Upchurch & Sims-Knight, 2001). In other words, if feedback replaces the practice of self-assessment, it may not be optimal. This is why, at times, delaying feedback is better.

Furthermore, immediate feedback on the result not only helps the student to maintain attention and motivation in the ongoing task but also may reduce the likelihood of errors consolidating in memory (Skinner, 1958; Herrnstein et al., 1993). Conversely, when the feedback focuses on processes (FP) and metacognitive strategies (FM), it is more effective to introduce a slight delay, giving the student the chance to review their procedures, reason, and search their memory (Clariana et al., 2000).

As for the frequency of feedback, the general guideline is that it should neither be too frequent nor too scarce. As the student progresses in their learning process, feedback should be less frequent. Continuous feedback is not desirable because it can make the student dependent (Schmidt et al., 1989), but if it is too infrequent, its potential as a learning enhancer will be lost.

Feedback, in a sense, could be seen as external metacognitive support, guided by someone with the expertise to identify the student's weaknesses and provide the strategies they need to employ to remedy them. It is akin to the teacher acting as a "metacognitive guide." Therefore, feedback should be gradually phased out as the student progresses, allowing them to take control of regulating their own learning without depending on external help (Beed et al., 1991).

2. According to the Way in Which Feedback Is Provided

We saw that there are different types of feedback depending on the aspect of the task they refer to and the questions they seek to answer. Regarding which one is better, the fundamental principle is that the most effective feedback is the one aimed at helping the student know what to do to improve (Hattie & Clarke, 2019). In this context, feedback types focusing on the process (FP) and metacognition (FM) present the most possibilities for guiding students on improving their performance. These types provide generalizable strategies that not only help correct a specific task but also transfer the feedback to new tasks—research on feedback effectiveness indicates that these two types are the most effective (Hattie & Timperley, 2007). Additionally, feedback targeting the task outcome (FT) also has some significance, though not to the extent of the previous two. The issue with the latter is the way it is usually delivered—through quantitative grades—which, as we will see later, reduces its effectiveness.

It is worth mentioning that the effectiveness of these three types of feedback (FT, FP, and FM) amplifies when, instead of providing them explicitly from the start, they are delivered through hints (Finn & Metcalfe, 2010).

Since feedback always follows the teaching activity, we assume that the student learned how to perform the task before tackling it. Therefore, if we use feedback as a retrieval practice opportunity, using hints so that the student can recall the correct answer by making connections, instead of giving them the answer directly, we can leverage the benefits of this practice: greater consolidation and better structuring of what was learned. For example, if a student mistakenly uses "it's" instead of the possessive word in "The dog sleeps in *it's* bed," we can ask, "Does this word show ownership, or is it a contracted form?" "Could you replace it with *it is* in the sentence?" Naturally, when the student fails to recall what they learned, then it will be the right time to offer explicit feedback—akin to a form of "reteaching"—addressing what they do not remember or understand. (It is advisable, however, to reteach it differently from the initial instruction, using different examples, contexts, approaches, etc.)

The effectiveness of feedback also depends on its specificity—the more precise, the better. For example, a comment like "You need to be more systematic when doing these activities" probably will not mean anything to the student, so they will not know how to use it. It would be better to give them some indications of what it means to be *systematic*. Of course, feedback like "You need to improve your pronunciation" will not be too helpful either; as Dylan Wiliam bluntly puts it, it would be like telling a novice comedian "You need to be funnier." It is a correct comment but too ambiguous and does not tell the student how to improve (Wiliam, 2011). It is worth noting that the possibility of giving concrete feedback increases the more limited the learning goals of the activity on which this feedback is provided are.

Finally, research indicates that feedback addressing the qualities of the learner (FL) has almost no effectiveness according to studies (Hattie & Timperley, 2007). Nonetheless, as we will see later, the way it is used can have long-term consequences on students' belief systems, which, in turn, determine how students interpret the feedback and, therefore, how effective it will be for them. We will discuss this in the next point.

3. According to How Students Interpret Feedback

The effectiveness of feedback not only depends on the type of feedback we give or when we give it but also on how the student interprets it (Hattie & Clarke, 2019). It is not so much about whether they understand it or not (which is important as well) but about what they will do with it and what effect it will have on their motivation. As for the former, one thing is that we expend effort to provide some feedback, and another is that students do not even pay attention to it. Fortunately, there are measures we can take to address these situations, as we will explore in the "Grades and Feedback" section at the end of the chapter. As for the effect of feedback on motivation, it is discussed extensively in turn.

Feedback and Motivation

If there is one practice in teaching and learning processes that has a more evident emotional impact on the student, influencing their learning, it is feedback. Providing feedback with the well-intentioned goal of helping the student understand their performance level and improve it inevitably and implicitly impacts their motivation (Tricomi & DePasque, 2016). Therefore, feedback is a double-edged sword that must be handled skillfully to prevent it from having the opposite effect of what is intended. The probability of negative consequences is so high when it is not used effectively that, at times, it might be better not to provide it.

The impact of feedback on motivation is obvious to everyone. Hence, we often try to choose our words carefully when giving feedback to a student (or another person). After all, feedback aims to be constructive criticism, and criticism is never easy for the recipient, even when well intentioned. Moreover, we also often use feedback to encourage and motivate our students ("Well done!"). In the end, we all know that feedback will emotionally affect the recipient.

In conclusion, the way a student interprets feedback determines its effectiveness as a promoter (or detractor) of learning, due to its impact on motivation. So what determines whether feedback positively affects motivation or, at the very least, does not negatively impact it? First, it will depend on the student's belief system.

For feedback to realize its full potential (remember that its impact on learning is among the most significant), it is important that the student is not afraid to receive it. Those with a fixed mindset (believing that academic skills are innate and can hardly be changed) become highly sensitive to negative feedback—the type that reflects their shortcomings (Dweck, 1999). As you may recall, a fixed mindset is linked to stigmatizing errors because they are viewed as evidence of an inherent incapacity rather than as a circumstantial state of someone who has not yet reached learning. Given that addressing errors is necessary for remediation, students with a fixed mindset will not be prepared to benefit from feedback. In fact, it may only cause demotivation, even feelings of anger and rejection, leading them to focus their attention on protecting their image. This makes them ignore the content of the feedback, its usefulness, and its well-intentioned nature.

Therefore, to ensure that students turn feedback into an ally of their learning, it is crucial to work on their beliefs (Hattie & Clarke, 2019). Openly discussing the nature of errors from a growth mindset perspective and even explicitly teaching students how to leverage feedback may help them develop a positive learning culture that enhances the potential of that feedback. A positive learning culture is a belief system shared by the school community that places self-efficacy and a growth mindset at its core. Establishing such a culture requires time and coordinated efforts across various members of the school community, operating at multiple levels. Indeed, the nature of our feedback can contribute to building or undermining the desired learning culture based on the type of beliefs that this feedback implicitly favors.

Earlier, we mentioned that feedback addressing the student's qualities in relation to the task performed (FL) has no effect on their learning. I must now clarify that it does not serve as a performance enhancer for the student in the current task (statistically speaking!). Still, it has a significant, more general effect on their long-term performance because it influences the student's belief system (Mueller & Dweck, 1998). Thus, this type of feedback can refer to the student's ability ("You're very good at this") or to the effort they have put in to complete the task ("I congratulate you for the hours you've put in"). While it is advisable to minimize the use of this type of feedback whenever possible, evidence indicates that if used, it is much better to focus on effort and always avoid emphasizing skill. Effort-oriented feedback contributes to fostering a growth mindset, while skill-oriented feedback promotes a fixed mindset (Table 1).

In any case, as mentioned before, it is preferable to limit the use of this type of feedback (FL) as it may be misinterpreted by the student. It is worth remembering that students with a fixed mindset believe that only the less skilled need to put in an

Table 1 Examples of feedback that appeal to the qualities of the student, according to their contribution to a fixed or growth mindset (Adapted from Mueller & Dweck, 1998).

Feedback Promoting a Fixed Mindset	Feedback Promoting a Growth Mindset
When the task result is positive . . .	
Well done! You're clearly good at this.	Congratulations! You've done a great job!
You are an outstanding student.	You are hardworking and your grades speak to it.
You did it! I told you that you were clever and that you had it in you!	I like how you approached the problem from different perspectives until you solved it.
You are a great student.	You are a great student because you put in effort, work hard, and seek help when needed to learn what you set out to achieve.

Feedback Promoting a Fixed Mindset	Feedback Promoting a Growth Mindset
When the task result is negative...	
Don't worry, not everyone is good at everything. Each person is good at different things.	It's normal, you're learning. It's impossible to do it right on the first try. Keep working like this and you'll see how you improve.
You made a great effort. I congratulate you.	It seems like we will have to find another way of doing things. How about trying this?
You didn't do it well.	This didn't turn out well. Where do you think you went wrong? What do you think we could do to improve it?
It seems like you're not very good at this.	It seems like you're not very good at this . . . yet.

effort. Therefore, they might perceive a "congratulations on the effort" as an indication that we believe they lack sufficient skill, and that is why we choose to praise their effort and not their ability. Thus, it is always better to direct feedback toward the task itself and not on the qualities of the student ("Good job!"). However, it is important to note that feedback like "Good job!" only serves as motivation; for feedback to be more effective, it must be more specific.

Finally, considering the unpredictable emotional impact of feedback, it is important to carefully evaluate the necessity of providing it and determine how to deliver it, when given in public. When feedback is given in a public setting, the student inevitably focuses their attention on what that feedback means for their reputation in front of their peers. Paradoxically, some students may not want to be perceived as good students by their friends, so even with the best of intentions, public feedback can sometimes have the opposite effect to what is desired (Sharp, 1985). But the general rule is to avoid providing feedback in public whenever it is not indispensable (Wiliam, 2011).

Positive and Negative Feedback

What results in greater learning benefits for students—positive feedback or negative feedback? From a purely rational standpoint, negative feedback is better than positive feedback because it highlights weaknesses in a student's performance and provides guidance for improvement. However, we cannot overlook the emotional dimension of feedback. In fact, if the feedback is directed at the person's qualities (FL), and its effects are limited to influencing motivation, it is better for it to always be positive (Brockner et al., 1987). As for the other three types of feedback (FT, FP, and FM), whether a positive or negative perspective is more suitable depends on the student's expertise level in the skill being assessed.

When a student is starting to acquire a skill, positive feedback is more effective than negative feedback because it motivates them to persist in their efforts. Conversely, when a student has attained a certain level of expertise, negative feedback becomes much more effective (Fishbach et al., 2010). This could be linked to the fact that when a student begins to learn something new, their initial intrinsic motivation is typically very low, given their yet-to-be-discovered interest in the subject, and their sense of self-efficacy (belief in their ability to learn it) is not yet formed. In cases of low intrinsic motivation and uncertain self-efficacy, positive feedback is more effective than negative feedback because the latter could easily undermine the student's expectations of achieving the learning goal. In contrast, when intrinsic motivation has grown—and hence commitment to learning goals is higher—and a positive sense of self-efficacy has been established, negative feedback is more effective for promoting improvements and more motivating to sustain effort (Fishbach et al., 2010).

Grades and Feedback

We have seen that when students do not have a belief system based on a growth mindset and a positive sense of self-efficacy, feedback directed at their qualities must be very delicately given. But so is feedback that only evaluates the outcome of their task (FT). This is the type of feedback represented by grades, undoubtedly the most prevalent in school educational practices (constituting 90% of feedback according to Airasian, 1997).

Although grades provide feedback on the task, students often interpret them as an assessment of their ability. That is, grades influence the construction of students' belief systems, especially in their view of themselves as students, their self-concept (Butler, 1987). So it is not uncommon to hear statements like "She's a student with just passing grades" or "She's an A-grade student." Grades often label and contribute to students labeling themselves, and this effect overshadows their potential function as feedback.

Regardless, grades play a significantly limited role in fostering learning, given that they function as a form of feedback that overlooks the third (and most important) question effective feedback should answer—they do not guide the student on what they can do to improve.

However, the main problem with grades, whether numerical or textual, is that they are often the most important feedback that the student receives throughout the learning process and, paradoxically, often only comes when the process is concluded. Feedback loses its meaning if the student does not have the opportunity to apply it to improve their performance. This is indeed something that students are aware of—consciously or unconsciously—and, therefore, they will hardly pay attention to exam corrections with the aim of learning if it marks the end of the learning process. Their focus will remain on the grade and how it contributes to shaping their reputation and belief system about themselves (Butler, 1988).

Providing feedback to students throughout the learning process, rather than only at the end, is crucial. To achieve this, it is useful to use periodic assessment tests, which may vary in type but should always allow us to provide feedback on the same learning goals. Ultimately, these tests repeatedly evaluate the same learning goals. With multiple assessment tests, students' anxiety decreases—as the risk in each one is diluted—and their attention to feedback increases—because they appreciate that they can apply it in the next assessment. However, in general, evidence advises against using grades for these tests if possible, recommending descriptive feedback instead. In this regard, Ruth Butler's influential study (1988) is noteworthy, where three groups of students received feedback in three different ways: only through grades, through grades and comments, and only through comments. The results showed that students who only received comments developed a greater interest in the evaluated task and scored higher in a subsequent surprise test. Conversely, students who only received grades did not show improvement, nor did those who received grades and comments. Only those who did not receive grades paid attention to the feedback. Grades tend to redirect students' focus toward thoughts related to their self-efficacy and reputation, diverting them from a detailed analysis of the performed task (Kluger & DeNisi, 1996). In addition, grades are interpreted as the end of the learning process, which demotivates them from learning from corrections.

In reality, research on how grades interfere with other more productive types of feedback is still inconclusive and leaves open the possibility that such interference occurs primarily when grades and comments are given simultaneously, as grades could hijack students' attention and give them the impression that the learning process is complete (Koenka et al., 2019). Thus, some researchers suggest not giving grades at the same time as comments but after students have had the opportunity to review these comments—and, above all, inform them of a future opportunity to apply the received feedback and correct errors—could minimize this negative effect. To sum up, while grades may not inherently cause the diminished effectiveness of more productive feedback, the attributions students make to them, often perceiving them as the conclusion of the learning process and a label of their ability, may be the underlying cause.

However, we cannot ignore that, for many teachers, grades serve an important function beyond mere certification: they often constitute a source of extrinsic motivation that prompts students to approach an activity seriously, either due to its academic impact or its influence on the student's reputation. In other words, when our attempts to generate intrinsic motivation for the task fall short, grades can be useful for generating extrinsic motivation (Koenka et al., 2019). We may not like this circumstance, but reality often asserts itself. What can we do in these cases? That is, how can we take advantage of this potential of grades as extrinsic motivation without causing students to overlook the more enriching feedback contained in our comments? I have already shared the general suggestion to deliver them after other types of feedback and, above all, not to associate them with the end of the learning process. I elaborate on two more concrete proposals in the next box.

Note: Using Grades Differently

Proposal 1. Grades on All Activities

First, I will outline the theoretical ideal of this proposal and then bring it down to a realistic scenario. Theoretically, grades can be very useful if used routinely in all student activities. This situation assumes that all activities inherently possess academic value. Importantly, students should be given the opportunity to repeat the activity and improve it after receiving the grade. Also, no activity should be considered complete until a satisfactory grade is achieved (the teacher must establish a coherent satisfactory grade). If this grade is not attained in any activity, even just one, the overall grade will not be positive.

This way, grades function as a tool informing the student about the outcome of their performance in very specific tasks, which they cannot abandon until reaching a desired level. Thus, the student understands that paying attention to the feedback provided in the form of comments or other guidance is the most effective way to progress.

For this approach to succeed, this feedback must focus on the process. That is, it should not immediately give the specific solution to the task at hand to the student but make them think about how to achieve it. While this approach may not always be feasible and may not be necessary for every task, simply highlighting errors can suffice in many cases.

The advantage of this practice is that it distributes feedback across the entire learning process, not just at the end. It also contributes to promoting a growth mindset, as the grade is not interpreted as a fixed label but as an assessment of a temporary situation open to improvement.

Certainly, you may consider the proposal theoretically interesting. Now, correcting such a large number of activities could become an unmanageable task. This is why this practice is much more viable when combining activities personally corrected by the teacher with those utilizing computer devices, enabling automatic correction or facilitating student self-assessment through a suitable sequence of clues and indications. While certain tasks demand the teacher's personalized feedback, others—especially those suitable for digital educational resources—can benefit from automatic correction or student self-assessment, whether created by the teacher or third parties.

In essence, the important aspect of this strategy is ensuring that students have opportunities to improve their performance.

Proposal 2. Assessment Tests That Are Corrected Twice

The second proposal is simpler than the previous one, involving the use of grades only in specific assessment tests. After completing the activity, students will receive corrections without grades, accompanied only by comments. Similar to the previous proposal, these comments should focus on the process, providing indications and hints on how to improve the outcome of the activity. Subsequently, students will have the opportunity to use that feedback to redo the test or undertake a very similar one. The second round of correction will then include the grade.

The debate about grades is complex and, ultimately, is overshadowed by administrative requirements. Grades serve as the tool used to certify a level of performance achieved, and whether we like it or not, they end up being required of us.

In whatever form they take, grades are always a way of indirectly measuring acquired learning. This is the role they supposedly fulfill during summative assessment activities, which are tests aimed at obtaining a final grade rather than providing real feedback. The next chapter discusses the possibility of revealing and measuring learning—that is, assessment—and how to use this information to contribute to learning. As we will see, assessment requires feedback to be useful in promoting learning. However, without assessment, there can be no feedback.

Assessment

5.3

A Key Process in Teaching and Learning

In the previous chapter, we explored the enormous impact that effective feedback can have on our students' learning. However, feedback is not possible without first carrying out another important process in teaching and learning: assessment. Indeed, to provide feedback on performance in a task and how to improve, it is necessary to create opportunities and methods for assessing that performance. Without assessment, there can be no feedback.

Nevertheless, this is not the only reason why we assess. In fact, it usually is not the sole purpose (Crooks, 1988). When we talk about assessment, we often think of the tests we subject students to at the end of each learning sequence to determine if they have achieved the desired objectives. Typically, these tests mark the end of a learning process, so they do not directly impact that process. In other words, this type of assessment does not contribute to learning; it only aims to estimate the level of learning achieved. For this reason, assessment is often perceived as distinct from the learning process (Graue, 1993).

In any case, whether we use assessment to obtain information and provide feedback or to certify the level of performance achieved, all forms of assessment impact the learning process (Crooks, 1988). For example, the design of assessment tests and the criteria established for assessment influence how students approach the learning process. It is important to note that learning, in the way we wish students to learn, is not always the same as preparing for an assessment test. Many times, it is not.

In this chapter, I will delve into the science of assessment and stress the importance of designing assessments appropriately, irrespective of their purpose. I will then discuss educational practices that explicitly rely on assessment to improve the learning process. This part of the chapter will intricately connect with the topics covered in the two previous chapters to address the importance of so-called *formative assessment* or *assessment for learning*. Finally, I will take this opportunity to remind the reader, for the last time, of the significant implicit effect that assessment has on the consolidation of learning—an aspect that is often overlooked.

Assessment Parameters

When we assess any student activity, we are essentially measuring their performance and, indirectly, their learning (Koretz, 2008). Despite any reservations we may have about the concept of "measurement" in education, the truth is that every time we assign a grade of any type (not only numerical), we are making a measurement. Therefore, evaluative activities are instruments we use to gauge the level of achievement of our students with respect to learning goals. This last point is crucial: evaluative tests are limited to measuring the performance achieved for specific predetermined learning objectives; they do not aim to identify anything else that students may have learned incidentally during the process.

Obviously, while written exams are the most common form of assessment tests (Doval, 2014), these tests can take many forms—any activity can be used to assess the learning achieved with respect to the set objectives. Indeed, not all written exams are alike, far from it. The key is that the type of test aligns with the intended evaluation.

Certainly, there are different assessment models, depending on the type of task the student must perform and how their performance is measured (Ahmed & Pollitt, 2010). In some tasks it is easier to quantitatively measure performance, while in others assessment is necessarily more qualitative. For example, assessing spelling accuracy in a dictation exercise allows for a more quantitative evaluation compared to assessing a commentary on a literary text. Using a sports analogy, sometimes we can measure performance similar to the measurements in high jump, and at other times, our role resembles that of judges in rhythmic gymnastics.

In any case, before even considering how to measure learning, it is useful to be familiar with some technical concepts related to evaluative tests, which allow us to reflect on their suitability, scope, and limitations as measuring instruments. These concepts are as follows:

- **Validity**. The validity of a test refers to whether it really measures what it intends to measure or, in other words, whether the results provided by the test are interpreted as what they truly are.

    When we talk about the validity of an assessment test, we address whether the test is properly aligned with the learning objectives, for example. Alignment is crucial for several reasons. First, without proper alignment, students may become demotivated when they realize they are not being evaluated on what they have worked on. Second, this misalignment can lead students to prepare in a way that deviates from the learning goals, as the test allows them to succeed without conforming to those objectives. In other words, students are guided by what will be evaluated. Therefore, if we aim for them to develop reasoning skills, apply what they have learned, interpret data, and so forth, but our exams primarily focus on reproducing factual knowledge, that is all they will learn. For example, if our goal is for students to conceptualize the cell as the structural and functional unit of living organisms but the assessment test involves tasks like labeling a cell diagram or reciting from memory the differences between eukaryotic and prokaryotic cells, students may simply memorize those facts without giving them the meaning we supposedly intended them to have.

The validity of a test also depends on whether the interpretation we make of the grades is appropriate—whether we correctly interpret what the results are telling us and use them accordingly. Validity is not really a property of tests but of the inferences we draw from the results they provide. I will elaborate on this later.

- **Reliability.** A test is considered reliable if the grade it assigns to a specific student is replicable and consistent. For example, the reliability of a test would be low if the grade given by one teacher is quite different from that given by another. A test that produces highly disparate results depending on the grader will have little reliability and, consequently, lack validity. However, achieving maximum levels of reliability is not always possible, such as by designing tests that are corrected more "objectively," as this can also lose validity. This scenario occurs when what we end up evaluating is not precisely what we intended to assess, such as assessing written expression with a multiple-choice questionnaire.

- **Accuracy.** Accuracy refers to how close the measurement obtained by the test is to the actual value of what we intend to measure. Assuming the test really measures what we intend, how well calibrated is it to provide us with accurate information? Do the grades precisely reflect the level of learning regarding the learning goals set? This is what we mean when a test is "too easy" or "too difficult." For example, in an exam aimed at determining students' ability to solve any type of second-degree equation, if all statements are solved in the simplest way, the accuracy of the test will be compromised.

- **Precision.** Precision is a concept that primarily applies to grades rather than the test itself. It refers to the extent of the grading ranges that distinguish one student's performance from another. For example, a grade like 7.35 out of 10 exhibits high precision, whereas a "B" grade has lower precision. Determining the appropriate level of precision is important for interpreting the meaning of a grade. After all, what does it mean for a student to get a 7.35 instead of a 7? Is that difference really significant for interpreting their level of learning?

To better understand the concepts of validity, reliability, accuracy, and precision, we can use the analogy of a GPS navigator, an instrument that determines our position using geographical coordinates. First, the reading provided by a GPS is valid as long as it measures geographical position. If the GPS gives us the time, that measurement will not be valid; we cannot use it to draw conclusions about our geographical position, even though the GPS provides it. But it will also lack validity if the geographical position it indicates is not the current one but that of, say, 24 hours ago. Although this time it is a measurement of our geographical position, we cannot use it to interpret where we are right now, which is what we usually want.

Suppose that the GPS does indeed provide us with our geographical coordinates at this very moment. Not many years ago, when GPS technology was in its early stages, every time we checked our position on a GPS navigator, it would show a different position even if we had not moved. In this case, we would have a reliability problem because the instrument's measurement is not replicating even though what we want to measure has not changed.

Now suppose that the GPS is also reliable, meaning it is consistent with its measurements and always shows us the same coordinates when we are in a specific location. Still, it could be that the position it indicates is not correct. That is, imagine that the measurement is consistent, but consistently places us 100 meters north of where we are. In this case, we would have an accuracy problem.

Finally, precision is determined by the value of the measurement provided by the GPS. When the signal is weak, GPS navigators usually display a circle of a few meters in diameter to indicate that we are somewhere within that circumscribed area. The larger that area, the lower the precision.

In conclusion, when interpreting and using the information we can extract from evaluative activities, it is relevant to consider these concepts. Let's explore this further.

What Do Assessment Tests Really Measure?

Many teachers question whether it is possible to measure something as ethereal as learning. It is not an absurd question—after all, learning occurs in our brains and is not directly observable. But this does not mean it cannot be measured. Like many other phenomena, learning can be measured indirectly—by observing the student's performance in a specific task and making an estimation based on a change in their behavior or ability in relation to that task. After all, psychology defines learning as a change in behavior or performance caused by experience. This is precisely what assessment tests aim to accomplish (Koretz, 2008). Nonetheless, it is true that these tests are very limited measuring tools. Their limitations are explained by the concepts of validity, reliability, accuracy, and precision discussed earlier.

For example, it is evident that we cannot measure learning with the same precision as a thermometer allows us to measure temperature. But we can certainly establish ranges of a certain breadth corresponding to different performance levels. It is like not having a thermometer readily available and having to determine the different temperatures of 30 glasses of water with our hands, one by one. In this scenario, we could differentiate between different temperature ranges and classify them into a few categories, namely, very hot, hot, warm, cold, and very cold.

Assessment tests are also often subject to a significant margin of error (Koretz, 2008) because they usually do not comprehensively assess all the learning goals they supposedly assess. Instead, they make an estimate based on a sample. That is, in an exam, we do not ask students to explain everything they have learned; instead, we ask them to answer specific questions or solve particular problems, inferring their overall performance from that. Therefore, some students may receive an incorrect grade regarding the scope of the estimated learning goals because the exam's sample either benefited or disadvantaged them. For example, in an extreme case, a student who had only studied half of the material could receive the maximum grade if, by chance, the assessment test only included questions from that half. Understandably, some students cross their fingers hoping that certain questions do not come up in the exam.

Moreover, there will also be some measurement error if the student takes the test at a time when they are not feeling well or under adverse environmental conditions, such as noise. In any case, remember that all measurements, even those of physical variables like temperature, are always subject to some error. Regarding learning, we must assume that the error will inevitably be relevant.

Therefore, the debate about the sense of assessment as a method for measuring learning is not so much about whether we can measure learning but rather about understanding the limitations of tests. In this sense, the crucial question is what type of learning we are really measuring with these tests. Here is an example to better explain this: suppose that a student scores 8 out of 10 on a well-designed test in terms of reliability and accuracy. Typically, we would agree that the student has achieved a good level of learning. However, if a week later, the student takes the exact same test, this time unexpectedly, and scores a 4 (which would not be unusual), then what did that initial 8 really mean? Considering how memory and forgetting work, as well as the strategies that many students use during exams—effective in the short term but not in the long term—this would not be an isolated situation. So what are we measuring and validating with grades when this situation occurs quite frequently?

This situation tells us, no more and no less, that the assessment systems we commonly use often lack the most important criterion—validity. This is because what we interpret they are measuring (the meaning we give to grades) is not really what they measure. Grades often reflect a student's ability to pass exams and tell us little about what will remain in their long-term memory after the test, which is ultimately what we would like them to tell us. You may recall that when students concentrate their study just the day before the test, they can get very good results, but this learning is quickly lost (Rawson et al., 2013). We saw this in the chapter on memory processes.

Note: Reducing the Subjectivity of Grading

While not the only factor, one reason assessment tests may lose reliability is the subjectivity of the grader, inevitably influenced by the cognitive biases we all have. One of the most dangerous cognitive biases when judging a student's performance is the *halo effect* (Kahneman, 2011).

The halo effect leads us to extrapolate the intuitive impression a student makes on us to any aspect of their behavior or performance. This unconscious bias makes us rate their work more leniently or critically. For example, a polite and responsible student is likely to receive a more favorable score on any type of task compared to a student with more disruptive behavior in the classroom. To mitigate the halo effect when grading an assessment test (if the nature of the test allows it), a simple strategy is to refrain from checking who the student is before grading. Unfortunately, this is not possible in oral presentations.

But there's more. The halo effect involves the idea that initial impressions from a test influence subsequent ratings (just think about the predisposition caused by a messy or visually neglected assignment). This means that if a test has multiple questions or activities to grade, the first one we grade will influence our predisposition toward the following ones. An excellent answer to the first question may lead to more generous grading of subsequent questions, while starting on a negative note might make us more critical. To counter this unconscious bias, we can try to grade the tests activity by activity, reviewing the same activity for all students consecutively, instead of grading all the activities for each student in succession. Nonetheless, from the second activity onward, we must be cautious and avoid noting the grade or the number of corrections made in the previous activities of the same test, because this could also impact our evaluation. Getting rid of cognitive biases is undeniably challenging, if not impossible.

Assessing Transfer

It is not uncommon for a teacher to express some frustration that their students "are not interested in learning, but in passing." This dichotomy is possible when assessment tests do not precisely measure what we intend them to measure. We saw how this paradox can occur if the test is not well aligned with our learning goals. But it also happens simply when students can pass the test through an intensive study session just before taking it, which does not lead to the type of learning we desire for them.

To resolve this dichotomy, as much as possible, designing tests that require the acquisition of meaningful knowledge to be passed is key—knowledge not easily obtained in a single study session. Certainly, this is easier said than done. In this regard, the types of tests that yield better results are those that assess the ability to transfer learning, that is, the ability to apply what has been learned in new contexts (Bransford et al., 2000). Two types of learning—one superficial and another more meaningful—may seem equivalent when assessed through tests based on reproducing literal knowledge. However, their differences become apparent when tests assess the ability to transfer. In these tests, knowledge is not an end in itself but a means to carry out specific tasks, and it is the resolution of these tasks that is evaluated. These tasks or processes were extensively discussed in the chapter on transfer of learning, so I will not repeat them here. When we evaluate the performance of these tasks, we are not only assessing what students know but also what they can do with what they know.

Nevertheless, it is relevant to mention one of the simplest formulas to determine if a test assesses the transfer of learning. Basically, consider whether it would make sense for students to take the test while having access to their notes or textbooks. Although not all transfer tests exhibit this, tests that still make sense as an assessment tool even when students can refer to their notes tend to focus on the ability to transfer what has been learned to new situations. A word of caution: designing this type of test is not easy.

Assessment as a Learning Tool

Despite the difficulties and limitations of assessment, this process is crucial for promoting learning, especially when used expressly for that purpose.

You are likely familiar with the difference between *summative assessment* and *formative assessment*. However, for clarity, let me briefly explain. In essence, these are the two most important functions of assessment. On one hand, when assessment is merely used to make a final judgment about a student's performance in relation to specific learning goals, it is called *summative assessment*. On the other hand, when assessment aims to gather information about the student's progress to decide what to do next to help them achieve learning goals, we refer to it as *formative assessment* or *assessment for learning* (Scriven, 1967).

To be more precise and include all practices that would fall under the umbrella of formative assessment, here is the definition suggested by Dylan Wiliam (2011), one of the foremost researchers in this field:

> An assessment functions formatively to the extent that evidence about student achievement is elicited, interpreted, and used by teachers, learners, or their peers to make decisions about the next steps in instruction that are likely to be better, or better founded, than the decisions they would have made in the absence of that evidence.

Let's briefly analyze this definition. First, it is important to appreciate that what determines whether an assessment is formative is what we do with the information it provides, not the assessment itself. Any evaluative test can be used for formative purposes, although when designing a test, it is worth considering what its function is, as there may be significant differences (Wiliam & Black, 1996).

The second point is that it is essential to note that both teachers and students can make an assessment activity be formative. In fact, students can create their own tests while studying to identify weaknesses in their performance and focus their efforts on those areas. Alternatively, they can reflect on assessments given by teachers (Chappuis & Stiggins, 2002), although they probably only do so if these assessments do not represent the end of the learning sequence. But it should be noted that merely reflecting on their performance is not sufficient for the practice to be considered formative assessment; the definition of formative assessment requires that reflection leads to decision-making that translates into concrete actions to improve performance if necessary. If a student reflects on their work but this reflection does not result in changes in their learning process, it will not be very effective. Of course, this implies that the student must have new opportunities to apply those changes.

Teachers, on the other hand, can use the information from assessments to provide feedback and decide what to do in the next lesson, among other things. As in the previous case, decision-making based on the interpretation of assessment results is a necessary condition for the assessment to be formative. If we do not use the information obtained to decide what to do next, then we are not conducting formative assessment. Sometimes the decision we make may not alter the preestablished plan for the didactic sequence, but at least we will have evidence that this is indeed the best plan. Other times, of course, the evidence will suggest making changes to reinforce some aspect that was not entirely clear or that requires rethinking. This does not mean that the decisions we make based on the information from assessment will necessarily be better; it probably will not always be the case. But at least they will be better informed (Wiliam, 2011).

Nevertheless, you may have noticed that the definition of formative assessment is so broad that it encompasses very different practices. Here are some examples that fall under the framework of formative assessment:

- When, at the end of the school year, teachers analyze students' academic results to review the educational program for the next school year or when the management team and faculty make adjustments to the educational project of the school based on such analysis

- When, after an exam, the teacher returns it with comments and dedicates a session to review it with the whole class, preparing students for a new exam in the next session

- When students use a rubric to assess their work and have the opportunity to improve aspects they did not find satisfactory

- When a student tests their performance by practicing with exams they created themselves and then reinforces the study of questions that were more challenging or had deficiencies in their answers

- When the teacher presents an activity in class and, noticing that most students are not performing well, decides to stop it and review the procedures or concepts involved in that activity

- When, after the final exam of a unit, the teacher discovers that the students' performance is generally poor and decides to extend the unit to try to address the most important shortcomings before starting the next unit

While these are just a few examples of educational practices that align with the principles of formative assessment, we can already appreciate the enormous diversity of procedures that fit into this concept. Without a doubt, these practices vary considerably, so much so that it is worth distinguishing between them, because their effectiveness as tools to improve the learning process varies considerably. Indeed, not all formative assessment practices are equally effective. What variables make formative assessment an effective method for helping students in their learning process? Let's now look at some important details that, in light of the evidence, we should keep in mind to get the most out of formative assessment.

Formative Assessment Variables

The first variable distinguishing various formative assessment practices is qualitative. It refers to who receives the information provided by the evaluative activity, who makes decisions regarding the results, and who is affected by those decisions. As seen in the earlier examples, sometimes formative assessment is used to make modifications in the planning for the next school year. Here, the recipient and user of the information is the teacher, and the changes do not affect the students who were assessed but rather those in the following academic year. In this regard, it goes without saying that formative assessment is more effective when it informs not only the teacher about how to adjust their lessons for the next occasion but also the student being assessed about their performance and, especially, how to improve it. Effectiveness is heightened when formative assessment includes providing feedback to the student being assessed (Wiliam, 2011). While this may seem obvious, it is worth emphasizing, considering there are formative assessment practices (as shown in the earlier examples) that do not include this aspect.

Moreover, there are also significant differences depending on who interprets the information and makes decisions about what to do next. On one hand, when the teacher takes on this role, the information enables them to adapt their instruction on the spot, undoubtedly contributing to improving the learning process. Additionally, the teacher can provide quality feedback to the student about what and how to improve. But this does not guarantee that the student will interpret the feedback constructively or even use it. Therefore, since learning is ultimately the student's responsibility, formative assessment is more efficient when the student makes decisions about what to do next. Neus Sanmartí (2007) points out that only the person who made the mistakes can correct them, with the assistance provided by teachers. Thus, the situation with the highest potential occurs when the teacher provides feedback and the student makes decisions for their learning based on that feedback. Nevertheless, as discussed in the chapter on metacognition, it is desirable for formative assessment to progress toward a situation where the student takes responsibility for their own assessment, develops methods to monitor their performance, and makes decisions on how to guide their learning. Since I already discussed self-regulated learning in the previous section of the book, I will not dwell on the importance of students developing their metacognitive skills here, notably including the ability to self-assess and guide their learning process based on the results of that self-assessment.

Another important variable that distinguishes various formative assessment practices is the length of a complete cycle, from collecting evidence about students' performance to the practical application of decisions derived from its interpretation—that is, how long it takes between assessment and using the obtained information. Dylan Wiliam (2011) proposes three categories for formative assessment in this context: long-cycle, medium-cycle, and short-cycle.

Long-cycle formative assessment is used, for instance, to decide on changes to be made in the planning and activities for the upcoming school year. It also includes changes that school leadership and teachers plan to implement in the school's educational project to enhance results in the following years.

Medium-cycle formative assessment occurs during the course of a teaching unit and is employed on specific occasions to determine whether revisiting a concept or procedure before progressing is appropriate, or if one can move on to the next lesson in the unit (or if the unit can be considered completed). This type of assessment involves evaluative activities of a certain significance and provides opportunities to engage the student in their own evaluation.

Finally, short-cycle formative assessment is done "on the fly," minute by minute, during a lesson, aiming to verify if what is currently being worked in class is being adequately "processed" by the students—that is, if the students understand it and can put it into practice or explain it.

It is evident that the length of the formative assessment cycle correlates with the frequency of employing this practice. Generally, a shorter cycle implies higher frequency. This aspect is undoubtedly important to differentiate its effectiveness.

As you may imagine, formative assessment, in principle, proves more effective with a shorter cycle and more frequent practice. The OECD itself emphasizes this aspect of formative assessment, defining it as "frequent, interactive assessment of student progress and understanding to identify learning needs and adjust teaching appropriately" (OECD, 2008). In any case, experts recommend combining all its variants—short, medium, and long cycles—as each plays a distinct role (Wiliam, 2011).

Short-cycle activities are obviously not exams or assignments understood in the traditional sense, even if used for formative purposes. Instead, they are practices related to interactive instruction, as discussed in the first chapter of this section on teaching. These practices involve the teacher posing questions to the class—applying effective methods to get answers from all students or a representative sample—or proposing activities in which students must exchange their conclusions and reasoning with the teacher and their peers. As noted earlier, the key to these practices lies in the quality of the questions and the methods we use to achieve maximum participation without compromising motivation.

Short-cycle formative assessment also has the advantage of limiting the learning objectives evaluated in each activity to a few very specific ones, increasing its reliability and allowing for more precise and useful feedback for the student.

Nevertheless, short-cycle formative assessment has a weakness that we cannot underestimate. As you may recall, our brain exhibits a peculiar feature—good performance in the short term may not cause learning in the long run (Soderstrom & Bjork, 2015). Many times, the fact that students can demonstrate that they have learned what we just explained or practiced does not guarantee that this learning will endure much beyond a few hours. It is not uncommon to find that students have forgotten what we verified they had learned perfectly in the previous lesson. Therefore, short-cycle formative assessment is more beneficial when we allow some time to pass between the learning episode and the assessment. For example, conducting the assessment at the beginning of the next session proves more effective than doing so at the end of the same session. Otherwise, short-cycle formative assessment will be marred by the typical illusions of knowing that result from immediately checking what has just been learned. Remember that learning strategies are not distinguished so much by their effectiveness in the short term as by their effect on long-term memory.

Finally, one of the most important variables of formative assessment is the quality of feedback. It is not for nothing that feedback is at the heart of formative assessment. In fact, even summative assessment implies it—academic grades themselves function as a (very poor) form of feedback.

Since I dedicated the entire previous chapter to discussing the nuances of feedback and talked about the impact of grades on the learning process, I will not dwell on it here. However, I encourage the reader to revisit that discussion, giving particular attention to aspects related to grades. Incorporating formative assessment into educational practice implies making decisions about how we traditionally provide feedback. In essence, formative assessment involves reflecting on the role and use of grades in the educational landscape.

Evidence on the Effectiveness of Formative Assessment

There is no doubt that formative assessment, as a tool to enhance learning, is firmly grounded in a robust theoretical framework. Adjusting instruction or study based on whether students have reached the expected mastery and having the opportunity to provide feedback on how to reinforce their weaknesses seems like a reasonable formula for success. This is indeed supported by research that has analyzed the effectiveness of this educational practice—although with nuances.

One of the most cited studies in this regard is the review conducted by Black and Wiliam in 1998, where they compiled reports from hundreds of studies conducted during the previous decade and subjected them to a meticulous analysis. Despite the methodological limitations of the studies analyzed, the authors of the review conclude that the reported research shows that formative assessment improves learning, and the improvements in performance "appear to be quite considerable . . . amongst the largest ever reported for educational interventions."

However, strictly speaking, these studies, as well as those conducted to date, are not significant enough for us to assert with complete scientific rigor that formative assessment is as effective as we would expect—and wish—it to be (Martínez Rizo, 2012). Despite the results of the experiences analyzed allowing reasonably optimistic expectations in this regard, to this day, given the limitations of the evidence obtained, it would still be appropriate to act with caution (much as it might disappoint us).

Indeed, although the theoretical framework is flawless, theory is not the same as practice. Since formative assessment depends on numerous variables and it is not easily applicable, it remains to be seen how scalable its deployment in classrooms is without compromising effectiveness. Additionally, it should be noted that implementing changes such as those required by formative assessment, affecting practices as deeply rooted as those related to assessment, poses considerable challenges. The results obtained to date are nonetheless very promising, but more research—employing more efficient designs and methodologies—is needed to achieve more conclusive results in real classroom contexts. This will also help determine the factors that influence whether its effects on learning are greater or lesser (Dunn & Mulvenon, 2009; Kingston & Nash, 2011).

The Contribution of Assessment to the Consolidation of Learning

The function of assessment as a certifying tool of learning (summative function) and its usefulness for obtaining information to decide how to adjust the learning process (formative function) are obvious to us all. However, we often overlook an intrinsic property of assessment that directly impacts learning, a consequence of how our memory works. Indeed, assessment involves retrieving what was learned, and as you may recall, this process strengthens memory—increasing the likelihood that we can recall it again in the future. In other words, when we retrieve something from memory, we enhance our ability to retrieve it again later. It is no wonder that the effect that retrieval produces on memory is also known as the "testing effect" (Roediger & Karpicke, 2006).

In the chapter on memory processes, I discussed the effectiveness of retrieval practice, emphasizing its role in not only improving the ability to remember factual information but also in promoting understanding and the ability to transfer learning (Karpicke, 2012; Carpenter, 2012). Retrieval forces us to structure and make sense of what we learned to explain it effectively. In this process, we must reconstruct what was learned from what we remember and what we already knew previously. This reconstruction, therefore, is done by connecting previous knowledge with the most recent, and that contributes to consolidating learning and making it more meaningful. Each instance of retrieval is a new act of learning.

In short, the effectiveness of retrieval in assessing learning, combined with the potential of feedback from formative assessment, makes assessment one of the most effective tools for promoting learning.

Nevertheless, for these benefits of assessment to materialize, it is necessary to alter our conception, especially that of students, of assessment activities or tests. Thus, it will be crucial to identify them as a routine aspect of the learning process, rather than a sword of Damocles held over students, serving only to judge their performance definitively and irreversibly. Only in this way can evaluative tests be integrated into the classroom as frequently as formative assessment demands. Perhaps the key lies in clearly emphasizing the distinction between tests intended to promote and guide learning and those that merely serve to fill in the academic record.

Appendix: Pseudoscientific Myths About Learning

Educational Neuromyths

In the latter half of the 20th century, there has been a growing interest in bridging the gap between the science of how we learn and educational practice. On one hand, the scientific community has increasingly directed its attention toward educational matters, gradually integrating insights into real educational contexts. On the other hand, the educational community has eagerly welcomed the possibility of supporting its practices with scientific evidence (Pickering & Howard-Jones, 2007).

However, the existing communicative gap between researchers and teachers has given rise to various pseudoscientific myths in schools, with emphasis on the proliferation of neuromyths (OECD, 2002). Coined by neurosurgeon Alan Crockard in the 1980s, the term *neuromyth* was first employed to describe unfounded ideas about the brain within medical culture (Crockard, 1996). In the educational context, neuromyths correspond to misunderstandings or misinterpretations of scientific findings about the brain describing certain teaching and learning processes, often resulting in questionable practical applications in the classroom. Neuromyths often rely on preconceived and intuitive ideas about how we learn and are frequently the result of unintentional distortions influenced by our confirmation bias (Pasquinelli, 2012).

In 2002, the OECD issued a report on neuroscience and education, alerting to the growing prevalence of learning-related neuromyths within the educational community and the potential risks associated with it. However, it was not until 2012 that a group of researchers (Dekker et al., 2012) conducted an analysis of the prevalence of some of these neuromyths among a significant sample of primary and secondary school teachers, specifically in the United Kingdom and the Netherlands.

The findings showed that some neuromyths were highly prevalent in the educational community of these countries. Some of the most widely held misconceptions are included in Table 1.

Further studies conducted in other countries yielded very similar results (Ferrero et al., 2016). Interestingly, the data show a positive correlation between an interest in neuroscience research and belief in neuromyths (Dekker et al., 2012).

The drawbacks of the widespread acceptance of educational myths are apparent. If our true aim is to guide our educational practices based on scientific evidence—precisely because we value the contribution of this approach to our work—it is crucial that we have reliable information. Neuromyths and other misconceptions about learning lead us to believe that our decisions and efforts align with evidence-based

Table 1   **Prevalence of some neuromyths in a sample of 137 teachers from the United Kingdom (UK) and 105 teachers from the Netherlands (NL).**

Neuromyth	Prevalence UK	Prevalence NL
People learn better when they receive information in their preferred learning style (auditory, visual, kinesthetic. . .).	93%	96%
Environments that are rich in stimuli enhance the brains of preschool children.	95%	56%
Certain differences in dominance of one cerebral hemisphere over the other help explain some of the differences among students.	91%	86%
We only use 10% of our brain.	48%	46%
There are critical periods in childhood after which it is no longer possible to learn certain things.	33%	52%

practices when, in reality, they do not. The associated opportunity cost is not trivial; we lose valuable time that could be devoted to more effective activities. This becomes even worse when it involves financial expenditures (several companies propose solutions based on these neuromyths), and, most importantly, when their impact on learning, far from being neutral, becomes detrimental (Pasquinelli, 2012).

Certainly, this does not mean that only practices backed by scientific evidence are valid. But there is a difference between advocating ideas based on intuition and experience and claiming they have scientific backing when they do not. If our interest lies in understanding the scientific evidence that underlies certain educational practices, then it is obvious that we want to know what science actually says about them, irrespective of our initial opinions, and avoid falling into the traps of biased interpretations.

Next, I will briefly summarize the scientific evidence regarding some of the most prevalent neuromyths in education, as listed in Table 1.

Learning Styles

The belief that each person has a distinct learning style, as if our brains have various mechanisms to learn the same type of things, and each person has some mechanisms more developed than others, is widespread. This idea is often associated with supposed sensory differences, leading to the categorization of students as visual, auditory, or kinesthetic learners. While there are many versions of learning styles, the sensory-based distinction, known as VAK, is the most common.

Certainly, the idea that the alleged peculiarities of an individual's brain determine how they learn most effectively is intriguing and, if true, would have significant implications for education. Consequently, many scientists have investigated and tested whether this intuition is valid or not, with a large number of studies putting it to the test. However, overall, the evidence does not support the concept of learning styles (Pashler et al., 2009; Coffield et al., 2004). For example, if we present information visually to a group of students and then subject them to an exam, hypothetically, we could determine who the "visual" learners are based on their results, right? If we then present the same information auditorily to the same group of students and test them again, we should expect different students to excel. But this is not the case; the same students excel as in the visual learning assessment. In other words, the type of approach does not reverse the students' results based on their supposed sensory advantage—the results remain the same (Kirschner, 2017).

These studies have covered all types of learning styles, not just the VAK sensory styles, although the latter have been the most researched. In all cases, the results have been similar (Pashler et al., 2009). Of course, this does not mean that there are no differences between students. In this book, we have discussed various circumstances that indeed make a difference between one student and another, notably prior knowledge, motivation, and self-regulation strategies. However, the brain's better ability to remember is not one of them.

Studies indicate that we do not inherently possess predefined learning styles that make us better at learning when we receive information or study in one way or another—all of us benefit from the same strategies, as long as we are motivated to implement them. Of course, for students with sensory deficits, they will need to rely on the available senses.

Certainly, many teachers have encountered situations where it seemed that some students grasped a concept better when presented with a different explanation. But this does not necessarily mean that their nature as learners is different. What happens when information is presented in several ways is simply an increase in the likelihood that more students understand what they are learning because they have more opportunities to do so—they have more clues to connect the dots. This does not mean that some students preferentially benefit from visual or auditory explanations; rather, they benefit from having more options.

In fact, the more modalities, examples, and sensory references we employ, the more we enhance learning for all students, as they can make more connections with their prior knowledge (Riener & Willingham, 2010). Moreover, if they can use two senses at once, such as when we explain something while using images, animations, and the like, they better utilize the working memory space, which is essential for optimizing learning (Clark & Paivio, 1991).

While individuals can no doubt differ in the sharpness of their visual or auditory memory, among other factors, this should not be confused with the ability to learn exclusively through these memories. Visual memory recalls the appearance and location of objects, while auditory memory remembers the physical features of auditory stimuli (tone, pitch, intensity, etc.). Yet, most of what is taught in school is in the form of meanings, and sight and hearing are just vehicles to convey them to students. Of course, for certain learning objects, an exact visual or auditory representation is essential. For example, a student with good visual memory might have an advantage in learning inherently visual material, such as the locations of capitals on a map of

Europe. Similarly, a student with good auditory memory might more easily learn the correct accent in a foreign language. However, most of what we want children to learn is based on meaning, so their superior memory in a specific sensory modality will not give them an advantage just because the material is presented in their favored modality. Whether the information is presented auditorily or visually, the student must extract and store its meaning (Willingham, 2005).

On the other hand, many people label themselves "visual learners" (or auditory, etc.) because, when they learn, they preferentially use methods that rely on this sensory modality. In reality, these preferences are not innate learning styles; rather, they are learning strategies that individuals have spontaneously developed. These are not styles; they are preferences created by habit (Willingham, 2018), and not all strategies are equally effective. In fact, all humans are inherently visual, and the best memorization techniques are grounded in this fact (as long as what we want to learn can be visually represented, of course). Learning these techniques would benefit anyone, even those who believe they have another modality (Cuevas & Dawson, 2018).

Finally, the best sensory option is almost always determined by the learning object. That is, depending on what we need to learn, a visual, auditory, kinesthetic, or another approach may prove more suitable. For example, understanding how to use a microscope would be less effective with an explanatory text about its use lacking images and hands-on experience with the microscope.

Believing in learning styles is not merely an anecdotal matter; it has significant consequences. The belief that there are no general principles that help us learn better makes us ignore the findings of research on how the brain learns—that such principles do indeed exist (Bjork et al., 2013). Some of these principles have been discussed in this book. Students who have spontaneously developed learning strategies aligned with these principles have, unknowingly, gained an advantage over others. Studies indicate that all students can benefit from using these strategies.

Critical Periods and Enriched Environments

Another prevalent myth among the educational community is the notion that stimulating environments enhance the brains of preschool children. This conception often pairs with the belief that certain things must be learned during the early years of childhood; otherwise, the window of opportunity to learn them will vanish. Overall, the neuromyth asserts that exposing children to stimulating environments during the early years of childhood is crucial to take advantage of a supposed window of opportunity that will determine their intellectual performance in the future (Bruer, 1999).

The origin of these beliefs is easily traceable; it stems from a misinterpretation of some well-known scientific research on the development and functioning of the nervous system. Specifically, it combines the distortion of four key findings in neuroscience.

- First, we now understand that the brain has the capability to modify its structure in response to experience, a phenomenon known as *neuroplasticity*. Specifically, neurons, the brain cells specialized in transmitting electrical signals, alter the amount and efficiency of their connections—called *synapses*—based on the stimuli they receive. These structural changes in the brain, induced by experience, essentially represent the physical manifestation of learning (Draganski et al., 2004). Therefore, neuronal interconnectivity is often interpreted as synonymous with greater ability.

- Second, it turns out that during the first 15 months of a person's life, some regions of the cerebral cortex undergo an unprecedented proliferation of synapses. Subsequently, synaptic pruning occurs—a process eliminating neuronal connections that have barely been used while strengthening those that persist. As a result, the adult's cerebral cortex has a lower synaptic density than that of an infant (Tau & Peterson, 2010).

- Third, we know that certain neuronal circuits in the cerebral cortex need to receive specific stimuli to develop properly, and this happens in the early years of life. Hence, it is said that there are sensitive periods when the brain requires certain experiences for correct development. The end of these sensitive periods usually coincides with the completion of synaptic pruning processes (Tau & Peterson, 2010).

- Finally, several experiments indicate that individuals raised in stimulating environments develop higher synaptic density in their brains and show greater learning abilities (Rosenzweig et al., 1972).

By combining these four findings, which I have intentionally simplified, it is not difficult to fall into the neuromyth at hand. The regrettable implication is thinking that it would be convenient to take advantage of the window of opportunity represented by sensitive periods to stimulate the child, reduce synaptic pruning, and achieve maximum neuronal interconnectivity—to make them learn as much as possible.

Why is this conclusion not accurate? Well, as is often the case, the answer lies in the details that are frequently omitted when oversimplifying. Let's go step by step. First, it is crucial to distinguish between two types of neuroplasticity. On one hand, there is *experience-dependent* neuroplasticity, and on the other, there is *experience-expectant* neuroplasticity. Although both involve neuroplasticity, they are functionally distinct processes (Greenough et al., 1987).

Experience-dependent neuroplasticity refers to how the brain learns—namely, the mechanism by which it encodes information from the environment or adjusts its circuits to improve the performance of coordinated activities (such as learning a new skill). It is not a process specific to brain development but rather the brain's way of operating to learn and enhance responses to environmental conditions.

In contrast, experience-expectant neuroplasticity is a process specific to the development of the cerebral cortex. Certain brain regions, primarily sensory and motor, require specific stimuli and experiences to complete their maturation during the early years of life. For example, the circuits in the cerebral cortex responsible for visual information processing need visual stimuli to configure themselves. But the stimuli necessary to satisfy this process are those readily available to anyone simply by opening their eyes (in a well-lit environment, of course). In a similar fashion, circuits that control basic body movements adjust through the normal motor activity that any baby engages in. Essentially, this type of plasticity is only involved in developmental processes common to all humans and resulting from basic stimuli. The experiences a child needs to develop such sensory and motor skills are easily attainable in any environment.

In conclusion, we should not confuse this aspect of postnatal development processes of some brain circuits with the notion that more stimuli make a child smarter. In fact, neuroplasticity related to acquiring semantic knowledge and learning all kinds of skills dependent on experience occurs throughout life, not just in the early years. One exception worth noting is language acquisition, which has a critical period of about 12 years during which the brain exhibits a particular ease of learning through mere social interaction (Kuhl, 1994; Kuhl et al., 2003). However, this does not mean that after the age of 12 we cannot learn any other language.

What about studies suggesting that individuals raised in stimulating environments have more developed brains? Does this imply the need to expose children to increasingly stimulating environments? The origin of this evidence lies in the research conducted by Mark Rosenzweig and colleagues with laboratory rats and other rodents in the 1960s (Rosenzweig et al., 1972; Diamond et al., 1964). It is important to note that the studies were conducted with rodent animals, posing obvious challenges when extrapolating findings to humans.

In their experiments, Rosenzweig's team reared rats in two different environments (Figure 1). On one hand, rats were individually raised and housed in cages without physical objects ("impoverished environment"). On the other hand, rats were housed in groups, placed in cages with toys and objects that were replaced regularly ("enriched environment"). Subsequently, the researchers dissected the rodents and examined their brains. The findings revealed that rats raised in a more stimulating environment had thicker cerebral cortices and higher neurochemical activity. Similar results were later replicated by other researchers who also observed a higher

Impoverished environment   Enriched environment

FIGURE 1   Rats' rearing environments in Rosenzweig's experiments (1972).

density of neuronal connections in rats raised in enriched environments (Greenough et al., 1987). Moreover, these rats displayed increased agility and demonstrated quicker learning abilities, such as navigating a maze (Bruer & Greenough, 2001).

However, public opinion soon unreservedly reinterpreted these results with rodents. The assumption was that if enriched environments produced smarter rats with larger brains, then we should expose our babies to numerous stimuli to enhance their cognitive abilities. Yet, aside from the considerable leap of faith involved in extrapolating between rodents and humans, there is another significant error in such an interpretation. To truly grasp the scope of these experiments, it is crucial first to understand the meaning researchers attributed to the concepts of "impoverished environment" and, especially, "enriched environment." It is key to appreciate that the term "enriched environment" was coined solely because it was richer in stimuli than the impoverished environment, representing a situation of extreme deprivation for the rodents. Neither of the two environments resembled anything close to the natural environment of rats; both represented confinement situations that only differed because the enriched one included the presence of other rats and some toys. Undoubtedly, life in freedom offers much more stimulating challenges.

Thus, the implication of these studies is not that increased stimuli lead to greater brain development, but rather the opposite—deprivation of stimuli results in less developed brains. These experiments cannot tell us what happens once the threshold of stimulation offered by mere life in the natural environment is reached.

Fundamentally, the described works contribute to the notion that experiences modulate the brain's structure, meaning that learning emerges from the proliferation of connections between neurons. Subsequent studies revealed that the observed changes in the rat's brain occur at any age in response to environmental experiences (Van Praag et al., 2000). Therefore, it is a phenomenon related to experience-dependent neuroplasticity, which is not subject to sensitive periods.

Finally, the idea of "reducing synaptic pruning" by exposing the baby to as many stimuli as possible before the end of the sensitive period also lacks coherence. Synaptic pruning is a natural and necessary process inherent in the development of the cerebral cortex. For the brain to operate efficiently, it must select the appropriate synaptic connections and reinforce them with all available resources—having more connections does not enhance brain efficiency. For example, in a hereditary disorder known as fragile X syndrome, affected individuals suffer from intellectual disabilities despite having a higher-than-average synaptic density (Irwin et al., 2001). There is no simple relationship between the number of synapses and an individual's intelligence.

Moreover, synaptic pruning occurs at different rates across different cerebral cortex regions and extends for many years, well into the 20s (Huttenlocher, 1979). The regions that finish maturation earlier in the process are sensory and motor, which, as mentioned earlier, only require very basic stimuli for proper development.

All in all, this does not mean that there are no differences between the environments where children are raised, which later impact their ability to learn. We already mentioned that the deprivation of certain stimuli can have long-term consequences.

In the case of humans, in addition to sensory deprivation—which would only be possible in subhuman rearing conditions—social and affective deprivation in the early years of life also seems to have detrimental effects. Studies with children who have experienced such unfortunate situations indicate that a lack of early socialization can have effects that are difficult to fully reverse (O'Connor et al., 1999; 2000).

Apart from extreme situations, differences in children's environments can also affect their learning abilities when they start school (Dawson et al., 2000). For example, environments providing emotional and cognitive support, as discussed in the chapter on self-control, seem linked to better self-regulation skills (Schroeder & Kelley, 2010; Grolnick & Farkas, 2002).

Another relevant difference lies in the richness of the language to which a child is exposed daily from early childhood. Mastery of language is crucial for later learning, especially reading comprehension. Some studies suggest that, by the age of three, there can be significant differences in the vocabulary acquired by children depending on their environment (Hart & Risley, 1995), leading to substantial differences in their learning capabilities. In this case, again, it is a matter of the prior knowledge with which children come to school.

Brain Potential

While the origin of this neuromyth remains uncertain, we have all heard it at some point: the notion that "we only use 10% of the brain." Despite its incorrect attribution to Albert Einstein (a physicist, not a neurologist), this myth has permeated all kinds of cultural products (Beyerstein, 2004). Its widespread dissemination is likely due to the captivating and comforting idea of "hidden potential" it implies. In any case, this myth has infiltrated popular culture despite lacking any scientific evidence. On the contrary, everything we know about how the brain works is incompatible with this notion.

First, from an evolutionary perspective, it is inconceivable that an organ constituting 2% of body weight but consuming 20% of the energy is underutilized. If we only needed 10% of the brain, natural selection would have favored individuals with much smaller and more efficient brains (Beyerstein, 1999). Evolutionary pressures do not allow for any unnecessary elements.

Second, people who suffer brain injuries always experience consequences. If we only used 10% of the brain, the chances of suffering consequences after an illness or accident would be much lower. The sequelae of these patients have, in fact, taught us that various regions of the brain perform very specific functions (recall the case of Henry Molaison, discussed in the chapter on different memory types). Fortunately, some of these functions can be assumed by different regions if the original ones have been damaged (Kleim & Jones, 2008). The point is that each set of neurons in the brain serves some function, and none are redundant.

Moreover, neuroimaging techniques, allowing us to observe the brains of healthy individuals in action, reveal that the entire brain is active most of the time. Even during sleep, activity is recorded in all brain regions (Kajimura et al., 1999). This is because every action requires the involvement of multiple brain regions, each contributing its specific function.

To use an analogy, we could envision the brain as a neuronal symphony orchestra that never stops playing, where all its musicians—neurons—intervene continuously. However, certain groups of musicians or even soloists may have greater prominence depending on the part of the symphony they are playing—that is, according to the task being carried out at any given moment. If any group of musicians were to fail, whichever group it may be, the symphony would be compromised.

Perhaps one might argue that the 10% myth does not refer to only 10% of neurons being active at any given moment but rather that all work below their potential, at 10% of their capacity. According to this, the intensity of neuronal activation determines cognitive performance. However, if this were the case, it does not make much sense that the brains of gifted individuals do not necessarily show higher activation levels than those of normal individuals, as shown by some neuroimaging studies (Mrazik & Dombrowski, 2010). In short, this neuromyth is untenable in light of the evidence.

Cerebral Laterality and Dominant Hemispheres

The fact that multiple parts of the brain work together to enable us to carry out any action leads us to debunk another prevalent neuromyth, especially among the educational community. In fact, this neuromyth is extensively exploited by all kinds of businesses and individuals offering products and services supposedly grounded in scientific knowledge of the brain. I am referring to the notion that each hemisphere of the brain is responsible for specific tasks, and that differences in the dominance of one hemisphere over the other could explain variations among students (Lindell & Kidd, 2011).

Specifically, this neuromyth claims that the left hemisphere is responsible for logical-analytical reasoning and verbal language, while the right hemisphere handles visuospatial perception, emotional experience, creativity, and nonverbal language, including musical language. According to this idea, individuals can be classified based on which hemisphere dominates over the other, supposedly granting them greater ease with certain knowledge and skills—"left-brained" individuals are thought to be verbal, analytical, and logical, while "right-brained" individuals are considered artistic, emotional, and creative (interestingly, language and mathematics proficiency would depend on the same hemisphere). Consequently, this myth encourages us to provide different learning experiences to each student based on their dominant hemisphere to facilitate learning according to their natural preferences. Some variations of the myth also assert that specific exercises are necessary to balance the development of both hemispheres, suggesting that there are activities that selectively strengthen one hemisphere or the other.

First, this neuromyth partly overlaps with that of learning styles. As mentioned earlier, there is no conclusive evidence that different educational approaches benefit some students over others based on presumed innate features, supposedly leading them to learn better when information is presented to them in a certain way (we are always talking about students without any relevant disorders).

Second, this neuromyth rests on a misunderstanding of the phenomenon of cerebral lateralization. Lateralization is a feature of the brains of vertebrates (not just humans) where some areas of the brain (those that are a minority) are not anatomically and functionally symmetrical, but there are differences between one hemisphere and the other. Returning to the analogy of the brain and the symphony orchestra, we could imagine an arrangement where most musicians, depending on the instrument they play, are distributed equally and symmetrically on either side of the stage; six violins on one side and six on the other, four cellos on the left, and four on the right, and so on. But then there would be some exceptions—for example, the oboes exclusively on the left side while the flutes are in the same position on the right side.

However, although some parts of the brain are not symmetrical, this does not mean that they operate independently. To carry out any task, the participation of multiple brain regions located in both hemispheres is necessary. Oboes alone cannot play any orchestral symphony.

Indeed, the two hemispheres always work in an integrated manner, continuously communicating through a vast bundle of 250 million nerve fibers known as the corpus callosum (Nielsen et al., 2013). Neuroscientific evidence unequivocally indicates that all individuals, from the most logical and analytical to the most emotional and creative, use both hemispheres of the brain simultaneously when performing any task.

Even in the case of language articulation—the most clearly lateralized task of the human brain—the activation and interaction of multiple processes in both hemispheres are necessary (Lindell, 2006). Ample evidence shows that any creative task relies on the integration of processes on both sides of the brain. According to a report by the OECD (2007), "No scientific evidence . . . indicates a correlation between the degree of creativity and the activity of the right hemisphere."

For example, a study examining brain activity using neuroimaging techniques (Carlsson et al., 2000) revealed that the performance of creative tasks, such as suggesting new uses for a common object, was accompanied by activation in both hemispheres. Furthermore, individuals who showed more creativity exhibited greater activation on both sides of the brain compared to those with lower creativity. Thus, instead of supporting the idea that creativity depends on the right hemisphere, these results rather suggest that creativity depends on a greater overall activation of the brain—a hypothesis supported by the study of brain activity in individuals with highly creative professions (artists) compared to individuals with less creative professions (Gibson et al., 2009).

Ultimately, no task depends exclusively on one hemisphere, and therefore, no exercise can allow us to strengthen exclusively one hemisphere. In fact, there is no rigorous evidence that any of the products or solutions offered to "balance" the hemispheres are effective, just as there is no evidence to validate the claims of so-called "brain training" solutions (Owen et al., 2010).

Finally, the notion that there is a "dominant hemisphere" determining our abilities may, once again, be a distortion of the meaning of the original scientific term. In neuroscience, this concept—when used without specifying a concrete function—simply refers to the hemisphere that, as a result of the lateralization process occurring during brain development, ends up hosting some specialized regions that contribute to language articulation (typically the left hemisphere in most people). In other words, the term *dominant hemisphere* always applies to what the neuromyth wrongly claims as the logical-analytical-verbal one. Therefore, suggesting that a person's dominant hemisphere can be either one or the other is incorrect.

In conclusion, cerebral lateralization is an intriguing phenomenon from medical, neurobiological, and evolutionary perspectives, but it cannot be employed in the pedagogical context to justify the classification of students based on their presumed learning styles. Therefore, any reference to it in the field of education should be treated with caution as it may lead into pseudoscientific territory. Of course, this does not mean that there cannot be neurological disorders affecting learning as a result of defects related to lateralization, but the effectiveness of supposedly remedial methods remains to be seen.

The prevalence of these and other pseudoscientific myths about the brain and learning underscores the need for careful consideration when encountering information from media, conferences, courses, and educational solution companies. As noted in the first chapter, a keen interest in scientific findings and cautious skepticism about claims must go hand in hand, along with the knowledge that nothing is ever as straightforward as it may initially seem. In this regard, I hope to have contributed to providing the reader with tools to recognize the importance of rigor in this fascinating field of research.

REFERENCES

Ahmed, A., & Pollitt, A. (2010). The support model for interactive assessment. *Assessment in Education: Principles, Policy and Practice, 17*(2), 133–167.

Airasian, P. W. (1997). *Classroom assessment.* McGraw-Hill.

Alfieri, L., Brooks, P. J., Aldrich, N. J., & Tenenbaum, H. R. (2011). Does discovery-based instruction enhance learning? *Journal of Educational Psychology, 103*(1), 1–18.

Alloway, T. P. (2006). How does working memory work in the classroom? *Educational Research and Reviews, 1*(4), 134–139.

Alloway, T. P., & Alloway, R. G. (2010). Investigating the predictive roles of working memory and IQ in academic attainment. *Journal of Experimental Child Psychology, 106*(1), 20–29.

Alloway, T. P., & Alloway, R. G. (2014). *Understanding working memory.* SAGE Publications.

Ambrose, S. A., Bridges, M. W., DiPietro, M., Lovett, M. C., & Norman, M. K. (2010). *How learning works: Seven research-based principles for smart teaching.* John Wiley & Sons.

Anderson, C. A., Anderson, K. B., Dorr, N., DeNeve, K. M., & Flanagan, M. (2000). Temperature and aggression. In M. P. Zanna (Ed.), *Advances in experimental social psychology* (Vol. 32, pp. 63–133). Elsevier.

Anderson, J. R. (1982). Acquisition of cognitive skill. *Psychological Review, 89*(4), 369–406.

Anderson, L. W. (Ed.), Krathwohl, D. R. (Ed.), Airasian, P. W., Cruikshank, K. A., Mayer, R. E., Pintrich, P. R., Raths, J., & Wittrock, M. C. (2001). *A taxonomy for learning, teaching, and assessing: A revision of Bloom's Taxonomy of Educational Objectives* (complete edition). Longman.

Anderson, M., & Della Sala, S. (2012). Neuroscience in education: An (opinionated) introduction. In S. Della Sala & M. Anderson (Eds.), *Neuroscience in education: The good, the bad and the ugly* (pp. 3–12). Oxford University Press.

Ando, J., Ono, Y., & Wright, M. J. (2001). Genetic structure of spatial and verbal working memory. *Behavior Genetics, 31*(6), 615–624.

Anzai, Y. (1991). Learning and use of representations for physics expertise. In K. A. Ericsson & J. Smith (Eds.), *Toward a general theory of expertise* (pp. 64–92). Cambridge University Press.

Arnsten, A. F. (2009). Stress signalling pathways that impair prefrontal cortex structure and function. *Nature Reviews Neuroscience, 10*(6), 410–422.

Aronson, J., Fried, C. B., & Good, C. (2002). Reducing the effects of stereotype threat on African American college students by shaping theories of intelligence. *Journal of Experimental Social Psychology, 38*(2), 113–125.

Arzi, H. J., Ben-Zvi, R., & Ganiel, U. (1986). Forgetting versus savings: The many facets of long-term retention. *Science Education, 70*(2), 171–188.

Atkinson, R. C., & Shiffrin, R. M. (1968). Human memory: A proposed system and its control processes. In K. W. Spence & J. T. Spence (Eds.), *Psychology of learning and motivation* (Vol. 2, pp. 89–195). Academic Press.

Atkinson, R. K., Derry, S. J., Renkl, A., & Wortham, D. (2000). Learning from examples: Instructional principles from the worked examples research. *Review of Educational Research, 70*(2), 181–214.

Atkinson, R. K., Renkl, A., & Merrill, M. M. (2003). Transitioning from studying examples to solving problems: Effects of self-explanation prompts and fading worked-out steps. *Journal of Educational Psychology, 95*(4), 667–686.

Ausubel, D. P. (1962). Learning by discovery. *Educational Leadership, 20*(2), 113–117.

Babad, E. (1993). Pygmalion—25 years after interpersonal expectations in the classroom. In P. D. Blanck (Ed.), *Interpersonal expectations: Theory, research, and applications—Studies in Emotional and Social Interaction* (pp. 125–153). Cambridge University Press.

Baddeley, A., Eysenck, M. W., & Anderson, M. C. (2015). *Memory.* Psychology Press.

Baddeley, A. D., & Hitch, G. J. (1974). Working memory. In G. A. Bower (Ed.), *The psychology of learning and motivation* (pp. 47–89). Academic Press.

Bahník, Š., & Vranka, M. A. (2017). Growth mindset is not associated with scholastic aptitude in a large sample of university applicants. *Personality and Individual Differences, 117,* 139–143.

Bahrick, H. P. (1979). Maintenance of knowledge: Questions about memory we forgot to ask. *Journal of Experimental Psychology: General, 108,* 296–308.

Ballarini, F., Martínez, M. C., Pérez, M. D., Moncada, D., & Viola, H. (2013). Memory in elementary school children is improved by an unrelated novel experience. *PloS One, 8*(6), e66875.

Bandura, A. (1997). *Self-efficacy: The exercise of control.* Macmillan.

Barbieri, S. M., & Light, P. H. (1992). Interaction, gender and performance on a computer-based problem solving task. *Learning and Instruction, 2*(3), 119–213.

Barnett, S. M., & Ceci, S. J. (2002). When and where do we apply what we learn? A taxonomy for far transfer. *Psychological Bulletin, 128*(4), 612–637.

Barron, K. E., & Harackiewicz, J. M. (2001). Achievement goals and optimal motivation: Testing multiple goal models. *Journal of Personality and Social Psychology, 80*(5), 706–722.

Bartlett, F. C. (1932). *Remembering: A study in experimental and social psychology.* Cambridge University Press.

Baumeister, R. F. (2002). Ego depletion and self-control failure: An energy model of the self's executive function. *Self and Identity, 1*(2), 129–136.

Baumeister, R. F., Campbell, J. D., Krueger, J. I., & Vohs, K. D. (2003). Does high self-esteem cause better performance, interpersonal success, happiness, or healthier lifestyles? *Psychological Science in the Public Interest, 4*(1), 1–44.

Baumeister, R. F., Vohs, K. D., & Tice, D. M. (2007). The strength model of self-control. *Current Directions in Psychological Science, 16*(6), 351–355.

Bayley, P. J., Hopkins, R. O., & Squire, L. R. (2006). The fate of old memories after medial temporal lobe damage. *Journal of Neuroscience, 26*(51), 13311–13317.

Beaver, K. M., Ratchford, M., & Ferguson, C. J. (2009). Evidence of genetic and environmental effects on the development of low self-control. *Criminal Justice and Behavior, 36*(11), 1158–1172.

Bechara, A., Tranel, D., Damasio, H., Adolphs, R., Rockland, C., & Damasio, A. R. (1995). Double dissociation of conditioning and declarative knowledge relative to the amygdala and hippocampus in humans. *Science, 269*(5227), 1115–1118.

Beed, P., Hawkins, M., & Roller, C. (1991). Moving learners toward independence: The power of scaffolded instruction. *Reading Teacher*, 44(9), 648–655.

Bernier, A., Carlson, S. M., & Whipple, N. (2010). From external regulation to self-regulation: Early parenting precursors of young children's executive functioning. *Child Development*, 81(1), 326–339.

Berry, D. C. (1983). Metacognitive experience and transfer of logical reasoning. *Quarterly Journal of Experimental Psychology Section A*, 35(1), 39–49.

Beyerstein, B. L. (1999). Whence cometh the myth that we only use ten percent of our brains. In S. Della Sala (Ed.), *Mind myths: Exploring popular assumptions about the mind and brain* (pp. 1–24). John Wiley & Sons.

Beyerstein, B. L. (2004). Do we really use only 10 percent of our brains? *Scientific American*, 290(6), 116.

Bian, L., Leslie, S. J., & Cimpian, A. (2017). Gender stereotypes about intellectual ability emerge early and influence children's interests. *Science*, 355(6323), 389–391.

Bielaczyc, K., Pirolli, P. L., & Brown, A. L. (1995). Training in self-explanation and self-regulation strategies: Investigating the effects of knowledge acquisition activities on problem solving. *Cognition and Instruction*, 13(2), 221–252.

Bjork, E. L., & Bjork, R. A. (2011). Making things hard on yourself, but in a good way: Creating desirable difficulties to enhance learning. In M. A. Gernsacher, R. W. Pew, L. M. Hough, & J. R. Ponerantz (Eds.), *Psychology and the real world: Essays illustrating fundamental contributions to society* (pp. 59–68). Worth Publishers.

Bjork, R. A. (1994). Memory and metamemory considerations in the training of human beings. In J. Metcalfe & A. Shimamura (Eds.), *Metacognition: Knowing about knowing* (pp. 185–206). MIT Press.

Bjork, R. A., & Bjork, E. L. (1992). A new theory of disuse and an old theory of stimulus fluctuation. In A. F. Healy, S. M. Kosslyn, & R. M. Shiffrin (Eds.), *From learning processes to cognitive processes: Essays in honor of William K. Estes* (Vol. 2, pp. 35–67). Lawrence Erlbaum Associates.

Bjork, R. A., Dunlosky, J., & Kornell, N. (2013). Self-regulated learning: Beliefs, techniques, and illusions. *Annual Review of Psychology*, 64, 417–444.

Black, P., & Wiliam, D. (1998). Assessment and classroom learning. *Assessment in Education: Principles, Policy and Practice*, 5(1), 7–74.

Blackwell L. S., Trzesniewski K. H., Dweck C. S. (2007). Implicit theories of intelligence predict achievement across an adolescent transition: A longitudinal study and an intervention. *Child Development*, 78(1), 246–263.

Blair, C., & Razza, R. P. (2007). Relating effortful control, executive function, and false belief understanding to emerging math and literacy ability in kindergarten. *Child Development*, 78(2), 647–663.

Bloom, B. S. (1956). *Taxonomy of educational objectives* (Vol. 1). David McKay.

Bloom, B. S. (1985). The nature of the study and why it was done. In B. S. Bloom (Ed.), *Developing talent in young people* (pp. 3–18). Ballantine Books.

Bong, M., & Skaalvik, E. M. (2003). Academic self-concept and self-efficacy: How different are they really? *Educational Psychology Review*, 15(1), 1–40.

Borkowski, J. G., Weyhing, R. S., & Carr, M. (1988). Effects of attributional retraining on strategy-based reading comprehension in learning-disabled students. *Journal of Educational Psychology*, 80(1), 46–53.

Bransford, J. D., Brown, A. L., & Cocking, R. R. (2000). *How people learn: Brain, mind, experience, and school.* National Academy Press.

Bransford, J. D., & Johnson, M. K. (1972). Contextual prerequisites for understanding: Some investigations of comprehension and recall. *Journal of Verbal Learning and Verbal Behavior,* 11(6), 717–726.

Bransford, J. D., & Schwartz, D. L. (1999). Chapter 3: Rethinking transfer: A simple proposal with multiple implications. *Review of Research in Education,* 24(1), 61–100.

Bransford, J. D., Vye, N., Kinzer, C. K., & Risko, V. (1990). Teaching thinking and content knowledge: Toward an integrated approach. In B. F. Jones & L. Idol (Eds.), *Dimensions of thinking and cognitive instruction* (Vol. 1, pp. 381–413). Lawrence Erlbaum Associates.

Brewer, J., Zhao, Z., Desmond, J. E., Glover, G. H., & Gabrieli, J. D. E. (1998). Making memories: Brain activity that predicts how well visual experience will be remembered. *Science,* 281(5280), 1185–1187.

Brockner, J., Derr, W. R., & Laing, W. N. (1987). Self-esteem and reactions to negative feedback: Towards greater generalizability. *Journal of Research in Personality,* 21(3), 318–333.

Brophy, J. E., & Good, T. L. (1974). *Teacher-student relationships: Causes and consequences.* Holt, Rinehart and Winston.

Brown, D. E., & Clement, J. (1989). Overcoming misconceptions via analogical reasoning: Abstract transfer versus explanatory model construction. *Instructional Science,* 18(4), 237–261.

Brown, R., & Kulik, J. (1977). Flashbulb memories. *Cognition,* 5(1), 73–99.

Bruer, J. T. (1999). *The myth of the first three years: A new understanding of early brain development and lifelong learning.* Free Press.

Bruer, J. T., & Greenough, W. T. (2001). The subtle science of how experience affects the brain. In D. B. Bailey, Jr., J. T. Bruer, F. J. Symons, & J. W. Lichtman (Eds.), *Critical thinking about critical periods* (pp. 209–232). Brookes Publishing.

Bruner, J. (1962). The art of discovery learning. In *On knowing: Essays for the left hand.* Harvard University Press.

Buckner, R. L., & Koutstaal, W. (1998). Functional neuroimaging studies of encoding, priming, and explicit memory retrieval. *Proceedings of the National Academy of Sciences of the United States of America,* 95(3), 891–898.

Budé, L., Imbos, T., van de Wiel, M. W., & Berger, M. P. (2011). The effect of distributed practice on students' conceptual understanding of statistics. *Higher Education,* 62(1), 69–79.

Bushman, B. J. (2002). Does venting anger feed or extinguish the flame? Catharsis, rumination, distraction, anger, and aggressive responding. *Personality and Social Psychology Bulletin,* 28(6), 724–731.

Bushman, B. J., Baumeister, R. F., & Phillips, C. M. (2001). Do people aggress to improve their mood? Catharsis beliefs, affect regulation opportunity, and aggressive responding. *Journal of Personality and Social Psychology,* 81(1), 17–32.

Butler, A. C. (2010). Repeated testing produces superior transfer of learning relative to repeated studying. *Journal of Experimental Psychology: Learning, Memory, and Cognition,* 36(5), 1118–1133.

Butler, R. (1987). Task-involving and ego-involving properties of evaluation: Effects of different feedback conditions on motivational perceptions, interest, and performance. *Journal of Educational Psychology,* 79(4), 474–482.

Butler, R. (1988). Enhancing and undermining intrinsic motivation: The effects of task-involving and ego-involving evaluation of interest and performance. *British Journal of Educational Psychology,* 58(1), 1–14.

Cahill, L., Babinsky, R., Markowitsch, H. J., & McGaugh, J. L. (1995). The amygdala and emotional memory. *Nature,* 377(6547), 295–296.

Cahill, L., & McGaugh, J. L. (1995). A novel demonstration of enhanced memory associated with emotional arousal. *Consciousness and Cognition,* 4(4), 410–421.

Calkins, S. D., Smith, C. L., Gill, K. L., & Johnson, M. C. (1998). Maternal interactive style across contexts: Relations to emotional, behavioral and physiological regulation during toddlerhood. *Social Development,* 7(3), 350–369.

Carey, L. J., Flower, L. G., Hayes, J. R., Schriver, K. A., & Haas, C. (1989). *Differences in writers' initial task representations (technical report no. 34).* Center for the Study of Writing, University of Berkeley and Carnegie Mellon University.

Carey, S. (1985). *Conceptual change in childhood.* MIT Press.

Carey, S. (1991). Knowledge acquisition: Enrichment or conceptual change? In S. Carey & R. Gelman (Eds.), *The epigenesis of mind: Essays on biology and cognition* (pp. 257–291). Lawrence Erlbaum Associates.

Carey, S. (1999). Sources of conceptual change. In E. Scholnick, K. Nelson, S. A. Gelman, & P. H. Miller (Eds.), *Conceptual development: Piaget's legacy* (pp. 293–326). Lawrence Erlbaum Associates.

Carlson, S. M., & Wang, T. S. (2007). Inhibitory control and emotion regulation in preschool children. *Cognitive Development,* 22(4), 489–510.

Carlsson, I., Wendt, P. E., & Risberg, J. (2000). On the neurobiology of creativity: Differences in frontal activity between high and low creative subjects. *Neuropsychologia,* 38(6), 873–885.

Carpenter, G. A. (2001). Neural-network models of learning and memory: Leading questions and an emerging framework. *Trends in Cognitive Sciences,* 5(3), 114–118.

Carpenter, S. K. (2012). Testing enhances the transfer of learning. *Current Directions in Psychological Science,* 21(5), 279–283.

Carpenter, S. K., & DeLosh, E. L. (2006). Impoverished cue support enhances subsequent retention: Support for the elaborative retrieval explanation of the testing effect. *Memory and Cognition,* 34(2), 268–276.

Carpenter, S. K., Pashler, H., & Cepeda, N. J. (2009). Using tests to enhance 8th grade students' retention of U. S. history facts. *Applied Cognitive Psychology,* 23(6), 760–771.

Carver, C. S., & Scheier, M. F. (1990). Origins and functions of positive and negative affect: A control-process view. *Psychological Review,* 97(1), 19–35.

Carver, C. S., & Scheier, M. F. (2001). *On the self-regulation of behavior.* Cambridge University Press.

Castles, A., Rastle, K., & Nation, K. (2018). Ending the reading wars: Reading acquisition from novice to expert. *Psychological Science in the Public Interest,* 19(1), 5–51.

Chapell, M. S., Blanding, Z. B., Silverstein, M. E., Takahashi, M., Newman, B., Gubi, A., & McCann, N. (2005). Test anxiety and academic performance in undergraduate and graduate students. *Journal of Educational Psychology,* 97(2), 268–274.

Chappuis, S., & Stiggins, R. J. (2002). Classroom assessment for learning. *Educational Leadership,* 60(1), 40–44.

Chase, W. G., & Simon, H. A. (1973). Perception in chess. *Cognitive Psychology,* 4(1), 55–81.

Chi, M. T. H. (2000). Self-explaining: The dual processes of generating inference and repairing mental models. In R. Glaser (Ed.), *Advances in instructional psychology: educational design and cognitive science* (Vol. 5, pp. 161–238). Lawrence Erlbaum Associates.

Chi, M. T., Feltovich, P. J., & Glaser, R. (1981). Categorization and representation of physics problems by experts and novices. *Cognitive Science*, 5(2), 121–152.

Chi, M. T., Bassok, M., Lewis, M. W., Reimann, P., & Glaser, R. (1989). Self-explanations: How students study and use examples in learning to solve problems. *Cognitive Science*, 13(2), 145–182.

Chi, M. T., De Leeuw, N., Chiu, M. H., & LaVancher, C. (1994). Eliciting self-explanations improves understanding. *Cognitive Science*, 18(3), 439–477.

Chinn, C. A., O'Donnell, A. M., & Jinks, T. S. (2000). The structure of discourse in collaborative learning. *Journal of Experimental Education*, 69(1), 77–97.

Clariana, R. B., Wagner, D., & Murphy, L. C. R. (2000). Applying a connectionist description of feedback timing. *Educational Technology Research and Development*, 48(3), 5–22.

Clark, J. M., & Paivio, A. (1991). Dual coding theory and education. *Educational Psychology Review*, 3(3), 149–210.

Clark, R. C., & Mayer, R. E. (2016). *E-learning and the science of instruction: Proven guidelines for consumers and designers of multimedia learning*. John Wiley & Sons.

Clark, R. C., Nguyen, F., and Sweller, J. (2006). *Efficiency in learning: Evidence-based guidelines to manage cognitive load*. Pfeiffer.

Clark, R. E., Kirschner, P. A., & Sweller, J. (2012). Putting students on the path to learning: The case for fully guided instruction. *American Educator*, 36(1), 6–11.

Coffield, F., Moseley, D., Hall, E., & Ecclestone, K. (2004). *Learning styles and pedagogy in post-16 learning: A systematic and critical review*. Learning and Skills Research Centre.

Cohen, E. G. (1994). Restructuring the classroom: Conditions for productive small groups. *Review of Educational Research*, 64(1), 1–35.

Cohen, J. R., & Lieberman, M. D. (2010). The common neural basis of exerting self-control in multiple domains. In R. Hassin, K. Ochsner, & Y. Trope (Eds.), *Self Control in Society, Mind, and Brain* (pp. 141–162). Oxford University Press.

Connor, C. M., Ponitz, C. C., Phillips, B. M., Travis, Q. M., Glasney, S., & Morrison, F. J. (2010). First graders' literacy and self-regulation gains: The effect of individualizing student instruction. *Journal of School Psychology*, 48(5), 433–455.

Corkin, S. (1968). Acquisition of motor skill after bilateral medial temporal-lobe excision. *Neuropsychologia*, 6(3), 255–265.

Cornford, I. R. (2002). Learning-to-learn strategies as a basis for effective lifelong learning. *International Journal of Lifelong Education*, 21(4), 357–368.

Cotton, K. (1988). Classroom questioning. *School improvement research series*, 5, 1–22.

Cowan, N. (2008). Sensory memory. In J. H. Byrne (Ed.), *Learning and memory: A comprehensive reference* (Vol. 2, pp. 23–32). Elsevier.

Craik, F. I. M., & Lockhart, R. S. (1972). Levels of processing: A framework for memory research. *Journal of Verbal Learning and Verbal Behavior*, 11(6), 671–684.

Credé, M., Tynan, M. C., & Harms, P. D. (2017). Much ado about grit: A meta-analytic synthesis of the grit literature. *Journal of Personality and Social Psychology*, 113(3), 492–511.

Crockard, A. (1996). Confessions of a brain surgeon. *New Science*, 2061, 68–69.

Croizet, J. C., & Claire, T. (1998). Extending the concept of stereotype threat to social class: The intellectual underperformance of students from low socioeconomic backgrounds. *Personality and Social Psychology Bulletin,* 24(6), 588–594.

Crooks, T. J. (1988). The impact of classroom evaluation practices on students. *Review of Educational Research,* 58(4), 438–481.

Cuevas, J., & Dawson, B. L. (2018). A test of two alternative cognitive processing models: Learning styles and dual coding. *Theory and Research in Education,* 16(1), 40–64.

Curtis, K. A. (1992). Altering beliefs about the importance of strategy: An attributional intervention 1. *Journal of Applied Social Psychology,* 22(12), 953–972.

Daneman, M., & Carpenter, P. A. (1980). Individual differences in working memory and reading. *Journal of Verbal Learning and Verbal Behavior,* 19(4), 450–466.

Dawson, G., Ashman, S. B., & Carver, L. J. (2000). The role of early experience in shaping behavioral and brain development and its implications for social policy. *Development and Psychopathology,* 12(4), 695–712.

De la Fuente, I. M., Bringas, C., Malaina, I., Fedetz, M., Carrasco-Pujante, J., Morales, M., Knafo, S., Martínez, L., Pérez-Samartín, A., López, J. I., Pérez-Yarza, G., & Boyano, M. D. (2019). Evidence of conditioned behavior in amoebae. *Nature Communications,* 10(1), 1–12.

De Lisi, R., & Golbeck, S. L. (1999). Implications of Piagetian theory for peer learning. In A. M. O'Donnell & A. King (Eds.), *Cognitive perspectives on peer learning* (pp. 3–37). Lawrence Erlbaum Associates.

Dekker, S., Lee, N. C., Howard-Jones, P., & Jolles, J. (2012). Neuromyths in education: Prevalence and predictors of misconceptions among teachers. *Frontiers in Psychology,* 3, 1–8.

Dewey, J. (1913). *Interest and effort in education.* Houghton Mifflin.

Diamond, A. (2013). Executive functions. *Annual Review of Psychology,* 64, 135–168.

Diamond, A., Barnett, W. S., Thomas, J., & Munro, S. (2007). Preschool program improves cognitive control. *Science,* 318(5855), 1387–1388.

Diamond, A., & Lee, K. (2011). Interventions shown to aid executive function development in children 4 to 12 years old. *Science,* 333(6045), 959–964.

Diamond, M. C., Krech, D., & Rosenzweig, M. R. (1964). The effects of an enriched environment on the histology of the rat cerebral cortex. *Journal of Comparative Neurology,* 123(1), 111–119.

Didau, D. (2018). *Making kids cleverer: A manifesto for closing the advantage gap.* Crown House Publishing.

Doval, H. O. (2014). El examen, herramienta fundamental para la evaluación certificativa. In N. M. Contreras Izquierdo (Ed.), *La enseñanza del español como LE/L2 en el siglo XXI* (pp. 553–562). Asociación para la Enseñanza del Español como Lengua Extranjera.

Draganski, B., Gaser, C., Busch, V., Schuierer, G., Bogdahn, U., & May, A. (2004). Neuroplasticity: Changes in grey matter induced by training. *Nature,* 427(6972), 311–312.

Duckworth, A. L. (2016). *Grit: The power of passion and perseverance.* Scribner.

Duckworth, A. L., & Eskreis-Winkler, L. (2013). True grit. *Observer,* 26(4). Retrieved from https://www.psychologicalscience.org/observer/true-grit

Duckworth, A. L., & Kern, M. L. (2011). A meta-analysis of the convergent validity of self-control measures. *Journal of Research in Personality,* 45(3), 259–268.

Duckworth, A. L., Peterson, C., Matthews, M. D., & Kelly, D. R. (2007). Grit: Perseverance and passion for long-term goals. *Journal of Personality and Social Psychology*, 92(6), 1087–1101.

Duckworth, A. L., & Seligman, M. E. (2005). Self-discipline outdoes IQ in predicting academic performance of adolescents. *Psychological Science*, 16(12), 939–944.

Duckworth, A. L., Quirk, A., Gallop, R., Hoyle, R. H., Kelly, D. R., & Matthews, M. D. (2019). Cognitive and noncognitive predictors of success. *Proceedings of the National Academy of Sciences*, 116(47), 23499–23504.

Dunbar, K. N., Fugelsang, J. A., & Stein, C. (2007). Do naïve theories ever go away? Using brain and behavior to understand changes in concepts. In M. C. Lovett & P. Shah (Eds.), *Thinking with data* (pp.193–205). Lawrence Erlbaum Associates.

Dunn, K. E. & Mulvenon, S. W. (2009). A critical review of research on formative assessment: The limited scientific evidence of the impact of formative assessment in education. *Practical Assessment Research and Evaluation*, 14(7), 1–11.

Dunning, D. (2004). *Self-insight: Roadblocks and detours on the path to knowing thyself*. Taylor & Francis.

Duschl, R. A., & Duncan, R. G. (2009). Beyond the fringe: Building and evaluating scientific knowledge systems. In S. Tobias & T. M. Duffy (Eds.), *Constructivist instruction: Success or failure?* (pp. 311–332). Routledge.

Duschl, R. A., Schweingruber, H. A., & Shouse, A. W. (Eds.). (2007). *Taking science to school: Learning and teaching science in grades K–8* (Vol. 500). Washington, DC: National Academies Press.

Dweck, C., Walton, G., & Cohen, G. (2014). *Academic tenacity: Mindsets and skills that promote long-term learning*. Bill and Melinda Gates Foundation. Retrieved from https://www.researchgate.net/publication/326191078_Teaching_Tenacity

Dweck, C. S. (1986). Motivational processes affecting learning. *American Psychologist*, 41(10), 1040–1048.

Dweck, C. S. (1999). *Self-theories: Their role in motivation, personality, and development*. Psychology Press.

Dweck, C. S. (2000). *Self-theories: Their role in motivation, personality, and development*. Psychology Press.

Dweck, C. S. (2008). *Mindset: The new psychology of success*. Random House Digital.

Dweck, C. S. (2015). Interview in Schools Week. Retrieved from https://schoolsweek.co.uk/why-mindset-is-not-a-tool-to-make-children-feel-good/

Dweck, C. S., & Leggett, E. L. (1988). A social-cognitive approach to motivation and personality. *Psychological Review*, 95(2), 256–273.

Ebbinghaus, H. (2013). Memory: A contribution to experimental psychology. *Annals of Neurosciences*, 20(4), 155–156.

Egan, D. E., & Schwartz, B. J. (1979). Chunking in recall of symbolic drawings. *Memory and Cognition*, 7(2), 149–158.

Eisenberg, N. (2005). Temperamental effortful control (self-regulation). In *Encyclopedia on early childhood development*. Retrieved from http://www.child-encyclopedia.com/temperament/according-experts/temperamental-effortful-control-self-regulation

Ekman, P. (1992). An argument for basic emotions. *Cognition and Emotion*, 6(3–4), 169–200.

Elliot, A. J. (1999). Approach and avoidance motivation and achievement goals. *Educational Psychologist*, 34(3), 169–189.

Erev, I., Luria, A., & Erev, A. (2006). On the effect of immediate feedback. In Y. Eshet-Alkalai, A. Caspi, & Y. Yair (Eds.), *Learning in the technological era. Proceedings of the Chais Conference* (pp. 26–30). Open University Press.

Ericsson, A., & Crutcher, R. (1990). The nature of exceptional performance. In P. Baltes, D. Featherman, & R. M. Lerner (Eds.), *Life-span development and behavior* (Vol. 10, pp. 187–217). Lawrence Erlbaum Associates.

Ericsson, A., & Pool, R. (2016). *Peak: Secrets from the new science of expertise* (pp. 167–168). Houghton Mifflin Harcourt.

Ericsson, K. A., Chase, W. G., & Faloon, S. (1980). Acquisition of a memory skill. *Science*, 208(4448), 1181–1182.

Ericsson, K. A., Krampe, R. T., & Tesch-Römer, C. (1993). The role of deliberate practice in the acquisition of expert performance. *Psychological Review*, 100(3), 363–406.

Evans, G. W., & Rosenbaum, J. (2008). Self-regulation and the income-achievement gap. *Early Childhood Research Quarterly*, 23(4), 504–514.

Ferrero, M., Garaizar, P., & Vadillo, M. A. (2016). Neuromyths in education: Prevalence among Spanish teachers and an exploration of cross-cultural variation. *Frontiers in Human Neuroscience*, 10, 496.

Festinger, L. (1957). *A theory of cognitive dissonance*. Stanford University Press.

Field, S. (1992). The effect of temperature on crime. *British Journal of Criminology*, 32(3), 340–351.

Finn, B., & Metcalfe, J. (2010). Scaffolding feedback to maximize long-term error correction. *Memory and Cognition*, 38(7), 951–961.

Fishbach, A. T., Eyal, T., & Finkelstein, S. R. (2010). How positive and negative feedback motivate goal pursuit. *Social and Personality Psychology Compass*, 4(8), 517–530.

Fisher, A. V., Godwin, K. E. & Seltman, H. (2014). Visual environment, attention allocation, and learning in young children: When too much of a good thing may be bad. *Psychological Science*, 25(7), 1362–1370.

Foerde, K., & Poldrack, R. A. (2009). Procedural learning in humans. In L. R. Squire (Ed.), *Encyclopedia of neuroscience* (pp. 1083–1091). Elsevier.

Foliano, F., Rolfe, H., Buzzeo, J., Runge, J., & Wilkinson, D. (2019). *Changing mindsets: Effectiveness trial*. Education Endowment Foundation. Retrieved from https://educationendowmentfoundation.org.uk/public/files/Projects/Evaluation_Reports/Changing_Mindsets.pdf

Fonseca, B. A., & Chi, M. T. (2011). Instruction based on self-explanation. In R. E. Mayer & P. A. Alexander (Eds.), *The handbook of research on learning and instruction* (pp. 296–321). Routledge Press.

Ford, M. E. (1992). *Motivating humans: Goals, emotions, and personal agency beliefs*. SAGE Publications.

Forman, E. A., & McPhail, J. (1993). Vygotskian perspective on children's collaborative problem solving activities. In E. A. Forman, N. Minick, & C. A. Stone (Eds.), *Contexts for learning: Sociocultural dynamics in children's development* (pp. 213–229). Oxford University Press.

Freedberg, M., Glass, B., Filoteo, J. V., Hazeltine, E., & Maddox, W. T. (2017). Comparing the effects of positive and negative feedback in information-integration category learning. *Memory and Cognition*, 45(1), 12–25.

Fried, L. (2010). Understanding and enhancing emotion and motivation regulation strategy use in the classroom. *International Journal of Learning*, 17(6).

Friend, R. (2001). Effects of strategy instruction on summary writing of college students. *Contemporary Educational Psychology*, 26(1), 3–24.

Fu, W. T., & Gray, W. D. (2004). Resolving the paradox of the active user: Stable suboptimal performance in interactive tasks. *Cognitive Science*, 28(6), 901–935.

Fugelsang, J. A., & Dunbar, K. N. (2005). Brain-based mechanisms underlying complex causal thinking. *Neuropsychologia*, 43(8), 1204–1213.

Furtak, E., et al. (2012). To teach or not to teach through inquiry: Is that the question? In Carver S. M., Shrager J. (Eds.), *The journey from child to scientist: Integrating cognitive development and the education sciences* (pp. 227–244). Washington, DC: American Psychological Association.

Garton, A. F. (1992). *Social interaction and the development of language and cognition*. Lawrence Erlbaum Associates.

Garton, A. F. (2004). *Exploring cognitive development: The child as problem solver*. Blackwell Publishers.

Gasca, L., & Gubern, R. (2001). *El discurso del cómic*. Cátedra.

Gathercole, S. E. (2008). Working memory. In J. H. Byrne (Ed.), *Learning and memory: A comprehensive reference* (Vol. 2, pp. 33–51). Elsevier.

Gathercole, S. E., & Alloway, T. P. (2007). *Understanding working memory: A classroom guide*. London: Harcourt Assessment.

Gathercole, S. E., Pickering, S. J., Ambridge, B., & Wearing, H. (2004). The structure of working memory from 4 to 15 years of age. *Developmental Psychology*, 40(2), 177–190.

Geake, J. (2008). Neuromythologies in education. *Educational Research*, 50(2), 123–133.

Geary, D. C. (2007). Educating the evolved mind: Conceptual foundations for an evolutionary educational psychology. In J. S. Carlson & J. R. Levin (Eds.), *Educating the evolved mind: Conceptual foundations for an evolutionary educational psychology* (pp. 1–99). Information Age Publishing.

Gentner, D., Loewenstein, J., & Thompson, L. (2004). Analogical encoding: Facilitating knowledge transfer and integration. In K. Forbus, D. Gentner, & T. Regier (Eds.), *Proceedings of the Annual Meeting of the Cognitive Science Society* (pp. 452–457). Cognitive Science Society.

Gibson, C., Folley, B. S., & Park, S. (2009). Enhanced divergent thinking and creativity in musicians: A behavioral and near-infrared spectroscopy study. *Brain and Cognition*, 69, 162–169.

Gick, M. L., & Holyoak, K. J. (1980). Analogical problem solving. *Cognitive Psychology*, 12(3), 306–355.

Gick, M. L., & Holyoak, K. J. (1983). Schema induction and analogical transfer. *Cognitive Psychology*, 15(1), 1–38.

Glaser, R. (1992). Expert knowledge and processes of thinking. In D. F. Halpern (Ed.), *Enhancing thinking skills in the sciences and mathematics* (pp. 63–75). Lawrence Erlbaum Associates.

Glerum, J., Loyens, M. M., Wijnia, L., & Rikers, R. M. (2019). The effects of praise for effort versus praise for intelligence on vocational education students. *Educational Psychology*, 1–17.

Goldsmith, H. H., Buss, K. A., & Lemery, K. S. (1997). Toddler and childhood temperament: expanded content, stronger genetic evidence, new evidence for the importance of environment. *Developmental Psychology*, 33(6), 891–905.

Gomes, C. M. A., Golino, H. F., & Menezes, I. G. (2014). Predicting school achievement rather than intelligence: Does metacognition matter? *Psychology*, 5(9), 1095–1110.

Good, C., Aronson, J., & Inzlicht, M. (2003). Improving adolescents' standardized test performance: An intervention to reduce the effects of stereotype threat. *Journal of Applied Developmental Psychology*, 24(6), 645–662.

Good, T. L., & Grouws, D. A. (1979). The Missouri Mathematics Effectiveness Project: An experimental study in fourth-grade classrooms. *Journal of Educational Psychology*, 71(3), 355–362.

Gottfredson, L. S. (1997). Why g matters: The complexity of everyday life. *Intelligence*, 24, 79–132.

Graue, M. E. (1993). Integrating theory and practice through instructional assessment. *Educational Assessment*, 1(4), 283–309.

Graziano, P. A., Reavis, R. D., Keane, S. P., & Calkins, S. D. (2007). The role of emotion regulation in children's early academic success. *Journal of School Psychology*, 45(1), 3–19.

Greenberg, D. L., & Verfaellie, M. (2010). Interdependence of episodic and semantic memory: Evidence from neuropsychology. *Journal of the International Neuropsychological Society*, 16(5), 748–753.

Greenough, W. T., Black, J. E., & Wallace, C. S. (1987). Experience and brain development. In M. H. Johnson, Y. Munakata, & R. O. Gilmore (Eds.), *Brain development and cognition: A reader* (2nd ed., pp. 186–216). Blackwell Publishers.

Grolnick, W. S., & Farkas, M. (2002). Parenting and the development of children's self-regulation. In M. H. Bornstein (Ed.), *Handbook of parenting* (pp. 89–110). Lawrence Erlbaum Associates.

Grolnick, W. S., & Ryan, R. M. (1989). Parent styles associated with children's self-regulation and competence in school. *Journal of Educational Psychology*, 81(2), 143–154.

Gross, J. J. (1998). Antecedent-and response-focused emotion regulation: divergent consequences for experience, expression, and physiology. *Journal of Personality and Social Psychology*, 74(1), 224.

Gross, J. J. (2002). Emotion regulation: Affective, cognitive, and social consequences. *Psychophysiology*, 39(3), 281–291.

Gross, J. J., & John, O. P. (2003). Individual differences in two emotion regulation processes: implications for affect, relationships, and well-being. *Journal of Personality and Social Psychology*, 85(2), 348–362.

Gross, J. J., & Thompson, R. A. (2007). Emotion regulation: Conceptual foundations. In J. J. Gross (Ed.), *Handbook of emotion regulation* (pp. 3–24). Guildford Press.

Grover, S., & Pea, R. D. (2013). Computational thinking in K–12: A review of the state of the field. *Educational Researcher*, 42(1), 38–43.

Gruber, M. J., Gelman, B. D., & Ranganath, C. (2014). States of curiosity modulate hippocampus-dependent learning via the dopaminergic circuit. *Neuron*, 84(2), 486–496.

Hacker, D. J., Bol, L., Horgan, D. D., & Rakow, E. A. (2000). Test prediction and performance in a classroom context. *Journal of Educational Psychology*, 92(1), 160–170.

Hagger, M. S., Wood, C., Stiff, C., & Chatzisarantis, N. L. (2010). Ego depletion and the strength model of self-control: A meta-analysis. *Psychological Bulletin*, 136(4), 495–525.

Halpern, D. F., Aronson, J., Reimer, N., Simpkins, S., Star, J. R., & Wentzel, K. (2007). *Encouraging girls in math and science*. National Center for Education Research.

Hambrick, D. Z., & Engle, R. W. (2002). Effects of domain knowledge, working memory capacity, and age on cognitive performance: An investigation of the knowledge-is-power hypothesis. *Cognitive Psychology*, 44(4), 339–387.

Hansen, D. A. (1989). Lesson evading and lesson dissembling: Ego strategies in the classroom. *American Journal of Education*, 97(2), 184–208.

Harackiewicz, J. M., Barron, K. E., Pintrich, P. R., Elliot, A. J., & Thrash, T. M. (2002). Revision of achievement goal theory: Necessary and illuminating. *Journal of Educational Psychology*, 94(3), 638–645.

Hart, B., & Risley, T. R. (1995). *Meaningful differences in the everyday experience of young American children*. Brookes Publishing.

Hattie, J. (2009). *Visible learning: A synthesis of meta-analyses relating to achievement*. Routledge.

Hattie, J., & Clarke, S. (2019). *Visible learning: Feedback*. Routledge.

Hattie, J., & Timperley, H. (2007). The power of feedback. *Review of Educational Research*, 77(1), 81–112.

Hayes, J. R. (1985). Three problems in teaching problem solving skills. In S. Chipman, J. W. Segal, & R. Glaser (Eds.), *Thinking and learning: Research and open questions* (Vol. 2, pp. 391–405). Lawrence Erlbaum Associates.

Haynes, T. L., Perry, R. P., Stupnisky, R. H., & Daniels, L. M. (2009). A review of attributional retraining treatments: Fostering engagement and persistence in vulnerable college students. In J. C. Smart (Ed.), *Higher education: Handbook of theory and research* (Vol. 24, pp. 227–272). Springer, Dordrecht.

Heider, F. (1958). *The psychology of interpersonal relations*. John Wiley & Sons.

Herman, P., & Gomez, L. M. (2009). Taking guided learning theory to school: Reconciling the cognitive, motivational, and social contexts of instruction. In S. Tobias & T. M. Duffy (Eds.), *Constructivist instruction* (pp. 62–81). Routledge.

Herrnstein, R. J., Loewenstein, G. F., Prelec, D., & Vaughan, W. (1993). Utility maximization and melioration: Internalities in individual choice. *Journal of Behavioral Decision Making*, 6(3), 149–185.

Hidi, S., & Harackiewicz, J. M. (2000). Motivating the academically unmotivated: A critical issue for the 21st century. *Review of Educational Research*, 70(2), 151–179.

Hidi, S., & Renninger, K. A. (2006). The four-phase model of interest development. *Educational Psychologist*, 41(2), 111–127.

Hmelo-Silver, C. E., Duncan, R. G., & Chinn, C. A. (2007). Scaffolding and achievement in problem-based and inquiry learning: A response to Kirschner, Sweller, and Clark. *Educational Psychologist*, 42(2), 99–107.

Hochanadel, A., & Finamore, D. (2015). Fixed and growth mindset in education and how grit helps students persist in the face of adversity. *Journal of International Education Research*, 11(1), 47–50.

Hodges, J. R., & Patterson, K. (2007). Semantic dementia: A unique clinicopathological syndrome. *Lancet Neurology*, 6(11), 1004–1014.

Hofer, S. B., Mrsic-Flogel, T. D., Bonhoeffer, T., & Hübener, M. (2009). Experience leaves a lasting structural trace in cortical circuits. *Nature*, 457, 313–317.

Hofmann, S. G. (2008). Cognitive processes during fear acquisition and extinction in animals and humans: Implications for exposure therapy of anxiety disorders. *Clinical Psychology Review*, 28(2), 199–210.

Hofmann, W., Schmeichel, B. J., & Baddeley, A. D. (2012). Executive functions and self-regulation. *Trends in Cognitive Sciences*, 16(3), 174–180.

Howes, C., Matheson, C. C., & Hamilton, C. E. (1994). Maternal, teacher, and child care history correlates of children's relationships with peers. *Child Development*, 65(1), 264–273.

Huttenlocher, P. R. (1979). Synaptic density in human frontal cortex-developmental changes and effects of aging. *Brain Research*, 163(2), 195–205.

Hyde, T. S., & Jenkins, J. J. (1973). Recall for words as a function of semantic, graphic, and syntactic orienting tasks. *Journal of Verbal Learning and Verbal Behavior*, 12(5), 471–480.

Inzlicht, M., & Ben-Zeev, T. (2000). A threatening intellectual environment: Why females are susceptible to experiencing problem-solving deficits in the presence of males. *Psychological Science*, 11(5), 365–371.

Irwin, S. A., Patel, B., Idupulapati, M., Harris, J. B., Crisostomo, R. A., Larsen, B. P., Kooy, F., Willems, P. J., et al. (2001). Abnormal dendritic spine characteristics in the temporal and visual cortices of patients with fragile-X syndrome: A quantitative examination. *American Journal of Medical Genetics*, 98(2), 161–167.

Jack, R. E., Garrod, O. G., & Schyns, P. G. (2014). Dynamic facial expressions of emotion transmit an evolving hierarchy of signals over time. *Current Biology*, 24(2), 187–192.

James, W. (1890). *The principles of psychology*. Henry Holt and Company.

Jamieson, J. P., Mendes, W. B., Blackstock, E., & Schmader, T. (2010). Turning the knots in your stomach into bows: Reappraising arousal improves performance on the GRE. *Journal of Experimental Social Psychology*, 46(1), 208–212.

Jeng, M. (2006). A selected history of expectation bias in physics. *American Journal of Physics*, 74, 578–583.

Johnson, D. W., & Johnson, R. T. (1994). Collaborative learning and argumentation. In P. Kutnick & C. Rogers (Eds.), *Groups in schools* (pp. 66–86). Cassell Education.

Johnson, D. W., & Johnson, R. T. (1999). Making cooperative learning work. *Theory into practice*, 38(2), 67–73.

Johnson, D. W., & Johnson, R. T. (2009). An educational psychology success story: Social interdependence theory and cooperative learning. *Educational Researcher*, 38(5), 365–379.

Joormann, J., & Gotlib, I. H. (2010). Emotion regulation in depression: Relation to cognitive inhibition. *Cognition and Emotion*, 24(2), 281–298.

Judd, C. H. (1908). The relation of special training to general intelligence. *Educational Review*, 36, 28–42.

Jussim, L. (1989). Teacher expectations: Self-fulfilling prophecies, perceptual biases, and accuracy. *Journal of Personality and Social Psychology*, 57(3), 469–480.

Jussim, L., & Harber, K. D. (2005). Teacher expectations and self-fulfilling prophecies: Knowns and unknowns, resolved and unresolved controversies. *Personality and Social Psychology Review*, 9(2), 131–155.

Kahneman, D. (2011). *Thinking, fast and slow*. Macmillan.

Kahneman, D., & Tversky, A. (1972). Subjective probability: A judgment of representativeness. *Cognitive Psychology*, 3(3), 430–454.

Kajimura, N., Uchiyama, M., Takayama, Y., Uchida, S., Uema, T., Kato, M., Sekimoto, M., et al. (1999). Activity of midbrain reticular formation and neocortex during the progression of human non-rapid eye movement sleep. *Journal of Neuroscience*, 19(22), 10065–10073.

Kalyuga, S., Chandler, P., Tuovinen, J., & Sweller, J. (2001). When problem solving is superior to studying worked examples. *Journal of Educational Psychology*, 93(3), 579–588.

Kang, S. H. K. (2016). The benefits of interleaved practice for learning. In J. C. Horvath, J. Lodge, & J. Hattie, *From the laboratory to the classroom* (pp. 91–105). Routledge.

Karimi Jozestani, L., Faramarzi, S., & Yarmohammadian, A. (2016). The effectiveness of training metacognition-based study skill on the students' achievement motivation, self-efficacy, satisfaction with school and resilience. *Interdisciplinary Journal of Virtual Learning in Medical Sciences*, 7(2), e12151.

Karpicke, J. D. (2012). Retrieval-based learning: Active retrieval promotes meaningful learning. *Current Directions in Psychological Science*, 21(3), 157–163.

Karpicke, J. D., & Blunt, J. R. (2011). Retrieval practice produces more learning than elaborative studying with concept mapping. *Science*, 331(6018), 772–775.

Karpicke, J. D., Butler, A. C., & Roediger, H. L. (2009). Metacognitive strategies in student learning: Do students practise retrieval when they study on their own? *Memory*, 17(4), 471–479.

Karpicke, J. D., & Roediger, H. L. (2007). Expanding retrieval practice promotes short-term retention, but equally spaced retrieval enhances long-term retention. *Journal of Experimental Psychology: Learning, Memory, and Cognition*, 33(4), 704–719.

Karpicke, J. D., & Roediger, H. L. (2008). The critical importance of retrieval for learning. *Science*, 319(5865), 966–968.

Karreman, A., Van Tuijl, C., van Aken, M. A., & Deković, M. (2006). Parenting and self-regulation in preschoolers: A meta-analysis. *Infant and Child Development*, 15(6), 561–579.

Keppel, G. (1964). Facilitation in short-and long-term retention of paired associates following distributed practice in learning. *Journal of Verbal Learning and Verbal Behavior*, 3(2), 91–111.

Kim, C. M., & Pekrun, R. (2014). Emotions and motivation in learning and performance. In J. Spector, M. Merril, J. Elen, & M. Bishop (Eds.), *Handbook of research on educational communications and technology* (pp. 65–75). Springer.

King, A. (1994). Guiding knowledge construction in the classroom: Effects of teaching children how to question and how to explain. *American Educational Research Journal*, 31(2), 338–368.

King, A. (2002). Structuring peer interaction to promote high-level cognitive processing. *Theory into Practice*, 41(1), 33–39.

Kingston, N., & Nash, B. (2011). Formative assessment: A meta-analysis and a call for research. *Educational Measurement: Issues and Practice*, 30(4), 28–37.

Kirschner, P. A. (2017). Stop propagating the learning styles myth. *Computers and Education*, 106, 166–171.

Kirschner, P. A., Sweller, J., & Clark, R. E. (2006). Why minimal guidance during instruction does not work: An analysis of the failure of constructivist, discovery, problem-based, experiential, and inquiry-based teaching. *Educational Psychologist*, 41(2), 75–86.

Klatte, M., Bergström, K., & Lachmann, T. (2013). Does noise affect learning? A short review on noise effects on cognitive performance in children. *Frontiers in Psychology*, 4, 578.

Kleim, J. A., & Jones, T. A. (2008). Principles of experience-dependent neural plasticity: Implications for rehabilitation after brain damage. *Journal of Speech, Language, and Hearing Research*, 51(1), S225–S239.

Kluger, A. N., & DeNisi, A. (1996). The effects of feedback interventions on performance: A historical review, a meta-analysis, and a preliminary feedback intervention theory. *Psychological Bulletin*, 119(2), 254–284.

Koenka, A., et al. (2019). A meta-analysis on the impact of grades and comments on academic motivation and achievement: a case for written feedback. *Educational Psychology* 41(7):1–22

Koole, S. L. (2009). The psychology of emotion regulation: An integrative review. *Cognition and Emotion*, 23(1), 4–41.

Koretz, D. M. (2008). *Measuring up*. Harvard University Press.

Kruger, A. C. (1992). The effect of peer and adult-child transactive discussions on moral reasoning. *Merrill-Palmer Quarterly*, 38(2), 191–211.

Kuhl, P. K. (1994). Learning and representation in speech and language. *Current Opinion in Neurobiology*, 4(6), 812–822.

Kuhl, P. K., Tsao, F. M., & Liu, H. M. (2003). Foreign-language experience in infancy: Effects of short-term exposure and social interaction on phonetic learning. *Proceedings of the National Academy of Sciences*, 100(15), 9096–9101.

Kuhn, D. (2007). Is direct instruction an answer to the right question? *Educational Psychologist*, 42(2), 109–113.

Kulik, J. A., & Kulik, C. C. (1988). Timing of feedback and verbal learning. *Review of Educational Research*, 58(1), 79–97.

Kunda, Z. (1990). The case for motivated reasoning. *Psychological Bulletin*, 108(3), 480–498.

LaBerge, D., & Samuels, S. J. (1974). Toward a theory of automatic information processing in reading. *Cognitive Psychology*, 6(2), 293–323.

Lachman, R., Lachman, J. L., & Butterfield, E. C. (1979). *Cognitive psychology and information processing: An introduction*. Lawrence Erlbaum Associates.

Lajoie, S. P. (2005). Extending the scaffolding metaphor. *Instructional Science*, 33(5–6), 541–557.

Lamborn, S. D., Mounts, N. S., Steinberg, L., & Dornbusch, S. M. (1991). Patterns of competence and adjustment among adolescents from authoritative, authoritarian, indulgent, and neglectful families. *Child Development*, 62(5), 1049–1065.

Laney, C., Heuer, F., & Reisberg, D. (2003). Thematically-induced arousal in naturally-occurring emotional memories. *Applied Cognitive Psychology*, 17(8), 995–1004.

LeDoux, J. E. (2000). Emotion circuits in the brain. *Annual Review of Neuroscience*, 23(1), 155–184.

Leibenstein, H. (1950). Bandwagon, snob, and Veblen effects in the theory of consumers' demand. *The Quarterly Journal of Economics*, 64(2), 183–207.

Leslie, S. J., Cimpian, A., Meyer, M., & Freeland, E. (2015). Expectations of brilliance underlie gender distributions across academic disciplines. *Science*, 347(6219), 262–265.

Levy, B. (1996). Improving memory in old age through implicit self-stereotyping. *Journal of Personality and Social Psychology*, 71(6), 1092–1107.

Li, Y., & Bates, T. C. (2019). You can't change your basic ability, but you work at things, and that's how we get hard things done: Testing the role of growth mindset on response to setbacks, educational attainment, and cognitive ability. *Journal of Experimental Psychology: General*, 148(9), 1640–1655.

Lindell, A. K. (2006). In your right mind: Right hemisphere contributions to human language processing and production. *Neuropsychology Review*, 16(3), 131–148.

Lindell, A. K., & Kidd, E. (2011). Why right-brain teaching is half-witted: A critique of the misapplication of neuroscience to education. *Mind, Brain, and Education*, 5(3), 121–127.

Locke, J. (1894). *Of the conduct of understanding*. Clarendon Press.

Lord, C. G., Ross, L., & Lepper, M. R. (1979). Biased assimilation and attitude polarization: The effects of prior theories on subsequently considered evidence. *Journal of Personality and Social Psychology*, 37(11), 2098–2109.

Lovett, M. (2001). A collaborative convergence on studying reasoning processes: A case study in statistics. In S. Carver & D. Klahr (Eds.), *Cognition and instruction: Twenty-five years of progress* (pp. 347–384). Lawrence Erlbaum Associates.

Luria, A. R. (1968). *The mind of the mnemonist: A little book about a vast memory*. Basic Books.

Maier, S. F., & Seligman, M. E. (1976). Learned helplessness: Theory and evidence. *Journal of Experimental Psychology: General*, 105(1), 3–46.

Manns, J. R., Hopkins, R. O., & Squire, L. R. (2003). Semantic memory and the human hippocampus. *Neuron*, 38(1), 127–133.

Markant, D. B., Ruggeri, A., Gureckis, T. M., & Xu, F. (2016). Enhanced memory as a common effect of active learning. *Mind, Brain, and Education*, 10(3), 142–152.

Martin, V. L., & Pressley, M. (1991). Elaborative-interrogation effects depend on the nature of the question. *Journal of Educational Psychology*, 83(1), 113–119.

Martínez Rizo, F. (2012). Investigación empírica sobre el impacto de la evaluación formativa. *Revisión de literatura. Revista Electrónica de Investigación Educativa*, 14(1), 1–15.

Mayer, R. E. (2002). Rote versus meaningful learning. *Theory into Practice*, 41(4), 226–232.

Mayer, R. E. (2004). Should there be a three-strikes rule against pure discovery learning? The case for guided methods of instruction. *American Psychologist*, 59(1), 14–19.

Mayer, R. E. (2009). Constructivism as a theory of learning versus constructivism as a prescription for instruction. In S. Tobias & T. M. Duffy (Eds.), *Constructivist instruction: Success or failure* (pp. 184–200). Routledge.

Mayer, R. E., & Wittrock, M. C. (1996). Problem-solving transfer. In D. C. Berliner & R. C. Calfee (Eds.), *Handbook of Educational Psychology* (pp. 47–62). Macmillan.

McClelland, M. M., & Cameron, C. E. (2011). Self-regulation and academic achievement in elementary school children. *New Directions for Child and Adolescent Development*, 133, 29–44.

McCloskey, M., Wible, C. G., & Cohen, N. J. (1988). Is there a special flashbulb-memory mechanism? *Journal of Experimental Psychology: General*, 117(2), 171–181.

McGaugh, J. L. (2013). Making lasting memories: Remembering the significant. *Proceedings of the National Academy of Sciences*, 110 (suppl. 2), 10402–10407.

McRae, K., Gross, J. J., Weber, J., Robertson, E. R., Sokol-Hessner, P., Ray, R. D., Gabrieli J. D., et al. (2012a). The development of emotion regulation: An fMRI study of cognitive reappraisal in children, adolescents and young adults. *Social Cognitive and Affective Neuroscience*, 7(1), 11–22.

McRae, K., Jacobs, S. E., Ray, R. D., John, O. P. & Gross, J. J. (2012b). Individual differences in reappraisal ability: Links to reappraisal frequency, well-being, and cognitive control. *Journal of Research in Personality*, 46(1), 2–7.

Mega, C., Ronconi, L., & De Beni, R. (2014). What makes a good student? How emotions, self-regulated learning, and motivation contribute to academic achievement. *Journal of Educational Psychology*, 106(1), 121–131.

Meichenbaum, D. H., & Goodman, J. (1971). Training impulsive children to talk to themselves: A means of developing self-control. *Journal of Abnormal Psychology*, 77(2), 115–126.

Merton, R. K. (1948). The self-fulfilling prophecy. *The Antioch Review*, 8(2), 193–210.

Miller, G. A. (1956). The magical number seven, plus or minus two: Some limits on our capacity for processing information. *Psychological Review*, 63(2), 81–97.

Mischel, W., Shoda, Y., & Peake, P. K. (1988). The nature of adolescent competencies predicted by preschool delay of gratification. *Journal of Personality and Social Psychology*, 54(4), 687–696.

Mischel, W., Shoda, Y., & Rodriguez, M. I. (1989). Delay of gratification in children. *Science*, 244(4907), 933–938.

Morris, A. S., Silk, J. S., Steinberg, L., Myers, S. S., & Robinson, L. R. (2007). The role of the family context in the development of emotion regulation. *Social Development*, 16(2), 361–388.

Morris, C. D., Bransford, J. D., & Franks, J. J. (1977). Levels of processing versus transfer appropriate processing. *Journal of Verbal Learning and Verbal Behavior*, 16(5), 519–533.

Mousavi, S. Y., Low, R., & Sweller, J. (1995). Reducing cognitive load by mixing auditory and visual presentation modes. *Journal of Educational Psychology*, 87(2), 319–334.

Mrazik, M., & Dombrowski, S. C. (2010). The neurobiological foundations of giftedness. *Roeper Review*, 32(4), 224–234.

Mueller, C. M., & Dweck, C. S. (1998). Praise for intelligence can undermine children's motivation and performance. *Journal of Personality and Social Psychology*, 75(1), 33–52.

Muenks, K., Yang, J. S., & Wigfield, A. (2018). Associations between grit, motivation, and achievement in high school students. *Motivation Science*, 4(2), 158–176.

Muijs, D., & Reynolds, D. (2017). *Effective teaching: Evidence and practice*. SAGE Publishing.

Muraven, M. (2012). Ego depletion: Theory and evidence. In R. M. Ryan (Ed.), *The Oxford handbook of human motivation* (pp. 111–126). Oxford University Press.

Neisser, U., Boodoo, G., Bouchard Jr., T. J., Boykin, A. W., Brody, N., Ceci, J. S., Halpern, D. F., et al. (1996). Intelligence: Knowns and unknowns. *American Psychologist*, 51(2), 77–101.

Nickerson, R. S. (1998). Confirmation bias: A ubiquitous phenomenon in many guises. *Review of General Psychology*, 2(2), 175–220.

Nielsen J. A., Zielinski B. A., Ferguson M. A., Lainhart J. E., Anderson J. S. (2013). An evaluation of the left-brain vs. right-brain hypothesis with resting state functional connectivity magnetic resonance imaging. *PLoS One*, 8(8), e71275.

Nielson, K. A., & Arentsen, T. J. (2012). Memory modulation in the classroom: Selective enhancement of college examination performance by arousal induced after lecture. *Neurobiology of Learning and Memory*, 98(1), 12–16.

Nielson, K. A., Yee, D., & Erickson, K. I. (2005). Memory enhancement by a semantically unrelated emotional arousal source induced after learning. *Neurobiology of Learning and Memory*, 84(1), 49–56.

Nunes-Carraher, T. N., Carraher, D. W., & Schliemann, A. D. (1985). Mathematics in the streets and in schools. *British Journal of Developmental Psychology*, 3(1), 21–29.

Oakes, J. (1985). *Keeping track: How schools structure inequality*. New Haven: Yale University Press.

O'Connor, T. G., Bredenkamp, D., Rutter, M., & English and Romanian Adoptees (ERA). Study Team. (1999). Attachment disturbances and disorders in children exposed to early severe deprivation. *Infant Mental Health Journal*, 20(1), 10–29.

O'Connor, T. G., Rutter, M., Beckett, C., Keaveney, L., Kreppner, J. M., & English and Romanian Adoptees Study Team. (2000). The effects of global severe privation on cognitive competence: Extension and longitudinal follow-up. *Child Development*, 71(2), 376–390.

Ochsner, K. N., Bunge, S. A., Gross, J. J. & Gabrieli, J. D. (2002). Rethinking feelings: An fMRI study of the cognitive regulation of emotion. *Journal of Cognitive Neuroscience*, 14(8), 1215–1229.

Organisation for Economic Co-operation and Development (OECD) (2002). *Understanding the brain: Towards a new learning science*. OECD.

Organisation for Economic Co-operation and Development (OECD) (2007). *Understanding the brain: The birth of a learning science*. OECD.

Organisation for Economic Co-operation and Development (OECD) (2008). Assessment for learning. The case of formative assessment. *CERI International Conference "Learning in the 21st Century: Research, Innovation and Policy."* Retrieved from https://www.oecd.org/site/educeri21st/40600533.pdf

Oswald, M. E., & Grosjean, S. (2004). Confirmation bias. In R. F. Pohl (Ed.), *Cognitive illusions: A handbook on fallacies and biases in thinking, judgement and memory* (pp. 79–96). Psychology Press.

Owen, A. M., Hampshire, A., Grahn, J. A., Stenton, R., Dajani, S., Burns, A. S., Howard, R. J., et al. (2010). Putting brain training to the test. *Nature*, 465(7299), 775–778.

Paas, F., Renkl, A., & Sweller, J. (2003). Cognitive load theory and instructional design: Recent developments. *Educational Psychologist*, 38(1), 1–4.

Paige, J., & Simon, H. (1966). Cognition processes in solving algebra word problems. In B. Kleinmuntz (Ed.), *Problem solving* (pp. 119–151). John Wiley & Sons.

Paivio, A. (1971). *Imagery and verbal processes*. Holt, Rinehart, and Winston.

Paivio, A. (1991). Dual coding theory: Retrospect and current status. *Canadian Journal of Psychology*, 45(3), 255.

Pajares, F. (1997). Current directions in self-efficacy research. In M. Maehr & P. R. Pintrich (Eds.), *Advances in motivation and achievement* (Vol. 10, pp. 1–49). JAI Press.

Pashler, H., McDaniel, M., Rohrer, D., & Bjork, R. A. (2009). Learning styles: Concepts and evidence. *Psychological Science in the Public Interest*, 9(3),105–119.

Pasquinelli, E. (2012). Neuromyths: why do they exist and persist? *Mind, Brain, and Education*, 6(2), 89–96.

Patel, V. L., & Groen, G. J. (1991). The general and specific nature of medical expertise: A critical look. In K. A. Ericsson & J. Smith (Eds.), *Towards a general theory of expertise. Prospects and limits* (pp. 93–125). Cambridge University Press.

Patrick, H., Mantzicoupoulos, P., & Sears, D. (2012). Effective classrooms. In K. R. Harris, S. Graham, & T. Urdan. (Eds.). *APA educational psychology handbook*. (pp. 443–469). American Psychological Association.

Paunesku, D. (2013). *Scaled-up social psychology: Intervening wisely and broadly in education* (Tesis doctoral, Stanford University). Retrieved from https://web.stanford.edu/~paunesku/articles/paunesku_2013.pdf

Paunesku, D., Walton, G. M., Romero, C., Smith, E. N., Yeager, D. S., & Dweck, C. S. (2015). Mindset interventions are a scalable treatment for academic underachievement. *Psychological Science*, 26(6), 784–793.

Pavlov, I. P. (1927). Conditioned reflexes: An investigation of the physiological activity of the cerebral cortex (G. V. Anrep, Trans.). Oxford University Press.

Peeck, J., Bosch van den, A. B., & Kruepeling, W. J. (1982). The effect of mobilizing prior knowledge on learning from text. *Journal of Educational Psychology*, 74, 771–777.

Pekrun, R., Frenzel, A. C., Goetz, T., & Perry, R. P. (2007). The control-value theory of achievement emotions: An integrative approach to emotions in education. In P. A. Schulz & R. Pekrun (Eds.), *Emotion in education* (pp. 13–36). Academic Press.

Pekrun, R., & Linnenbrink-Garcia, L. (2014). Introduction to emotions in education. In *International handbook of emotions in education* (pp. 11–20). Routledge.

Perkins, D. N., & Salomon, G. (1992). Transfer of learning. *International Encyclopedia of Education* (2nd ed.). Pergamon Press.

Phelps, E. A. (2006). Emotion and cognition: Insights from studies of the human amygdala. *Annual Review of Psychology*, 57, 27–53.

Philippot, P., Chapelle, G., & Blairy, S. (2002). Respiratory feedback in the generation of emotion. *Cognition and Emotion*, 16(5), 605–627.

Piaget, J. (1959). *The language and thought of the child* (3rd ed.). Routledge and Kegan Paul.

Piaget, J. (1968). *Genetic epistemology*. Columbia University Press.

Pickering, S. J., & Howard-Jones, P. (2007). Educators' view on the role of neuroscience in education: Findings from a study of UK and international perspectives. *Mind, Brain, and Education*, 1, 109–113.

Pintrich, P. R. (2003a). Motivation and classroom learning. In W. M. Reynolds & C. E. Miller (Eds.), *Handbook of psychology* (Vol. 7, pp. 103–122). John Wiley & Sons.

Pintrich, P. R. (2003b). A motivational science perspective on the role of student motivation in learning and teaching contexts. *Journal of Educational Psychology*, 95(4), 667–686.

Pintrich, P. R., Marx, R. W., & Boyle, R. A. (1993). Beyond cold conceptual change: The role of motivational beliefs and classroom contextual factors in the process of conceptual change. *Review of Educational Research*, 63(2), 167–199.

Platón (2003). *Libro VII de La República*. Tilde.

Poldrack, R. A. (2012). The future of fMRI in cognitive neuroscience. *Neuroimage*, 62(2), 1216–1220.

Poldrack, R. A., & Packard, M. G. (2003). Competition among multiple memory systems: Converging evidence from animal and human brain studies. *Neuropsychologia*, 41(3), 245–251.

Posner, G.J., et al. (1982). Accommodation of a scientific concept: toward a theory of conceptual change. *Science Education* 66(2): 211–227.

Prince, M. (2004). Does active learning work? A review of the research. *Journal of Engineering Education*, 93(3), 223–231.

Raudenbush, S. W. (1984). Magnitude of teacher expectancy effects on pupil IQ as a function of the credibility of expectancy induction: A synthesis of findings from 18 experiments. *Journal of Educational Psychology*, 76(1), 85–97.

Rawson, K. A., Dunlosky, J., & Sciartelli, S. M. (2013). The power of successive relearning: Improving performance on course exams and long-term retention. *Educational Psychology Review*, 25(4), 523–548.

Renkl, A., Atkinson, R. K., & Große, C. S. (2004). How fading worked solution steps works: A cognitive load perspective. *Instructional Science*, 32(1–2), 59–82.

Reusser, K. (1988). Problem solving beyond the logic of things: Contextual effects on understanding and solving word problems. *Instructional Science*, 17, 309–338.

Riener, C., & Willingham, D. (2010). The myth of learning styles. *Change: The magazine of higher learning*, 42(5), 32–35.

Rienzo, C., Rolfe, H., & Wilkinson, D. (2015). *Changing mindsets: Evaluation report and executive summary.* Education Endowment Foundation.

Rimfeld, K., Kovas, Y., Dale, P. S., & Plomin, R. (2016). True grit and genetics: Predicting academic achievement from personality. *Journal of Personality and Social Psychology,* 111(5), 780–789.

Rimm-Kaufman, S. E., Early, D. M., Cox, M. J., Saluja, G., Pianta, R. C., Bradley, R. H., & Payne, C. (2002). Early behavioral attributes and teachers' sensitivity as predictors of competent behavior in the kindergarten classroom. *Journal of Applied Developmental Psychology,* 23(4), 451–470.

Robertson, J. S. (2000). Is attribution training a worthwhile classroom intervention for K–12 students with learning difficulties? *Educational Psychology Review,* 12(1), 111–134.

Roediger III, H. L., Agarwal, P. K., McDaniel, M. A., & McDermott, K. B. (2011). Test-enhanced learning in the classroom: long-term improvements from quizzing. *Journal of Experimental Psychology: Applied,* 17(4), 382–395.

Roediger III, H. L., & Pyc, M. A. (2012). Inexpensive techniques to improve education: Applying cognitive psychology to enhance educational practice. *Journal of Applied Research in Memory and Cognition,* 1(4), 242–248.

Roediger III, H. L., Zaromb, F. M., & Goode, M. K. (2008). A typology of memory terms. In J. H. Byrne (Ed.), *Learning and Memory: A Comprehensive Reference* (Vol. 1, pp. 11–24). Elsevier.

Roediger, H. L., & Butler, A. C. (2011). The critical role of retrieval practice in long-term retention. *Trends in Cognitive Science,* 15(1), 20–27.

Roediger, H. L., & Karpicke, J. D. (2006). Test-enhanced learning: Taking memory tests improves long-term retention. *Psychological Science,* 17(3), 249–55.

Rohrer, D., & Taylor, K. (2006). The effects of overlearning and distributed practise on the retention of mathematics knowledge. *Applied Cognitive Psychology,* 20(9), 1209–1224.

Rohrer, D., & Taylor, K. (2007). The shuffling of mathematics problems improves learning. *Instructional Science,* 35(6), 481–498.

Romero, C., Master, A., Paunesku, D., Dweck, C. S., & Gross, J. J. (2014). Academic and emotional functioning in middle school: The role of implicit theories. *Emotion,* 14(2), 227–234.

Rosenshine, B. (2010). *Principles of Instruction. Educational Practices Series-21.* UNESCO International Bureau of Education.

Rosenthal, R., & Jacobson, L. (1968). Pygmalion in the classroom. *The Urban Review,* 3(1), 16–20.

Rosenzweig, M. R., Bennett, E. L., & Diamond, M. C. (1972). Brain changes in response to experience. *Scientific American,* 226, 22–29.

Rowland, C. A. (2014). The effect of testing versus restudy on retention: A meta-analytic review of the testing effect. *Psychological Bulletin,* 140(6), 1432–1463.

Rubin, D. C., & Kozin, M. (1984). Vivid memories. *Cognition,* 16(1), 81–95.

Sadler, D. R. (1989). Formative assessment and the design of instructional systems. *Instructional Science,* 18(2), 119–144.

Sakakibara, A. (1999). A longitudinal study of a process for acquiring absolute pitch. *The Japanese Journal of Educational Psychology,* 47, 19–27.

Sakakibara, A. (2014). A longitudinal study of the process of acquiring absolute pitch: A practical report of training with the chord identification method. *Psychology of Music,* 42(1), 86–111.

Salden, R. J., Paas, F., & van Merriënboer, J. J. G. (2006). A comparison of approaches to learning task selection in the training of complex cognitive skills. *Computers in Human Behavior,* 22(3), 321–333.

Saleh, M., Lazonder, A. W., & de Jong, T. (2007). Structuring collaboration in mixed-ability groups to promote verbal interaction, learning, and motivation of average-ability students. *Contemporary Educational Psychology*, 32(3), 314–331.

Salkind, N. J. (2016). *Statistics for people who (think they) hate statistics*. SAGE Publishing, Inc.

Sanmartí, N. (2007). *10 ideas clave: Evaluar para aprender*. Editorial Graó.

Schiefele, U., Krapp, A., & Winteler, A. (1992). Interest as a predictor of academic achievement: A meta-analysis of research. In K. A. Renniger, S. Hidi, & A. Krapp (Eds.), *The role of interest in learning and development* (pp. 183–212). Lawrence Erlbaum Associates.

Schmeichel, B. J., Demaree, H. A., Robinson, J. L., & Pu, J. (2006). Ego depletion by response exaggeration. *Journal of Experimental Social Psychology*, 42(2), 95–102.

Schmeichel, B. J., & Tang, D. (2014). The relationship between individual differences in executive functioning and emotion regulation: A comprehensive review. *The Control Within: Motivation and Its Regulation*, 133–152.

Schmidt, R. A., Young, D. E., Swinnen, S., & Shapiro, D. C. (1989). Summary knowledge of results for skill acquisition: Support for the guidance hypothesis. *Journal of Experimental Psychology: Learning, Memory, and Cognition*, 15(2), 352–359.

Schneps, M., & Sadler, P. (1988). *A private universe*. Pyramid Films.

Schoenfeld, A. H. (1987). What's all the fuss about metacognition. In A. H. Schoenfeld (Ed.), *Cognitive science and mathematics education* (pp. 189–215). Lawrence Erlbaum Associates.

Schommer-Aikins, M. (2002). An evolving theoretical framework for an epistemological belief system. In B. K. Hofer & P. R. Pintrich (Eds.), *Personal epistemology: The psychology of beliefs about knowledge and knowing* (pp. 103–118). Lawrence Erlbaum Associates.

Schroeder, V. M., & Kelley, M. L. (2010). Family environment and parent-child relationships as related to executive functioning in children. *Early Child Development and Care*, 180(10), 1285–1298.

Schunk, D. H. (1989). Self-efficacy and achievement behaviors. *Educational Psychology Review*, 1(3), 173–208.

Schunk, D. H. (1991). Self-efficacy and academic motivation. *Educational psychologist*, 26(3–4), 207–231.

Schunk, D. H., & Hanson, A. R. (1985). Peer models: Influence on children's self-efficacy and achievement. *Journal of Educational Psychology*, 77(3), 313–322.

Schunk, D. H., Pintrich, P. R., & Meece, J. L. (2013). *Motivation in education: Theory, research, and applications* (4th ed.). Pearson.

Schwartz, D. L., Lin, X. J., Brophy, S., & Bransford, J. D. (1999). Toward the development of flexibly adaptive instructional designs. In C. M. Reigeluth (Ed.), *Instructional-design theories and models: A new paradigm of instructional theory* (Vol. 2, pp. 183–213). Lawrence Erlbaum Associates.

Schwartz, M. S., Sadler, P. M., Sonnert, G., & Tai, R. H. (2008). Depth versus breadth: How content coverage in high school science courses relates to later success in college science coursework. *Science Education*, 93, 798–826.

Scoville, W. B., & Milner, B. (1957). Loss of recent memory after bilateral hippocampal lesions. *Journal of Neurology, Neurosurgery, and Psychiatry*, 20(1), 11.

Scriven, M. (1967). The methodology of evaluation. In R. W. Tyler, R. M. Gagné, & M. Scriven (Eds.), *Perspectives of curriculum evaluation* (Vol. 1, pp. 39–83). Rand McNally.

Senn, D., & Marzano, R. J. (2015). *Organizing for learning: Classroom techniques to help students interact within small groups.* Learning Sciences International.

Séré, M. G. (1986). Children's conceptions of the gaseous state, prior to teaching. *European Journal of Science Education,* 8(4), 413–425.

Sharp, P. (1985). Behaviour modification in the secondary school: A survey of students' attitudes to rewards and praise. *Behavioral Approaches with Children,* 9(4), 109–112.

Shuman, V., & Scherer, K. R. (2015). Psychological structure of emotions. In *International encyclopedia of the social and behavioral sciences* (pp. 526–533). Elsevier.

Simpson, M., & Arnold, B. (1982). Availability of prerequisite concepts for learning biology at certificate level. *Journal of Biological Education,* 16(1), 65–72.

Sisk, V. F., Burgoyne, A. P., Sun, J., Butler, J. L., & Macnamara, B. N. (2018). To what extent and under which circumstances are growth mind-sets important to academic achievement? *Two meta-analyses. Psychological Science,* 29(4), 549–571.

Skibbe, L. E., Connor, C. M., Morrison, F. J., & Jewkes, A. M. (2011). Schooling effects on preschoolers' self-regulation, early literacy, and language growth. *Early Childhood Research Quarterly,* 26(1), 42–49.

Skinner, B. F. (1958). Teaching machines. *Science,* 128, 969–977.

Slavin, R. E. (1991). Are cooperative learning and untracking harmful to the gifted? *Educational Leadership,* 48(6), 68–71.

Slavin, R. E. (1995). *Cooperative learning: Theory, research, and practice* (2nd ed.). Allyn & Bacon.

Slavin, R. E. (2013). Cooperative learning and achievement: Theory and research. In W. M. Reynolds, G. E. Miller, & I. B. Weiner (Eds.), *Handbook of psychology* (2nd ed., Vol. 7, pp. 199–212). John Wiley & Sons.

Slavin, R. E. (2018). *Educational psychology: Theory and practice.* Pearson.

Smith, C., Maclin, D., Grosslight, L., & Davis, H. (1997). Teaching for understanding: A study of students' pre-instruction theories of matter and a comparison of the effectiveness of two approaches to teaching about matter and density. *Cognition and Instruction,* 15(3), 317–393.

Smith, M. A., & Karpicke, J. D. (2014). Retrieval practice with short-answer, multiple-choice, and hybrid tests. *Memory,* 22(7), 784–802.

Smith, S. M. (1982). Enhancement of recall using multiple environmental contexts during learning. *Memory and Cognition,* 10(5), 405–412.

Smith, S. M., Glenberg, A., & Bjork, R. A. (1978). Environmental context and human memory. *Memory and Cognition,* 6(4), 342–353.

Smith, S. M., & Vela, E. (2001). Environmental context-dependent memory: A review and meta-analysis. *Psychonomic Bulletin and Review,* 8(2), 203–220.

Soderstrom, N. C., & Bjork, R. A. (2015). Learning versus performance: An integrative review. *Perspectives on Psychological Science,* 10(2), 176–199.

Sowell, E. R., Peterson, B. S., Thompson, P. M., Welcome, S. E., Henkenius, A. L., & Toga, A. W. (2003). Mapping cortical change across the human life span. *Nature Neuroscience,* 6(3), 309–315.

Spellman, K. V., Deutsch, A., Mulder, C. P. H., & Carsten-Conner, L. D. (2016). Metacognitive learning in the ecology classroom: A tool for preparing problem solvers in a time of rapid change? *Ecosphere,* 7(8), e01411.

Spencer, S. J., Logel, C., & Davies, P. G. (2016). Stereotype threat. *Annual Review of Psychology*, 67, 415–437.

Spilich, G. J., Vesonder, G. T., Chiesi, H. L., & Voss, J. F. (1979). Text processing of domain-related information for individuals with high and low domain knowledge. *Journal of Verbal Learning and Verbal Behavior*, 18(3), 275–290.

Squire, L. R. (2004). Memory systems of the brain: A brief history and current perspective. *Neurobiology of Learning and Memory*, 82(3), 171–177.

Squire, L. R. (2009). The legacy of patient HM for neuroscience. *Neuron*, 61(1), 6–9.

Squire, L. R., & Zola, S. M. (1998). Episodic memory, semantic memory, and amnesia. *Hippocampus*, 8(3), 205–211.

Stangor, C., & McMillan, D. (1992). Memory for expectancy-congruent and expectancy-incongruent information: A review of the social and social developmental literatures. *Psychological Bulletin*, 111(1), 42–61.

Stavy, R. (1991). Children's ideas about matter. *School Science and Mathematics*, 91(6), 240–244.

Steele, C. M. (1997). A threat in the air: How stereotypes shape intellectual identity and performance. *American Psychologist*, 52(6), 613–629.

Steele, C. M., & Aronson, J. (1995). Stereotype threat and the intellectual test performance of African Americans. *Journal of Personality and Social Psychology*, 69(5), 797–811.

Steinberg, L., Elmen, J. D., & Mounts, N. S. (1989). Authoritative parenting, psychosocial maturity, and academic success among adolescents. *Child Development*, 60(6), 1424–1436.

Stewart, J., Cartier, J. L., & Passmore, C. M. (2005). Developing understanding through model-based inquiry. In M. S. Donovan, D. Bransford (Eds.), *How students learn: Science in the classroom* (pp. 515–565). National Academies Press.

Stipek, D., & Gralinski, J. H. (1996). Children's beliefs about intelligence and school performance. *Journal of Educational Psychology*, 88(3), 397–407.

Stipek, D. J. (1996). Motivation and instruction. In D. C. Berliner & R. C. Calfee (Eds.), *Handbook of educational psychology* (pp. 85–113). Macmillan.

Strayhorn Jr, J. M. (2002). Self-control: Toward systematic training programs. *Journal of the American Academy of Child and Adolescent Psychiatry*, 41(1), 17–27.

Swanson, J., Valiente, C., Lemery-Chalfant, K., & O'Brien, T. C. (2011). Predicting early adolescents' academic achievement, social competence, and physical health from parenting, ego resilience, and engagement coping. *Journal of Early Adolescence*, 31(4), 548–576.

Sweller, J. (1988). Cognitive load during problem solving: Effects on learning. *Cognitive Science*, 12, 257–285.

Sweller, J. (1994). Cognitive load theory, learning difficulty, and instructional design. *Learning and Instruction*, 4(4), 295–312.

Sweller, J. (2006). The worked example effect and human cognition. *Learning and Instruction*, 16(2), 165–169.

Sweller, J. (2010). Element interactivity and intrinsic, extraneous and germane cognitive load. *Educational Psychology Review*, 22(2), 123–138.

Sweller, J., Ayres, P. L., Kalyuga, S., & Chandler, P. A. (2003). The expertise reversal effect. *Educational Psychologist*, 38(1), 23–31.

Sweller, J., Van Merriënboer, J. J. G., & Paas, F. (1998). Cognitive architecture and instructional design. *Educational Psychology Review*, 10(3), 251–296.

Talarico, J. M., & Rubin, D. C. (2003). Confidence, not consistency, characterizes flashbulb memories. *Psychological Science*, 14(5), 455–461.

Tangney, J. P., Baumeister, R. F., & Boone, A. L. (2004). High self-control predicts good adjustment, less pathology, better grades, and interpersonal success. *Journal of Personality*, 72(2), 271–324.

Tau, G. Z., & Peterson, B. S. (2010). Normal development of brain circuits. *Neuropsychopharmacology*, 35(1), 147–168.

Taylor, V. J., & Walton, G. M. (2011). Stereotype threat undermines academic learning. *Personality and Social Psychology Bulletin*, 37(8), 1055–1067.

Teasley, S. D. (1995). The role of talk in children's peer collaborations. *Developmental Psychology*, 31(2), 207–220.

Thorndike, E. L. (1923). The influence of first year Latin upon the ability to read English. *School Sociology*, 17, 165–168.

Thorndike, E. L., & Woodworth, R. S. (1901). The influence of improvement in one mental function upon the efficiency of other functions. (I). *Psychological Review*, 8(3), 247–261.

Thorndike, R. L. (1968). Reviewed work: Pygmalion in the classroom by Robert Rosenthal and Lenore Jacobson. *American Educational Research Journal*, 5(4), 708–711.

Tice, D. M., & Bratslavsky, E. (2000). Giving in to feel good: The place of emotion regulation in the context of general self-control. *Psychological inquiry*, 11(3), 149–159.

Tracy, J. L., & Robins, R. W. (2004). Putting the self into self-conscious emotions: A theoretical model. *Psychological Inquiry*, 15(2), 103–125.

Tricomi, E., & DePasque, S. (2016). The role of feedback in learning and motivation. In S. Kim, J. Reeve, & M. Bong (Eds.), *Advances in motivation and achievement: Recent developments in neuroscience research on human motivation* (pp. 175–202). Emerald Group Publishing Limited.

Tulving, E. (2002). Episodic memory: From mind to brain. *Annual Review of Psychology*, 53(1), 1–25.

Ullman, M. T. (2016). The declarative/procedural model: A neurobiological model of language learning, knowledge, and use. In G. Hickok & S. L. Small (Eds.), *Neurobiology of language* (pp. 953–968). Elsevier.

Ullman, M. T., & Lovelett, J. T. (2016). Implications of the declarative/procedural model for improving second language learning: The role of memory enhancement techniques. *Second Language Research*, 34(1), 39–65.

Upchurch, R., & Sims-Knight, J. (2001). What's wrong with giving students feedback? In *ASEE Annual Conference Proceedings*. American Society for Engineering Education. Retrieved from https://peer.asee.org/10027

Valentine, J. C., DuBois, D. L., & Cooper, H. (2004). The relation between self-beliefs and academic achievement: A meta-analytic review. *Educational Psychologist*, 39(2), 111–133.

Van Dillen, L. F., & Koole, S. L. (2007). Clearing the mind: A working memory model of distraction from negative mood. *Emotion*, 7(4), 715–723.

Van Overwalle, F., & De Metsenaere, M. (1990). The effects of attribution-based intervention and study strategy training on academic achievement in college freshmen. *British Journal of Educational Psychology*, 60(3), 299–311.

Van Praag, H., Kempermann, G., & Gage, F. H. (2000). Neural consequences of environmental enrichment. *Nature Reviews Neuroscience*, 1(3), 191–198.

Varvogli, L., & Darviri, C. (2011). Stress management techniques: Evidence-based procedures that reduce stress and promote health. *Health Science Journal*, 5(2), 74–89.

Vogel, S., and Schwabe, L. (2016). Learning and memory under stress: implications for the classroom. NPJ Science of Learning 1. Article number 29:1:16011.

Von Culin, K. R., Tsukayama, E., & Duckworth, A. L. (2014). Unpacking grit: Motivational correlates of perseverance and passion for long-term goals. *Journal of Positive Psychology*, 9(4), 306–312.

Vosniadou, S., & Brewer, W. F. (1992). Mental models of the earth: A study of conceptual change in childhood. *Cognitive Psychology*, 24(4), 535–585.

Vygotsky, L. S. (1978). *Mind in society*. Harvard University Press.

Wade, S. E. (1992). How interest affects learning from text. In K. A. Renninger, S. Hidi, & A. Krapp (Eds.), *The role of interest in learning and development* (pp. 255–277). Lawrence Erlbaum Associates.

Webb, N. M. (1992). Testing a theoretical model of student interaction and learning in small groups. In R. Hertz-Lazarowitz & N. Miller (Eds.), *Interaction in cooperative groups: The theoretical anatomy of group learning* (pp. 102–119). Cambridge University Press.

Webb, N. M. (2009). The teacher's role in promoting collaborative dialogue in the classroom. *British Journal of Educational Psychology*, 79(1), 1–28.

Wegner, D. M. (1994). Ironic processes of mental control. *Psychological review*, 101(1), 34–52.

Weiner, B. (1986). *An attributional theory of motivation and emotion*. Springer.

Weiner, B. (1990). History of motivational research in education. *Journal of Educational Psychology*, 82(4), 616–622.

Wertheimer, M. (1959). *Productive thinking*. Harper and Row.

White, B. Y., & Frederiksen, J. R. (1990). Causal models progressions as a foundation for intelligent learning environments. *Artificial Intelligence*, 42, 99–157.

Wigfield, A., & Eccles, J. S. (1992). The development of achievement task values: A theoretical analysis. *Developmental Review*, 12(3), 265–310.

Wigfield, A., & Eccles, J. S. (2000). Expectancy-value theory of achievement motivation. *Contemporary Educational Psychology*, 25(1), 68–81.

Wightman, D., & Lintern, G. (1985). Part-task training for tracking and manual control. Human Factors, *Journal of the Human Factors and Ergonomics Society*, 27, 267–283.

Wilen, W. W. (1991). *Questioning skills, for teachers. What research says to the teacher*. National Education Association.

Wiliam, D. (2011). *Embedded formative assessment*. Solution Tree Press.

Wiliam, D., & Black, P. (1996). Meanings and consequences: A basis for distinguishing formative and summative functions of assessment? *British Educational Research Journal*, 22(5), 537–548.

Willingham, D. T. (2002). Ask the cognitive scientist inflexible knowledge: The first step to expertise. *American Educator*, 26(4), 31–33.

Willingham, D. T. (2005). Ask the cognitive scientist: Do visual, auditory, and kinesthetic learners need visual, auditory, and kinesthetic instruction? *American Educator*, 29(2), 31.

Willingham, D. T. (2008). Critical thinking: Why is it so hard to teach? *Arts Education Policy Review*, 109(4), 21–32.

Willingham, D. T. (2008). What will improve a student's memory? *American Educator*, 32(4), 17–25.

Willingham, D. T. (2009). *Why don't students like school? A cognitive scientist answers questions about how the mind works and what it means for the classroom.* Jossey-Bass.

Willingham, D. T. (2012). Ask the cognitive scientist: Why does family wealth affect learning? *American Educator*, 36(1), 33–39.

Willingham, D. T. (2014). Strategies that make learning last. *Educational Leadership*, 72(2), 10–15.

Willingham, D. T. (2017). *The reading mind: A cognitive approach to understanding how the mind reads.* John Wiley & Sons.

Willingham, D. T. (2018). Ask the cognitive scientist: Does tailoring instruction to "learning styles" help students learn? *American Educator*, 42(2), 28–32.

Wing, J. M. (2006). Computational thinking. *Communications of the ACM*, 49(3), 33–35.

Wolters, C. A. (2004). Advancing achievement goal theory: Using goal structures and goal orientations to predict students' motivation, cognition, and achievement. *Journal of Educational Psychology*, 96(2), 236–250.

Wood, D., Bruner, J. S., & Ross, G. (1976). The role of tutoring in problem solving. *Journal of Child Psychology and Psychiatry*, 17(2), 89–100.

Yeager, D. S. (2018). *Re-analysis of descriptive statistics from Mueller & Dweck* (1998). Retrieved from https://osf.io/ngwn8

Yeager, D. S., & Dweck, C. S. (2012). Mindsets that promote resilience: When students believe that personal characteristics can be developed. *Educational Psychologist*, 47(4), 302–314.

Yeager, D. S., Hanselman, P., Walton, G. M., Murray, J. S., Crosnoe, R., Muller, C., Tripton, E., et al. (2019). A national experiment reveals where a growth mindset improves achievement. *Nature*, 573, 364–369.

Yerkes, R. M., & Dodson, J. D. (1908). The relation of strength of stimulus to rapidity of habit-formation. *Journal of Comparative Neurology and Psychology*, 18(5), 459–482.

Zimmerman, B. J. (2001). Theories of self-regulated learning and academic achievement: An overview and analysis. In B. J. Zimmerman & D. H. Schunk (Eds.), *Self-regulated learning and academic achievement: Theoretical perspectives* (pp. 1–37). Lawrence Erlbaum Associates.

Zimmerman, B. J., & Martinez-Pons, M. (1986). Development of a structured interview for assessing student use of self-regulated learning strategies. *American Educational Research Journal*, 23(4), 614–628.

Zins, J. E., Bloodworth, M. R., Weissberg, R. P., & Walberg, H. J. (2007). The scientific base linking social and emotional learning to school success. *Journal of Educational and Psychological Consultation*, 17(2–3), 191–210.